Fictions of the Self: 1550-1800

FICTIONS OF THE SELF: 1550-1800

Arnold Weinstein

PRINCETON UNIVERSITY PRESS

Library of Congress Cataloging in Publication Data will
be found on the last printed page of this book

Publication of this book has been aided by the Paul Mellon
Fund of Princeton University Press

This book has been composed in V-I-P Bembo

Printed in the United States of America
by Princeton University Press, Princeton, New Jersey

To Ann

Preface

The longer one lives, the more one is aware of connection and indebtedness. I decided to call this book "fictions of the self," because the very notion of an integral, unenmeshed human being is—psychically and socially—something of a fiction. This is no less the case professionally, and I am pleased to trace the origins of this study and to thank those who have helped me see it through. Many years ago, Robert Scholes and I both noted the lack of comparative studies dealing with 18th-century fiction; in the spring of 1974 we jointly taught at Brown University a graduate seminar on the major British and French novels of the period, and from that enterprise arose my desire to do this book. Individual studies of the novelists themselves, and of each national tradition, were not lacking, but I was attracted by the challenge of erecting a critical framework that could both illuminate the specificity of single texts and also say something about the "rise of the novel" in a pan-European context. Having studied the problems of character assertion in modern fiction, I was intrigued by the similar conflicts in 17th- and 18th-century novels: the varieties and problems of self-realization; the search for freedom, against the constraints of society and contingency.

In attempting to chart the self's career in early fiction, I have tried to balance and to interweave a variety of issues: (1) the development and rationale of two kinds of fictions, the mimetic and the generative, each corresponding to a particular mode of self-enactment; (2) the complementary and sometimes opposing roles that language and gesture play in self-realization; (3) a view of character that could both account for the diverse energies of the texts at hand, and also be of interest to us today.

To a number of my colleagues at Brown University I owe a debt of gratitude: Sears Jayne and Juan López-Morillas were kind enough to read through portions of my manuscript at an early stage and to give me their counsel; Mark Spilka and Robert Scholes looked over the entire book, and I benefited considerably from their thoughtful remarks; I am especially grateful to Reinhard Kuhn for taking my argument and my prose seriously at every turn and for offering me many valuable suggestions in the interests of clarity and persuasiveness.

My greatest debt, however, in this book as in the other projects I have undertaken is to my wife Ann. What I know of relationship and the dialectic between language and gesture comes largely from our life together. Finally, I am grateful for her support concerning the fundamental principle of this book and of my work: that the life of the mind—so splendidly at work and at play in literature—is shareable.

The practice used for foreign texts and translations is as follows. All material in the text itself will be given in English; the original Spanish, German, and French quotations will be provided at the end of the book. In some cases, the English translations are taken entirely from published English versions of these novels (e.g., Michael Alpert's translation of *Lazarillo* and the *Buscón* in the Penguin edition). In other cases, I have both used and amended existing translations (e.g., Walter Wallich's remarkable version of *Simplicissimus* in the Ungar series, Harry Steinhauer's very readable *Werther* in the Norton series, Richard Aldington's translation of *Les Liaisons dangereuses* in the Signet Classic, Jacques Barzun's rendering of *Le Neveu de Rameau* and J. M. Cohen's version of Rousseau's *Confessions*). Finally, where I felt that existing translations were inadequate, I translated all the material myself (*La Princesse de Clèves, La Vie de Marianne, Manon Lescaut*). These translations are followed by *italic* numbers; the originals appear at the end of the book.

Table of Contents

Fictions of the Self: 1550-1800

Introduction

TO BEGIN A BOOK is to express a fundamental faith in the power of the word. Writing about literature is doubly pious, for literature itself is an act of belief, a transcription of life into language. To be sure, it is possible, from a linguistic or semiotic perspective, to assert the contrary, that language is the *a priori* bedrock and structure of whatever reality we can know or possess. Yet, as living creatures who inhabit a physical and social world, as laymen with bodies as well as tongues, we cannot help distinguishing between things and the words that denote them. Most of us still believe, perhaps naively, in a reality out there which language magically—but servilely—names. It is clear, however, even to the most unphilosophical among us, that language is more than a servant, more than a bridge to things out there; a daily human drama is made of word achievements, of speech acts, of language as end rather than means. Language is precisely, and in countless ways, the replacement for things. We are all the users and beneficiaries of this verbal alchemy, for such transformations are hardly restricted to writers: language may well be the great enabler, one of the most potent resources that man has, not merely for communication, but for self-enactment.

Yet, the world is more than language; we all know basic areas of experience and forms of expression that are not verbal. As a record of life, literature must tell us about love, death, money, business, and politics; as a medium it can only *tell* us about these things. Can telling be enough? We know that language is bread-and-butter for the writer; but what about the starving child? the woman thief? the yearning lover? In these elemental struggles, common to many novels and seemingly beyond the precincts of linguistic play, there is to be found an astonishing dosage of words, of verbal responses to moral or material dilemmas. In examining the major British and Continental fictions of the 17th and 18th centuries, we will see two basic kinds of narrative: stories of impasse or conflict where no amount of words will do, and, on the other hand, novels in which verbal threads lead out of material labyrinths. I shall be designating these two kinds of fictions "mimetic" and "generative," and my concern is with the rationale of each: when are solutions gestural? when verbal?

There is drama here, perhaps the most elemental exchange process known to man. What coins do we deal in? Does language extend or lessen our estate? What provinces can we enter through words alone? Death, for example, can be available to us only as a concept, a word, a metaphor; literature can mediate for us here, allowing us a peculiar kind of appropriation and ersatz of the "real thing." But, what happens when words about love or freedom tend to replace love and freedom, when language itself fulfills, when speech acts become the only acts? The very presence of literature testifies to the appeal and beauty of such verbal displacement. Writers are wooed by the enabling powers of language, its capacity not only to "render" experience but also its indigenous virtues *as* experience. So, too, readers annex new realms each time they enter texts. Yet, who would be only a reader? How much experience is to be vicarious?

What do language and art enable? What do they cost? These are the elemental, pointedly economical questions which I want to address in this book. Within the novels at hand we shall see varieties of exchanges and trade-offs, as protagonists make their way through the world. Beyond the frame of the novels themselves, the larger question comes home to us as well: to what end language? in what sense is the novel an experience? For those of us who spend our lives with books, such a query has unmistakable personal, as well as professional, relevance. It is in this light that the study of fiction is especially advantaged. Although poetry doubtless privileges the generative power of language more than any other genre, only fiction gives us that fuller picture, that larger tableau which relegates language to relative status, thereby assessing it as tool while simultaneously exploiting it as medium. Fiction, then, encompasses projects that are more than verbal. Novels are capacious and may depict acts of love as well as declarations of love, thieving as well as talking, mingling of souls as well as self-reflections. In looking at fiction, the critic is privy to the entire range of human energies, the multiple projects and all the assorted data which constitute the fiction. The sum of those projects is, quite simply, the life-story; by life-story, I mean that entire eco-system which is ultimately constructed by the work of art. The novel, with its possibilities of temporal span and multiple situations, its capacity to depict setting, speech, and consciousness, is an ideal macrocosm for containing roads both taken and untaken, and for demonstrating varieties of self-enactment, both mimetic and generative.

The entity which permits us to bring all these elements into focus is, of course, the self. Whereas individuation is the condition of the human species, individualism is a phenomenon of history, certainly of literary history. The circumscribed human being, always radically on his own from a biological point of view, may or may not regard his own life as a special promise or a unique case. Tradition, religion, the influence of church or state, all these factors may favor a collective sense of reality, as opposed to a private one.

Primitive man may have had a vaguer sense of his own contours, may have distinguished less sharply between self and other. But, the instinct for survival, the capacity to cope, the sense of a beginning and an end, have always conferred a precious form and responsibility on human life. We do not live twice (even an after-life would be *after*); each single life carries out its negotiations with contingency, with all that is not itself. Identity, consistency, integrity, and fidelity are so many words for coercing the fluid *durée* of existence into a recognizable, hence a tolerable, form.

At what point does fiction depict private experience? How does one give their due to convention and context, and nonetheless discern a personal voice and a personal destiny in art? These questions are asked in the interests of economy, not biography. A novel can be seen either as an instance of particular conventions, or as a unique configuration of the protagonist's life story. A detail in the plot, an expression in the narrative, a reference to history: these specific givens may be either assigned to multiple sources (in which case, the novel is a potpourri, a mixed document), or they may be seen as elements of a character's destiny. It is all a matter of perspective. Is the picaresque novel in Spain a hide-and-seek document about *conversos*, or is it a tale of individual coping and cunning? Is *Simplicissimus* a historical account of the Thirty Years' War, or an imaginative account of how an individual retains integrity during endless crises? The pain in the chest or the pounding at the temples will offer a different interest to the sufferer and to the doctor. To view art and reality as character-ridden is to assert a hidden agenda, perhaps a hidden teleology: the world may not be anthropocentric, but surely our own drama, our fictive sense of things, the shape we take during our time, is limited to that ongoing interaction of self and world which is our life.[1]

In this study, I intend to illuminate that interaction by endowing fictional characters with the attribute of a self. To personalize print, to go from language to referent, to espy (or to infer) human drama in the context of cultural and verbal convention: these imaginative acts, far from being naive,

---

[1] No one has more acutely assessed the self as interface between consciousness and world than Borges. In his "New Refutation of Time," he sovereignly proves the unreality of time, only to conclude that such feats of philosophy can never alter the elemental fact we all suffer time and self until our death:

And yet, and yet—To deny temporal succession, to deny the ego, to deny the astronomical universe, are apparent desperations and secret assuagements. Our destiny (unlike the hell of Swedenborg and the hell of Tibetan mythology) is not horrible because of its unreality; it is horrible because it is irreversible and ironbound. Time is the substance I am made of. Time is a river that carries me away, but I am the river; it is a tiger that mangles me, but I am the tiger; it is a fire that consumes me, but I am the fire. The world, alas, is real; I, alas, am Borges.

("A New Refutation of Time," *Other Inquisitions*, 1937-1952, tr. Ruth L. Simms. New York: Simon and Schuster, 1968, pp. 186-187.)

make reading both challenging and enlightening. I will be viewing fictional characters as people, because I think there is everything to gain in such an orientation. How does one transform the grittiness of the world into the fable of a life? Far from being an aesthetic afterthought, the creation of form is at the very heart of both life and art. The shaping impulse is coextensive with life itself; not so much jars or statues, but our very identity, must be made. And there is considerable drama in such efforts. Characters in early fiction are, precisely and fascinatingly, having to fight for character. From Lazarillo to Tristram, self-assertion is the dominant, the despotic, note.

"Self," then, as I use it, is not a nostalgic, arrogant relic of a human-centered world or an orderly life; it is, rather, as Stevens would say, a supreme fiction, a necessary, generous, eye-opening rather than soporific fiction. The centrality of one's own life is unarguable. And the finer lives absorb more world into their circular nets, transforming discrete facts and inchoate details into biography. Life, defined this way, is a colonizing enterprise. My critical strategy is to assess the characters' critical strategy, to respect survival and affirmation as the most powerful and coherent drive known to man.

To demonstrate the interest and primacy of character in these early fictions, it is essential that I discern self-affirmation and self-realization wherever, and in whatever guise, they appear. Such discernment is hardly tantamount to moral approval, however, and I have no intention of defending egoists merely because they know how to marshall their energies. It will be seen, moreover, that blindness and hubris are not infrequent hallmarks of the most organized selves, and I trust that the ethical ramifications of the behavior in question will be visible to all. But my primary aim is to illuminate the characterological spectacle itself. Literature highlights the interplay of pressure and performance, and the fictions studied in this book display a rich spectrum of responsive affirmations: role-playing, love, death, control of others, day dreaming, and art.

Modern fiction is not lacking in texts that dramatize the negotiations between language and experience, but early fiction

is even more suggestive, because the fictional enterprise itself—not yet as complacent or transparent as it will become
in the 19th century—is new, open to question and experiment. The central notion of recounting a life in words is bristling and problematic in Quevedo, Goethe, Diderot, and
Sterne. All the texts studied here portray varieties of enactment and fulfillment, and in each case the narrative act itself
looms large as human resource. By pondering the connection
between self-enactment and language, I hope to reveal something important about both the rationale of fiction and the
kinds of avenues that are open to character.[2] The novel is born
and, in some sense, dies during the span of fictions that I assess.

"Early fiction" is an unhappy appellation, chosen only because century numbers are unbearably dry. Needless to say,
fiction does not start with *Lazarillo*, and the problematics of
the self have already appeared on the literary scene as well. An-
cient and medieval narratives might well qualify for a number
of my chapters, so a word is in order as to why I start where
I do, and why I end when I do. In the first place, as indicated,
I am working with a view of fiction that is essentially that of
the life-story, the individualist impetus that charges the texts
studied in the following chapters. Two of the great "epic" fictions of the 16th century are roughly contemporaneous with
the picaresque tales: *Don Quijote* and the books of Rabelais;
although each of these "texts" is, in its own way, a *summa*, the
primacy and fortunes of the self cannot be said to be their
main concern. Rabelais looks forward already to Sterne, and
his immense erudition and wordplay have been assessed in all

[2] I would like to acknowledge, at the outset, my debt to Erich Kahler's important study, *The Inward Turn of Narrative*, tr. Richard and Clara Winston
(Princeton: Princeton University Press, 1973). Kahler's book has much more
scope than mine, since he spends considerable time with classical material before coming to the novel proper; moreover, he discusses some of the 18th-
century novelists whom I treat as well. Nonetheless, I think it is clear that our
methods differ radically, and that I am making an argument for the use of
fictions in general, rather than tracing some kind of cultural or philosophical
evolution. Above all, the notion of self-enactment allows me to place in some
kind of dialectic the generative and mimetic uses of language which fiction
depicts and enables.

manner of ways, ranging from cultural documentation on to epistemological crisis. Yet, we need merely to see the movement from the episodic fables of the giants in the first two books to the more sweeping, paralyzing verbal queries of the third book, to realize that plot and character do not much interest Rabelais. With Cervantes, the case is different, and his imprint is clearly discernible in a good number of the writers I deal with; yet, he does not really touch the fundamental issue of coping and survival which is at the heart of the texts I treat. Like Rabelais, he is enormously aware of the generative power of language and fiction, so much aware that he creates a character who lives wholly in that constructed realm and hence clashes repeatedly with the world of contingency. Yet, such clashes are very different from the collisions that I intend to chart between self and society, self and other. The autonomy of the subjective is the impetus for Cervantes' novel, but it hardly provides that introspective new world to which the individual is increasingly going to withdraw, as the only free arena imaginable.

The final figure whose absence must be accounted for is Montaigne. Two centuries before Rousseau he undertakes the project of depicting the self in language, indeed the self as language. And, yet, one cannot claim the *Essais* to be a fiction, as one properly can for the *Confessions*. Man of leisure, aristocrat, Montaigne is marvelously cavalier with his narrative; his self-exposure has none of the tragic, re-writing urgency of Rousseau's account. Montaigne does not need a Last Judgment of readers; he does not rely on his *words* to remake and thereby redeem his life.

Hence the picaresque and baroque fictions initiate my study. In them the authority of the self becomes a central, problematic, issue. *Lazarillo* is more than an assemblage of folk-tale motifs, precisely because the unifying, containing locus of the action is the figure of the servant boy who seeks to impose his form. From this point on, the coherence and the economy of the life-story dictate the parameters of the novel.

I stop with Rousseau, because the story has essentially been told by then. The watershed that appears to come in the work of Flaubert and James, the displacement of interest from the fable itself to the enabling language and strategy which *presents* the fable, that crisis has taken place, I am suggesting, during the course of the fictions I have studied. Proust, Joyce, et al., add immeasurably to the picture, but the givens of the picture—the rationale of mimetic versus generative fictions, the privileged status of language in fiction, the increasing primacy of speech acts as the only kinds of assertion imaginable, the recourse to writing as ultimate self-enactment—are clearly and profoundly delineated in the early fictions that I study. At the beginning there is the seemingly characterless picaresque novel and at the end there is the seemingly plotless depiction of consciousness and language. Seen through my lens, these are all fictions of self-realization.

To examine the life-story according to its emphases, priorities and choices, to chart whether the enacted life of the protagonist is primarily social, passional or mental, is to propose criteria for literary criticism that have little to do with national boundaries or particular schools. The self pursues its goals and expends its energies as fully in *Lazarillo de Tormes* as in *Tristram Shandy*. As Proust puts it somewhat pathologically: "a hidden jewel turns up; when the amount of urine of the sick person diminishes, it is because he perspires more; the excretion must nonetheless take place" (*Sodome et Gomorrhe*, ed. Folio, p. 34). James hauntingly illustrates, in *The Sacred Fount*, that there is only one kind of energy, and the processes of acting and narrating are definitely related to each other dialectically. The picaresque *Lazarillo*, with its folklore elements and lack of inwardness, takes on a special meaning when contrasted with the generative, self-conscious art of Sterne. The life-story is still binding: how to survive or succeed? how to be free of constraint? Taken together, the anonymous Spanish tale and the sophisticated English fiction chart the *uses*—human as well as aesthetic—of mimetic versus generative narratives. In this light, narrative strategies are always living strategies.

Why do such a study? That is probably the most begged question in literary criticism, but my personal answer follows from what has already been stated: fiction illuminates large areas of human experience about which we are in the dark.

What is on record, in this case in Spain, France, England, and Germany from 1550 to the French Revolution, are a variety of "documents" which are essentially fields of force, *tableaux* of life lived and thought, pictures of what happened and, equally important, "what they cannot have told you." Fiction complements history because it yields a palimpsest, a multiple imprint of many hues and strains, a rare kind of EKG and EEG which shows the organism in its panoramic, more-than-social, otherwise unrecorded, life activities. The *Buscón*'s wordplay, Moll's disguises, Marianne's wit, Des Grieux's and Werther's stormy feelings, Merteuil's masks, the nephew's mimicry, Tristram's fabulation: seen together, these exploits aggrandize our sense of the human; they constitute a tribute to the self's powers of creation and preservation, and they form a picture, an invaluable fictive picture, of welcome even if unsettling resources.

To group texts along these lines runs the risk of making this kind of "comparative criticism" hopelessly unprincipled and impressionistic; yet, the cardinal rule of comparative literature is that literature is one, from which it follows that the arrangement and juxtaposition of materials is considerably more arbitrary and exciting than literary history customarily allows. Comparison itself is inherently scandalous, but, without it, there can be no knowledge. Works of art are, in the form the world knows them by, finite and delimited. To compare *The Sound and the Fury* to *Absalom, Absalom!* is but to walk a shorter distance on the same tightrope as one must when comparing Proust and Joyce, or E. E. Cummings and Calderón. The mind itself is the supreme comparative grab-bag, working fearlessly through association and devious connection, making a mockery of our specialties and taxonomies, linking literature to sausages and Peugeots. Given the unavoidable (delightful) infinite clutter of the world as it is, I have chosen to take small chances, to forge modest connections between *novels* written during a 200-year period, depicting a variety of life-stories. Like a successful metaphor, comparisons create both heat and light, unearth unsuspected parallels; in so doing, they may well illuminate the materials in question more sharply, more indelibly than an entire arsenal of so-called "background information" (which may be, ultimately, as foreign to art's special keenness, as the bowl is to the Béarnaise).

Hence, there will be little attention given, in this study, to the social and cultural matrix from which these books issue, other than what the texts themselves tell us; that matrix doubtless exists, but the novels themselves, orphans like Moll and Marianne, roam the world, radically unsponsored, and, like Moll and Marianne, must make it on their own, must become, as it were, their own papers. Despite universities and the enormous buffer zone of established criticism, the great books always have succeeded on this ground. The life of the self, the life of the book, the life of the reader—so many loaded analogies—exist in themselves as well as in context. The grand bluff of the academy frequently consists in saying that nothing exists on its own, that grids and coordinates must be established, that the single performance is indecipherable without the enabling knowledge of background and *oeuvre*. There is much that is substantial in this claim, but there is also much that is missed. We must know what we want to know. An appreciation of art as history, of text as document, requires the kind of expertise and pinning down which our specialists provide. But the reading of literature as document frequently falls prey to a strange kind of resurrectionist fervor, a desire to recapture, as totally as possible, the presumable significance of the work when written. My own bias should be evident: the work of art, especially fiction, depicts strategies for living which may be shaped by a specific age but which are rich in meaning for all ages. My concern is candidly with contemporary meanings. From *Lazarillo* to *Tristram*, fiction tells us about coping; rather than to a criticism that discerns "appropriate" meanings, I am committed to what today's reader can see in them. (I might add that the reader is always "today's reader," and that the historical critic is no less contemporary than the unenlightened student.) In the course of this study I would like to delineate and to assess strategies of self-realization which find in literature their most privileged and atemporal expression. It is that freer trajectory, that visible projection of energies, which I will be viewing as the animus of fiction. Such an investigation is at once more universal and more particular than either history or literary history. Background, biography and historical setting can take us—unless we are utterly simple-minded determinists—only so far in understanding the constellations produced in each fiction. The novel both is and often reflects precisely that untrammeled, uncensored, unconstrained expenditure of energy and desire which history and society rarely accommodate. If anything, these novels tell us about freedom, its whereabouts and its cost; our quarry then is rare and precious, because the bird, even when fictive, is dazzling when in flight.

"Flight" itself is richly ambivalent as a metaphor for fiction, suggesting as it does, evasion as well as transcendence. No fiction has ever made a life. Or prolonged it. Living, as James demonstrated so sweetly in "The Beast in the Jungle," is relentless. James, devotee though he was of the free-floating, self-authoritative imagination, never failed to give those two villains—Time and Matter—their due. The mind may defy Newtonian physics and logic (Uncle Toby can be in England and Namur at the same time), but the body does not enjoy such liberty. During their stay, human beings divide their time among countless activities, but none of them is, or can be, free. Everything counts and is counted. Yet we know very little about the choices that people make in this realm, the time or space or value allotted to loving, eating, speaking, or thinking. Few of us have lights about our own priorities, how much of our life takes shape in gesture, how much in word. In some profound sense, we do not know how and where people genuinely live, "live" in the sense of committed energies; and no statistics or demography are likely to shed light on such intimate matters. Many of us are haunted by the notion that our life is a dream, our pursuits solipsistic, our sensations unshared, our *vita* a farce. Herein lies the beauty of fiction; blessed with impurities and relatively free of poetics, it depicts, sensitively and ineluctably, that fuller human ecosystem which escapes graphs and charts. In a novel everything is on show, as it never is in life. These fictions may be seen as a type of *Spielraum*, an arena in which the energies of the individual are given form.

From my point of view, character is always center-stage, and all novels impart valuable living instructions to readers. Whereas the 19th century tirelessly centralizes character (so much so that everything in *Great Expectations* or *Père Goriot* will finally be ingested by the protagonist, transformed into his *Bildung*), the life-story in early fiction is more precarious and more devious. It is no accident that these novels are filled with outsiders and orphans, would-be rather than established individuals. Every text studied here depicts the appetite for selfhood, the desire not merely for survival, but also for integrity and even consistency. "Consistency," far more than the hobgoblin of small minds, demands that one's gestures and statements today have some bearing to yesterday's; we shall see that the Thirty Years' War and "making it in London" coerce the self into an endless repertory of masks and roles. Finally, early fiction dramatizes an elemental quest for freedom. The central question which Stein raises in *Lord Jim*, "how to be?" assumes an ontological urgency in these novels that is beyond mere moral considerations. Julien Sorel, Raskolnikov, and Pip *are*, and the thrust of their story consists in gauging the rightness of their behavior; Lazarillo, Marianne, Werther, and Tristram are bent on staying in the fiction at all, on maintaining existence itself: this primordial tension accounts for the extraordinary malleability of self, the profusion of mask and repertory, the seesaw of enactment through language as opposed to gesture, which I shall be assessing in the following chapters.

My first study is devoted to the marginal self depicted in picaresque and Baroque fictions: in different guises, Lazarillo, Quevedo's Buscón, and Grimmelshausen's Simplicius illustrate the remarkable elasticity of self when the setting is either starvation or war. These seemingly plot-oriented fictions attest to the suppleness of the individual, but they raise disturbing questions of integrity and identity: how many guises and disguises are tolerable? Is consistency (or even selfhood) a luxury item, necessitating sameness and fidelity where metamorphosis and denial are the order of the day? *La Princesse de Clèves*, bathed in an entirely different courtly atmosphere, depicts still more lethally the annihilation of self by the public world: Lafayette's novel is even more grisly than the raucous picaresque stories, and it lays bare the manner in which social extermination becomes a matter of language rather than of swords or duels.

In Defoe, Marivaux, and Fielding the self reigns triumphant, and this chapter constitutes the idyllic interlude of my study. *Moll Flanders* and *La Vie de Marianne* are both, oddly and interestingly, stories of people without "papers," without official claims to respectability. In each case we see how women succeed in a man's world, succeed not only through sexual exploits but even more importantly through a generative sense of self. Throughout all of Moll's disguises is a vigorous feeling of harmony and identity, the will to assume all her roles, to recognize her past, to achieve independence (her initial definition of "gentlewoman" is precisely that). It is the story itself, the "confession" to the reader (and to the priest at Newgate), that discloses and confirms an integrity unperceived (and too risky to show) in life. Marianne's case is an even more flagrant illustration of someone "becoming" her story. Marianne substantiates her claim to aristocracy before our very eyes, through wit and language; she is a success story of the self, a celebration of the orphan's ability to achieve recognition through performance alone, unaided by documents or by past. Fielding's Joseph Andrews triumphs too: endowed more modestly in the mental area than Marianne, less energetic and assertive than Moll, he shows us that his greatest virtue is his virtue: the purity and beauty of his body. Comic fiction though it is, *Joseph Andrews* is a test case for the open self, the unadorned, natural body that is coextensive with the soul.

Whereas Defoe, Marivaux, and Fielding are writing, in some sense, fairytales, stories where the self's appetites can be fully gratified and brought into harmony with society, the novels studied in my third chapter reveal the conflict between self-as-authority and society. Prévost's *Manon Lescaut*, Richardson's *Clarissa*, and Goethe's *Werther* all depict the impasse of self and setting, and that impasse is tragically personalized as well: the collision between self and other, the failed love story. These three novels point toward the antagonistic fictions of 19th-century Romanticism and Realism, both in an emotional and a social sense, as we see that the desires of the self cannot be brooked. This chapter closes with a study of Laclos' *Liaisons dangereuses* as the ultimate extension and perversion of the authorized self. Laclos presents the superman theme that is to reappear in Stendhal and Balzac, but he does so in an erotic and verbal context that goes beyond anything produced in the 19th century. Here we see the desire for total freedom, first shown as erotic manipulation but finally seen as self-creation: Merteuil uses both her language and her body as she wills, to become multiple and invulnerable. Such freedom, in a novel of social and human relations, is awesome and deadly.

In my final chapter I pick up all the threads that I have been developing, and I show that the ultimate arena for self-expression, creation, and enactment is the one of thought and language and consciousness. This realm is solipsistic, for the mind is a solitary place, but the avenues for expansion are endless. Diderot's *Neveu de Rameau*, Sterne's *Tristram Shandy*, and Rousseau's *Confessions* will be analyzed as consummate examples of literature offering the only life that can be lived. Here we confront the full appeal and the undeniable escapism of cathartic literature. "Virtual" and "vicarious" become terms of infinite value here; psychodrama replaces drama. The determinist prison of the body (those two villains—Matter and Time) can be transcended, because even the most maimed life can be a whole narrative, and consciousness may enjoy a freedom and simultaneity which life denies but which books can render. If the novels of collision point toward the 19th-century fictions of Dickens, Balzac, Stendhal, and Dostoevsky, these strange texts unmistakably point us to Proust, Joyce, Nabokov, Borges, and company. What I am arguing, indeed the entire rationale for my book, is that the generative fictions of solipsis and purely verbal creations must be placed next to mimetic and representational novels if we are truly to understand either set. If language offers possibilities of transcendence and fulfillment, it is because the self as well as the novelist has recourse to it as his greatest trump. In the face of the body's dissolution and time's erasure, language may be the only valid currency the self has; it may be only out of language that a self can be made.

The evolution which I am charting takes the self from marginal to flourishing to defiant on to internalized. We see in these novels, as we could never see elsewhere, an eloquent array of answers to Stein's question, "How to be?" Eloquent because something great begins to appear, surfaces, swells, and then, as it were, goes inside. What I have just articulated is clearly a metaphor for the drama of individualism, a phenomenon we know to be contemporaneous with the development of fiction. The individual goes through his repertory in the texts I discuss, and one can hardly separate the social, psychological, and aesthetic implications of his evolution. But we cannot fail to be moved by the changing role that art and language play in the ongoing process of self-enactment. Whereas "literature" stops in *Lazarillo*, so that he can get on with the material life and make good on his success story, Rousseau finds that language and art alone permit him to remake and redeem his life. Literature, in the beginning, is, like the self, marginal; literature, at the close, is, like the inner universe it both celebrates and retreats to, all.

It is possible that the great freedoms, the best life, admit of no restraint or compromise. In language are conquests and affirmations available nowhere else. But at what cost? In the shift from the tragic love story of *Manon Lescaut* to the quip of Diderot's philosopher, *"Mes pensées, ce sont mes catins* (My ideas are my trollops)," something crucial has transpired. Prévost's novel dramatizes a real pursuit, a mimetic love story, a quest of one person for another; the objects of Diderot's desire are not of the flesh but of the mind, and the gratification he seeks takes place there as well. Thought, consciousness, and language serve that unpoliced inner life where one can live most wholly, where "One's grand flights, one's Sunday baths,/One's tootings at the weddings of the soul/Occur,"[3] but those orgies are solitary happenings. What of love and society? That terribly real world *outside* the self, present and

---

[3] Wallace Stevens, "The Sense of the Sleight-of-hand Man," in *The Palm at the End of the Mind* (New York: Vintage Books, 1972), p. 168.

even omnipresent in all the fictions studied here, refuses to be the plaything of the mind, the creature of language and thought. Here is the enduring dialectic caught and mirrored in early fiction, repeated in modern fiction, experienced well beyond the precincts of literature itself: *where* do we live? Is our self-realization primarily verbal and mental, or is it encompassed in social gestures and human relations? Is language a tool, a world, or a retreat? Finally, what is truly betokened by the pattern of this study: as fiction moves from the mimetic *Lazarillo* to the generative *Tristram*, how can we assess the antics of the self? Are we perceiving a response to society or to death? Is this the play of history and culture, or is it more simply the self's drama in time? As moralistic as it may seem, novels have much to teach us about these matters. The dialectic between freedom and bondage is not altered by books, but we, as readers, may perceive in fiction a strange breathing room for life itself; and, in so doing, we may learn better to recognize our own dance.

... il est certain que l'époque actuelle est plutôt celle du numéro matricule.—Robbe-Grillet, *Pour un nouveau roman*

THE
MARGINAL
SELF

IT IS NOT fashionable to discuss character at all, but especially not in the picaresque novel. The protagonist of these fictions is more frequently assessed as lens, as means of viewing society bottom-side-up, exposing its foibles, etc. Hence, these tales are presumably short on psychological data and long on social satire and conventional role figures. But there is a strange urgency and energy in these fictions as well, an irresistible sense that the teller counts, that the story told is his story, not merely history.

One need not interpret the plight of Lazarillo, Pablos and Simplicius as existentialist crises,[1] in order to view these characters as selves rather than as figures. Their lack of interiority, their astonishing resiliency and protean capacity for rebirth— these attributes demarcate a larger, not a smaller, view of identity than we are accustomed to. The episodic tale, the dizzying metamorphoses and accommodations, make a mockery of our notions of consistency and integrity. But masks are never gratuitous, and even the character who plays out roles for their own sake (as is conceivably the case with Pablos) is

[1] See W. M. Frohock's persuasive article on the current "misreadings" of the picaresque in "The Failing Center: Recent Fiction and the Picaresque Tradition," *Novel* (Fall 1969), pp. 62-69. In particular, Frohock stresses the unexistentialist dimension of the "classic" picaresque texts, and suggests that we need a new term to describe those 20th-century fictions (*The Invisible Man, The Adventures of Augie March, The Tin Drum*, etc.) that are frequently hailed as modern descendants of the picaresque.

pursuing a strange kind of self-enactment. In *Lazarillo de Tormes*, *Simplicissimus*, and *La Vida del Buscón* we see a struggle to remain coherent, to remain at all. Here is the embryonic self, a living creature that must be first, and be something afterwards. Even in the sophisticated courtly fiction of Mme de Lafayette, with its annunciatory dosage of psychological analysis, there is no room for leisurely identity or for complacent consciousness. Life is, at every turn, coercive, and these fictions record the difficulty and the challenge of self-assertion. One is hard put to interpret the cumulative pattern at work here; the claims of self and the claims of life simply cut deeper than any moral framework we have: Lazarillo goes public and lives; the Princess remains private and dies. No code will tidy up or interpret this picture. The body and the soul, we learn, each have a life-and-death story.

The Marketplace: *Lazarillo de Tormes*

Lazarillo de Tormes is the proper text for initiating a study of the self's fortunes in fiction. This little book, without "papers" or acknowledged author, is the quintessential success story. Less established even than the orphans, Moll and Marianne, Lazarillo is the meekest of the meek, an obscure servant whose *"fortunas y adversidades"* catapulted him to fame with the reading public in 16th- and 17th-century Europe. As the prologue says, "it's a good thing that important events which quite accidentally have never seen the light of day should be made public"[1,2]; neither hero nor prince, Lazarillo achieves importance precisely by telling his story; it is indeed his use of the first person that constitutes those "important events" which can see the light of day only if literature is there to transcribe them. What irony there is in the opening phrase, is to be found in the innocuous clause, "made public"; for, as we shall see, Lazarillo is to move from naked consciousness to public voice, with all the ethical and narrative corollaries which attend such an evolution.

[2] *Two Spanish Picaresque Novels*, tr. Michael Alpert (Penguin Classics, 1969), p. 23. Subsequent translated quotations are drawn from Alpert and will be noted in the text.

It seems apt to view both the book and its title character as more or less embryonic stages in the development of fiction and of the self. Just as the infant begins life by crying, *Lazarillo de Tormes* is a powerful picture of the self as hunger. Not the spiritual or allegorical hunger of literature, the searching for an ideal rose or Kafka's artist who declined the offerings of his age, but strictly visceral, physical hunger, the gut kind.

The self as hunger is a terrifying lens to place on society. The world becomes nothing more than something to eat. Values do not hold up well under such an optic, and the satire in this slender book is corrosive. The world and its overlay of meanings (religion, honor, virtue) are, as it were, eaten away. This is comic and satiric. But the tougher truth of *Lazarillo de Tormes* is that the self as hunger, after revealing the fraud of the world, ceases to be; as it too becomes the pure matter that it has ever experienced around itself, there is a death of the spirit. Under the guise of a pre-picaresque tale, a would-be progenitor of the *Bildungsroman*, a fictionalized and temporalized arrangement of folklore motifs, we actually have—almost 300 years before Balzac and Flaubert—the *Urform* of the "sell-out," and what is sold goes by various names: soul, consciousness, character. The beauty of the novel lies in the way that transaction is depicted.

We begin with an ironic prologue which announces that literature may have merit and bring honor to its author, and that people write for a public. In the story proper we will discover that honor, of all types, is fraudulent, that this narration is ostensibly *not* for public usage, but destined to a powerful benefactor (*vuestra merced*), and that Lazarillo himself will progress from obscure servant to Town Crier. It is quite clear that all these terms are larded with ambiguity: can a life without merit be told with merit? is honor, in any form whatsoever, viable? what does it mean to go public? what is the itinerary between the consciousness of a hungry child and the list of wares of the Town Crier-Wine Merchant?

From the outset of the story, there is a persistent mix-up between values and food. Zaide, the black friend of the child's mother, at first frightens Lazarillo, "but when I saw that with him around there the food got better, I began to like him quite a lot" (p. 6).[2] With his first master, the blind man, Lazarillo displays his cunning solely in terms of sneaking food. The only moment of pure happiness in the novel occurs when the child is guzzling wine:

> I was sitting the same as always, taking in those sweep sips, my face turned toward the sky and my eyes slightly closed so I could really savor the delicious liquor. The dirty blind man saw that now was the time to take out his revenge on me, and he raised that sweet and bitter jug with both his hands and smashed it down on my mouth with all his might. As I say, he used all his strength, and poor Lázaro hadn't been expecting anything like this; in fact, I was drowsy and happy as always. So it seemed like the sky and everything in it had really fallen down on top of me. (pp. 13–14)[3]

The passage captures the ecstasy and the vulnerability of the child, and it describes the sky falling in with distinct apocalyptic overtones. Not only the earth, but the heavens themselves revolve around eating and drinking, but the child learns to be more prudent in his pilfering. Of course, eating can be an expansive social act; but in this text, given the first two masters' dispositions, it is solitary and monstrous, a perversion of relationship. The wine is stolen by carving a small hole and sealing it off with a piece of wax; when the jug is warm, the wax melts, the hole opens, the wine comes out.

If Lázaro tries to open up wine jugs with his first master, he concentrates on opening up a bread chest with the second one. This master, a priest, is as greedy as the blind man and has eyes as well. The child knows that his only salvation lies locked in the chest, and the scene where a tinker gives him the key is written in charged language: "The angelic tinker began to try out the keys on his chain, one after the other, and I was helping him with my feeble prayers. Then, when I least expected it, I saw the face of God, as they say, formed by the loaves of bread inside that chest" (p. 36).[4] What follows is a duel of almost epic proportions, as the priest tries to safeguard his precious bread and Lázaro daily assaults the chest under the guise of mice and snakes. This sequence of events is vir-

tually surrealist in tone, as the scene is reduced to the presence
of two desperate humans and a chest of bread. The boy is constantly making new holes in the chest and the priest assidu-
ously plugs them up. The motif itself is so repeated that it begins to take on compelling erotic and religious overtones:

> I was dying a slow death, and finally I got to the point that
> when I was alone the only thing I did was open and close
> the chest and look at the face of God inside (or at least that's
> how children put it). (pp. 38-39)[5]

After the mice ploy, the priest boards up the holes, and we
read, "Now, by closing up the holes in the chest, he's closing
the door to my happiness, too, and opening the one to my
troubles" (p. 40).[6] The chest itself is personified when Lázaro
attacks it at night: "It was really an old chest, and it had been
around for so many years that it didn't have any strength or
backbone left. It was so soft and worm-eaten that it gave in to
me right away and let me put a good-sized hole in its side so
I could relieve my own suffering. When I finished this, I
opened the slashed-up chest very quietly, and feeling around
and finding the cut-up loaf, I did the usual thing" (p. 42).[7]
These implications of mutilation and sacrifice take on a darker
hue as the pace quickens to a frenzy:

> He began to look around on the walls of the house again
> for nails and pieces of wood to keep them [mice] out. Then
> when night came and he was asleep, there I was on my feet
> with my knife in hand, and all the holes he plugged up dur-
> ing the day I unplugged at night. That's how things went,
> me following him so quickly that this must be where the
> saying comes from: "Where one door is closed, another
> opens." (p. 43)[8]

The finale comes when the priest shifts from the mice theory to a snake solution; by this time, the man is so agitated
that he cannot sleep at night, for fear that the snake is nearby.
Lázaro is magnificently given away by the hissing noise that
the key makes in his mouth (the only place he can hide it)
when he sleeps, and the hunt comes to its end with the mur-
derous assault on the sleeping, hissing boy-snake. I have de-

scribed this sequence in some detail, because the haunting language of holes and doors and keys enables us to put the hunger motif in proper perspective. These scenes depict a desperate need to fill oneself up, the need for a key to open things up, the urge to penetrate within and find gratification; also depicted is the grim, passionate resistance which Lázaro confronts. There is no relationship, almost no language (except for the hissing), between Lázaro and these two masters, but, in its place, a series of assaults and defenses, of raids on nourishment, which are stymied by plugged holes and closed chests. Doubtless the most violent image of the hungry self attempting to penetrate the other occurs when the blind man, suspecting Lázaro of stealing food, goes the limit to check it out:

> He got up and grabbed me by the head and got close so he could smell me. And he must have smelled my breath like a good hound. Really being anxious to find out if he was right, he held on tight and opened my mouth wider than he should have. Then, not very wisely, he stuck in his nose. And it was long and sharp. And his anger had made it swell a bit, so that the point of it hit me in the throat. So with all this and my being really frightened, along with the fact that the black sausage hadn't had time to settle in my stomach, and especially with the sudden poking in of his very large nose, half choking me—all these things went together and made the crime and the snack show themselves, and the owner got back what belonged to him. What happened was that before the blind man could take his beak out of my mouth, my stomach got so upset that it hit his nose with what I had stolen. So his nose and the black, half-chewed sausage both left my mouth at the same time. (p. 20)[9]

There can hardly be a more vivid image in literature of human violation. The cannibalism in Quevedo's *La Vida del Buscón* is far more cerebral than what we have here. Whereas Lázaro has sought to fill himself full, fulfilment, the blind man treats him like a thing, an orifice, a bread chest where he can get his own back. The result is a kind of creatural anarchy; rather than an inanimate chest or jug, the body becomes a potent counterforce, expelling both the invading beak and the black sausage as well.

I have been trying to suggest that the hunger scenes in the first two chapters, with their elaborate emphasis on food and orifices, enact a grotesque caricature of relationship. It is in this light that the third chapter, Lázaro and the *escudero*, may be seen as the climax of the story. Lázaro reaches his economic nadir, for not only does this master not feed him, but he is obliged to nourish his master. Not obliged, exactly, but rather by choice, Lázaro seeks to fill full another as well as himself. Many critics have remarked that this chapter signals the child's greatest moment of humanity and compassion; the Squire, burdened by a ridiculous honor code (*hidalguía*), amuses the boy, but he also touches him deeply, for he is genuinely poor:

> "This man," I said, "is poor. And no one can give what he doesn't have. But both the stingy blind man and that blasted miser of a priest did all right in God's name—one of them with a quick tongue and the other one with his hand-kissing. And they were starving me to death. So it's only right that I should hate them and feel sorry for this man."
> (p. 67)[10]

The grudging tone of the statement reflects the child's need to reassure himself that this new-found compassion is justifiable. The situation is pellucid: Lázaro's economic (and professional) career is at its lowest precisely when his moral character is fullest; the scene depicts a strange kind of ethical birth, one that is destined to be short-lived, one that is, in fact, a luxury item in the world that Lázaro inhabits. The author insists on the empty, quasi-haunted house with absolutely nothing in it except a pathetic bed and two people. No property and no food. Yet that house and that chapter are filled with language, dialogue, interest that is more than self-interest. We learn that the Squire "asked me a lot of questions about where I was from and how I'd happened to come to that city" (p. 54).[11] There is no violence in this chapter, but rather a gentle comic vision that is both delicate and mellow. The Squire talks to Lázaro, and he exposes both his excessive pride and vulnerability; to be sure, the Squire's sham gentility and play-acting (even to the extent of picking his teeth in public to appear to have eaten) are ridiculous, but they are also consummately civilized gestures. The elemental level of raw need, so vividly depicted in the experiences with the blind man and the priest, is rarefied and refined, and the self becomes more than hunger:

> So, for supper I began to eat my tripe and bread, while I was watching my poor master out of the corner of my eye. And he kept staring at my shirttail that I was using for a plate. I hope God takes as much pity on me as I felt for him. I knew just what he was feeling, since the same thing had happened to me lots of times—and, in fact, it was still happening to me. I thought about asking him to join me, but since he told me that he'd already eaten I was afraid he wouldn't accept the invitation. The fact is, I was hoping that the sinner would help himself to the food I had gone to the trouble of getting and that he'd eat the way he did the day before so he could get out of his own troubles. This was really a better time for it, since there was more food and I wasn't as hungry. (p. 64)[12]

Why is this vision of compassion and humanity abandoned? The *escudero* makes a comic exit, and the remaining chapters are utterly different in tone. It is important to understand that the entire tale, both before and after the experience with the Squire, shows why such a moral vision is doomed. There is nothing aberrant or surprising in Lázaro's consequent growth into hypocrite and face man. He has learned his lessons, and the reader should too. The first and foremost lesson is to keep your eyes open and focussed on what is in front of you, and it is perfect that a blind man should be his teacher. When the pair comes to a statue of a bull, the blind man tells the child to put his ear next to it so as to hear the great sound inside it:

> I put my ear next to it very simply, thinking he was telling the truth. And when he felt my head near the statue, he doubled up his fist and knocked my head into that devil of

a bull so hard that I felt the pain from its horns for three days. And he said to me, "You fool, now learn that a blind man's servant has to be one step ahead of the devil." And he laughed aloud at his joke.

It seemed to me that at that very instant I woke up from my childlike simplicity and I said to myself, "He's right. I've got to open my eyes and be on my guard. I'm alone now, and I've got to think about taking care of myself." (pp. 9-10)[13]

This is the determining event of Lázaro's life. When his head crashes into the stone, he has his first collision with reality. And he wakes up to realize that the self is alone and unprotected. Taking care means looking out for number one, and in *Lazarillo de Tormes* this kind of lifemanship leads to a world composed of matter alone. The symbolic and spiritual realms disappear when one has one's eyes open. The bread in the chest may be votive loaves, but it is just bread; only the children call it "the face of God," and Lázaro has awakened from his "childlike simplicity." In some systems the wine may be the blood of Christ, but not here; bread is to eat and wine is to drink, and their symbolic resonance is either parodied or nonexistent. This little tale is pregnant with things, things that are vividly and unforgettably present in the text: bread, wine, a chest, a bed, a black sausage, a stone statue. These things can be seen, touched, and smelled; the child with open eyes is quick to grant priority to these items because, otherwise, one might smash one's head against them. Some things, however, cannot be seen, touched, or smelled. God, honor, virtue, friendship, and love are singularly immaterial items. The person who sees only what is in front of him cannot see those other things; they cannot be physically *seen* at all. But maturation in this text means a reverence for matter and a disregard for anything else; Lazarillo's education consists in a rigorous and systematic denial of the symbolic or the transcendent. Just as everything of value can be seen, touched, or smelled, so too can it be bought or sold. The world is a marketplace, and there is nothing which cannot be exchanged. Thus we see why the poignant scene with the *escudero* cannot

bear fruit; to feel for another and to seek to fill up another testifies to an order of experience that is properly transcendent,
for it goes beyond one's own animal needs. But the logic and
lesson of this story is not to go from matter to spirit, but from
spirit to matter, from relationship with the Squire to accomplice for the Pardoner. Hunger yielded to generosity with
the Squire; the Pardoner can sell you Grace.

Much has been written about the unevenness of the last
four chapters, and even those who defend and justify their
place in the narrative do so apologetically. Raymond Willis
has convincingly argued for the artistic necessity of these last
chapters,[3] but I think one must go the whole route and insist
that Lazarillo's virtual disappearance from the narrative, his
shift from subject to witness and then false witness, is the fullest embodiment of the novel's meaning: Lazarillo, as moral
agent, dies, because the moral world has gone out of business.
The con-game world of the Pardoner and the Constable beckons already to the pyrotechnics instituted by the King and the
Duke while a helpless Huckleberry Finn watches on; it is the
fullest picture of the materialist world, the ultimate marketplace being the church, where salvation is bartered. Lázaro is
no longer hungry, and we seem to have come a long way
from wine jugs and bread chests, but the stage is merely larger
and the show is actually the same. Except that Lázaro is no
longer center-stage, but rather off to the side, conning us
somewhat like what the Pardoner and Constable are doing. In
the first three chapters Lázaro had given us *his* experience, of
hunger and of bizarre masters, that "complete picture of me"
which is the hallmark of the self in literature. One's experience is not merely in front of one's eyes, however, and some
degree of consciousness is necessary if one's experience is to
be narrated. In chapters four through seven, the inner view is
dropped, because it can no longer be afforded. The funeral
procession, so forcefully and comically presented as intended
for Lázaro himself in the third chapter, *is* in fact intended for
Lázaro: it heralds his forthcoming death as ethical consciousness.

[3] Raymond S. Willis, "Lazarillo and the pardoner," *Hispanic Review*, XXVII
(1959), *passim*.

The final chapter of the text concludes Lázaro's growth;
gone are the days of hunger and obscurity:

> I work in God's service—and yours, too [*vuestra merced*, to
> whom the story is being "told"]. What I do is announce the
> wines that are being sold around the city. Then, too, I call
> out at auctions and whenever anything is lost. And I go
> along with the people who are suffering for righteousness'
> sake and call out their crimes. I'm a town crier, to put it
> plainly. (p. 95)[14]

Lázaro has gone public. Américo Castro has suggested that
Lazarillo de Tormes is essentially the first modern novel because it gives us, as no preceding fiction does, "the illusion of
observing human life directly, without any intermediary, of
being invited to enter the individual's inner consciousness and
to contemplate his actions from that viewpoint."[4] How true
is this claim? That inner consciousness is the signature of the
self, and that "complete picture of me" which the prologue
promises would be inadequate without it. Such presence and
self-awareness are presented from the outset as Lázaro's cardinal virtue:

> I remember one time when my black stepfather was play-
> ing with the little fellow [Lázaro's brother], the child no-
> ticed that my mother and I were white but that my step-
> father wasn't, and he got scared. He ran to my mother and
> pointed his finger at him and said, "Mama, it's the bogey-
> man!" And my stepfather laughed: "You little son-of-a-
> bitch!"
> Even though I was still a young boy, I thought about the
> word my little brother had used, and I said to myself: How
> many people there must be in the world who run away
> from others when they don't see themselves. (p. 6)[15]

Lazarillo de Tormes records precisely the birth and death of
such vision. After the experience with the Squire, Lázaro no
longer sees himself, and, consequently, the reader can no
longer see in him. The hunger has finally been glutted, but the

---

[4] Américo Castro, Introduction to *La Vida de Lazarillo de Tormes*, ed.
Everett W. Hesse and Harry F. Williams (Madison, 1948).

inner voice is silenced. What remains is the auction. Life is a question of the right exchange. The child innocently told us, at the outset, that he liked his black stepfather better once he realized that he brought bread and meat and firewood. His mother completes the exchange: "So with his visits and the relationship going, right along, it happened that my mother gave me a pretty little black baby . . ." (p. 6).[16] The parity of the barter—a pretty black baby in exchange for food and warmth—is the same at the close of the text; Lázaro marries the Archpriest's "maid," and the deal is a good one:

> . . . besides the fact that she's a good woman, and she's hardworking and helpful, through my lord, the archpriest, I have all the help and favors I need. During the year he always gives her a few good-sized sacks of wheat, meat on the holidays, a couple loaves of bread sometimes, and his socks after he's through with them. He had us rent a little house right next to his, and on Sundays and almost every holiday we eat at his place. (p. 98)[17]

The towncrier lies to us about his private life, although the whole town knows the nature of their *ménage à trois*: "So, right up to today we've never said another word about the affair. In fact, when I see that someone wants to even start talking about it, I cut him short, and I tell him: 'Look, if you're my friend, don't tell me something that will make me mad because anyone who does that isn't my friend at all' " (p. 99).[18]

The exposure afforded to us through literature is over. Something crucial is happening here: the rewards of consciousness and language are snuffed out by material gain. Lázaro is the most primitive and successful character in my study, for he alone is content with such success. Already Pablos and Moll will sense that selfhood entails maintaining consciousness as well as riches; Lázaro's materialist trajectory will be quite simply turned on its head in the project of Rousseau: there the life itself will be eclipsed by its verbal rendition. And the result may well appear as monstrously imbalanced as it does here. The materialist education is over for Lazarillo. The self is abandoned, because its price is too high;

to honor its dictates of consciousness and spirit is to look inward rather than in front of you. Lazarillo has forgotten neither his hunger nor the statue. He is one of the most successful traders in Toledo: and people will not buy what they cannot see.

The Making of a Skin-Artist: *La Vida del Buscón*

Quevedo's *La Vida del Buscón* is a filthy book. It takes the materialist premise in *Lazarillo de Tormes* to its logical conclusion: spirit and transcendence not only yield to matter, but they are reduced to the lowest animal common denominator: excrement. The prominence of defecation, spitting, vomiting, and, of course, eating (up to, and even including one's own kind) makes the flesh and its appetites and frailties loom large in this text, and many find it too revolting to be taken seriously.[1] Yet, Quevedo's obsession with scatological phenomena is nonetheless the obsession of a poet, and it is clear that even the most repugnant scenes are doing double duty. What is the meaning of all the filth?

The boy Pablos' first encounter with "the lower elements" occurs as he is prancing on a horse, decked out in all finery, playing the role of the boy-king (*rey de gallos*) at Carnival time; things begin to look bad when the mangy horse steals a cabbage, and the vegetable women start hurling carrots and turnips at the poor king: "When I saw it was a turnip battle, not a cavalry charge, I got down; but they gave my poor horse such a clout that it reared up and fell down and brought me down with it into a pile of (excuse me) shit" (pp. 20-91).[2] Falling into shit is both a traumatic and a symbolic experience. Other episodes include a forced enema where the

---

[1] See, especially, the reading of M. Mohlo, in *Romans picaresques espagnols* (Paris: Edition de la Pleiade, 1968), LXXXIII-CIV.

[2] *Two Spanish Picaresque Novels*, tr. Michael Alpert (Penguin Classics, 1969), pp. 90-91. Subsequent translated quotations are drawn from Alpert and will be noted in the text. Alpert has freely translated the Spanish "Yo, viendo que era batalla nabal, y que no se habia de hacer a caballo, quise apearme" to create the antithesis between turnip battle and cavalry charge, but he is true to Quevedo's spirit in doing so.

boy unloads his insides on the face of the person giving it to
him (shades of Lazarillo!); a seemingly gratuitous trick played
on an old man wherein his hoarded candy box is emptied,
filled with sticks and stones and finally beshat; a gruesome
spitting sequence where the boy is so barraged by missiles of
phlegm that he is left "like an old man's spittoon" (p. 107);[3]
a night spent in jail, where the chamber pot is placed just behind Pablos' bed, and the tempestuous noises and smells (at-
tributed to both diarrhoea and constipation) keep him up all
night. The sequence which completes the pattern suggested
by the boy-king falling into shit, however, revolves around
the boy's university initiation. After being bespat and berated,
he is told by his master, in terms strongly reminiscent of Lazarillo's awakening: "Pablos, you've got to wake up. Watch
out for yourself. You know your father and mother can't do
it for you" (p. 108).[2] That night, when the boy goes to sleep,
we read "I pretended I was with my father and my brothers"
(p. 109);[3] sleep does not last long, however, for Pablos is
awakened by such a whipping that he hides under the bed,
and while he is there, "the bastard who slept next to me got
into my bed, crapped in it and covered the mess up" (p. 109).[4]
The boy returns to bed, and he falls into a tortured sleep: "I
twisted and turned while I was dreaming, so when I woke up
I was smothered in shit" (p. 109).[5] I think we can leave the
child in his dilemma and begin to assess what Quevedo is saying so brutally: the chivalric world is over, and turnip battles
replace cavalry charges; candy sweets, if you hoard them, are
likely to be dung-covered; the new student who wants to
communicate with the regulars at the University may use *his*
mouth for speaking, but they will use theirs for hurling gobs
of spit and phlegm; jail not only houses the lower elements,
but it stages a fecal performance of those elements; the child
who is "on his own" is safe nowhere, especially not in bed,
and the vulnerability of sleep and dreams—where memories
of the family poignantly return—betrays you to a second skin
of shit. This is materialism and pessimism with a vengeance.

There is still hunger, for it is a kind of staple item in the

[3] This splendid phrase is strictly Michael Alpert's doing; there is no Spanish
equivalent.

picaresque, a constant reminder that the belly has its own needs. But whereas the bread and the wine become, in *Lazarillo*, so preciously real and earthly that all transcendence disappears, hunger exists somewhat differently in the *Buscón*. Lázaro at least makes an even barter: a wife for food; Pablos, in his gluttony (as in his enema), is an eating machine run wild, and food and hunger become mere components of a mechanical operation ranging from ingestion through defecation and ending in decomposition:

> "Stuff" is the word, because I made a bigger hole in the gherkins than a bullet does in a jerkin! Up came the stew which I bolted down in a couple of mouthfuls. I didn't have anything against it but I was in such a hurry that I didn't feel sure of it even when I had it in my mouth. I swear by God that the old cemetery in Valladolid that can break down a body in twenty-four hours couldn't have got rid of a whole family's food for a day as fast as I did. It went as quick as an express letter. (pp. 163-164)[6]

This odd passage connotes some of the metamorphic frenzy of the novel. Change occurs at every level here: disguise, decomposition, ultimately the transformation of matter into language (the express letter). We also notice Quevedo's obsession with dehumanizing, mechanical processes themselves, a powerful reminder that the dynamics of metaphor and metamorphosis (so much a part of Quevedo's elaborate Baroque style) achieve an unsettling kind of parity, a stylistic "no man's land" wherein anything may become anything else. The body is a system that takes in and puts out, and people are no more than their bodies. What place can the soul possibly have within such a frame?

Perhaps the fullest vision of such a world is given in the scene at the uncle's feast. The relation between human beings and animals, the possible ways of filling oneself full, and the role of speech and thought in articulating that relationship, are vividly shown:

> Up came the food on a few chipped old plates and in broken jugs and pots. . . . They sat down to eat, with the beggar at the head of the table and the others all over the place.

. . . The mulatto noisily slurped down three glasses of red wine and the pig-keeper snatched the jug from me and drank more than all of us. . . . Five four-*real* pies came up. They took off the pastry and, holy-water sprinkler in hand, they all said a prayer and a *Requiem Aeternam* for the soul of the person to whom the meat in the pies had belonged originally.

"You remember, my boy," said my uncle, "what I wrote to you about your father."

I remembered.

They ate, but I was satisfied with the base of the pastry and that's the only part I eat now. In fact, whenever I eat pies I say a Hail Mary for the soul which once belonged to the meat in it.

They refilled two jugs time and time again and the mulatto and the beggar drank so much that when a plate of sausages like black men's fingers was brought up they asked why they were having stewed tubes of gunpowder. My uncle was so drunk that he stretched his arm out, took one, and said in a hoarse, cracked voice, with one eye half shut and the other swimming in wine:

"My boy, by the Host that God created in his likeness and image, I've never had better red meat in my life."

Then I saw the mulatto stretch out his arm, take the salt, and say:

"This soup is very hot."

And the pig-keeper took a fistful of salt, shoved the lot in his mouth, and said:

"This'll give me a thirst."

I began to laugh through my shame and anger. Then came soup, and the beggar picked up a bowl of it in both hands, saying:

"Cleanliness is next to Godliness."

Then he put the bowl to his cheek, poured it out, scalded himself and got himself into a filthy state from head to toe. When he saw the state he was in he stood up and, as his head was whirling, he steadied himself against the table, which was on wheels, overturned it, and messed up the others. Then he said that the pig-keeper had pushed him.

When the pigman saw the beggar coming for him, he stood up and cracked him on the head with his bone horn. They came to blows and in a clinch the beggar bit him on the cheek. What with his excitement and rage, the pig-keeper vomited everything he had eaten into the beggar's face. My uncle, who was more sober, asked why there were so many priests in his house. Seeing that things were getting noisier, I calmed them down, separated them and picked up the mulatto, who was weeping noisily. I laid my uncle down on his bed, but not before he had bowed to a wooden candlestick, thinking it was one of his guests. (pp. 143-145)[7]

The cannibalism implicit in this scene (the boy eating his dead father in the form of a paté) is so logical that it is not even shocking. The description of the "men" eating is bestial, and the food they eat is human figuratively as well as literally ("a plate of sausages like black men's fingers"). These characters, swilling their food and wine, overturning tables, quite naturally hit each other with bone horns and bite one another. Their perceptions are not merely blurred, but transformed, and we see a world of metamorphic, tumbling figures: the sausages look like black men's fingers, but also like tubes of gunpowder and even red meat to the uncle. The mulatto takes salt and calls it soup. The uncle ceremoniously bows to a wooden candlestick. There is a kind of formal anarchy here, a parity of names and things, an egalitarian liberation wherein the "humans" are mere elements of the composition, deprived of their centrality and their control. Amid this carnival and chaos, one thing remains constant, poised and hence grotesque: language. The human meat pies are gobbled up, but not without a prayer for the soul that once lived there. The sausage is called red meat "by the Host that God created in his likeness and image"; the beggar, pouring hot soup all over himself, nicely articulates: "Cleanliness is next to Godliness." Each of these speeches testifies to a spiritual realm behind the material world, but the scene itself is a denial of that realm. Where can "soul" exist among such creatures? Mouths more naturally hurl phlegm or bite necks than say prayer or express

reverence; the lip-service to the Godhead is just that: lip-service. And if soul is just a myth, a spurious window-dressing,
then the human being is only his body, and that body is more
genuinely red meat than the sausage the uncle mistakes for it.
So, the human meat pies are just meat pies. And, for Pablos
to eat his father would be most appropriate in this animal
kingdom.

Pablos refuses to go that far, but the carnality at the basis of
the human enterprise is indelibly depicted. On the way to his
uncle's, Pablos had met with a strange assortment of figures,
among them a ridiculous old priest-poet who had written a
play titled *Noah's Ark*:

> It was full of cocks, mice, donkeys, vixens and wild boar,
> just like Aesop's fables. I praised its plan and the language
> and he replied:
>
> "It's all my own work. Nobody else in the world has
> done anything like it, and novelty is the most important
> thing. If I can get it acted, it'll be famous."
>
> "How can it be put on," I asked, "if the parts are all ani-
> mals and they can't speak?"
>
> "That's the trouble. If it weren't for that it would be a
> marvelous thing. But I think I'll do it all with parrots,
> thrushes, and talking magpies, and I'll put monkeys in to
> do the funny turns between the acts." (p. 131)[8]

Pablos has a good laugh on the old man, but the reader must
surely recognize that *Noah's Ark* can easily be put on without
recourse to parrots and thrushes and magpies and monkeys;
Pablos and his fellows will do quite nicely, and they can even
quote chapter and verse while on their animal stage.

Filthy and bestial though it is, *La Vida del Buscón* is more
than pure matter. Its main character has extraordinary verbal
resources, wit and cunning, a delight in punning and in language itself, all of which confer a strangely cerebral tone to
the novel. Are we to relegate these characteristics to Quevedo
himself while condemning his protagonist as a brute? To do
so would be to overlook the dialectic between words and
things, the crucial connection between language and reality,
which the text everywhere evidences. It is a dialectic that the

boy himself learns early on. Spitzer, in his masterful study of Quevedo's style, has dealt at length with the autonomous, non-referential language that Quevedo uses (e.g., the description of Doctor Goat), and he has asserted that the text creates its internal world, what we today would call a world of *signifiants*: "Establishing between words relationships that contradict both reality and logic, creating, as it were, an 'intralinguistic' reality limited exclusively to the realm of language (thus an irreality from the point of view of the world beyond language), word play is perfectly appropriate to bring about deceiving appearances and also to undeceive."[4] Spitzer enlists Quevedo's verbal tricks and games in the service of the *desengaño* so characteristic of Spanish Baroque literature.

One can equally argue, however, that Pablos *learns* the style that Quevedo lends to him, that Pablos, as a character, needs and enjoys the verbal resources with which he is endowed. The creative use of language is an alternative to both shit and hunger, and Pablos needs all the help he can get. The famous scenes at the boarding school run by the *licenciado* Cabra illustrate such a need. Pablos' motto might well be: when starving, pun: "Then our masters ate an infinite meal, by which I mean it had no beginning and no end" (p. 94),[9] or "They had supper, we had supper; in fact nobody had supper" (p. 96).[10] There is an insistent relationship in this book between words and eating. We have already seen that mouths can bite and spit as well as open to utter speech; but, in some cases, it appears that we can truly eat our words: "I had to read out the first declension nominatives aloud to the others. I breakfasted on half of them, swallowing the words" (p. 97).[11] When the two boys are brought home, half dead of starvation, people are counseled not to speak in their room, "because every word echoed in our hollow stomachs" (p. 100).[12] We are obviously dealing here with a sophisticated Baroque language that delights in word play, but, beyond that, I think Quevedo is trying to show the *value* of gratuitous, generative language. Speech is for free, and it remains a priceless resource for even

[4] *Leo Spitzer, L'Art de Quevedo dans le Buscon* (Paris: Ediciones hispanoamericanas, 1972), translation of *Zur Kunst Quevedos in seinem Buscón*.

the most deprived *pícaro*. Pablos receives no food, but he set-
tles for the gratifications of thought and language. To fill oneself full with language is a peculiarly human talent (or folly),
and it "bespeaks" a kind of human achievement in a world
where other achievements are denied. If we ascribe the wit entirely to Quevedo, we impoverish the novel and reduce the
character to a vehicle.

Consider, for example, Pablos' description of his father's
leaving prison: "he left prison in such a proud state that he
went out with two hundred stripes on his body but not a single one gave him any rank" (p. 85).[13] In the Spanish a pun is
made to the detriment of cardinals, and most critics read the
passage in such a satirical light.[5] I would suggest that this kind
of language does, in fact, dignify the father (whose courage
and bearing always outlast the ironic presentation), that the
father can become, through the language of the boy—and
only through it—a kind of prince. Pablos' father is a prince in
much the same way that we have emperors of ice cream: the
need for royalty is deeper than the value of the kingdom, and
"ice cream" and "stripes" may tarnish or mock, but they cannot erase the title which language has fixed. Word play is always desperate play, a mode of assertion and affirmation by
linguistic means alone, a way of *saying* "yes" when that realm
of referents, matter and hunger, says "no."

Yet, verbal creation is not deified in this novel, because it is
as susceptible to excess and abuse as is the body. When Pablos
leaves Segovia and his master Don Diego for a new life, he
meets up with a gallery of grotesques. Each is a literalist, one
who takes or mistakes the word for the deed. There is a crack-
pot who would assist the King in capturing Ostend by simply
sucking up the sea with sponges; another is an academic
swordsman mouthing gibberish about circumference, quil-
lons, dividers, spirals, and angles, but who cannot even dis-
mount a horse, much less actually fence. Quevedo enjoys

[5] Here is one of the many instances where Alpert cannot possibly keep pace
with Quevedo; the fine "stripes" and "rank" capture the irony of punishment
and stature, but Quevedo has done still more by referring to the Church as
well: ". . . salio de la carcel con tanto honra, que le acompañaron doscientos
cardenales, sino que a ninguno llamaban eminencia."

having others misunderstand him by thinking that "angles" can be eaten and roasted, that "obtuse" and "angle" are people they have not met. Still another is the poet who thinks that Corpus Christi is the name of a saint, and a soldier who tries to pass a plague-scar for an honorable military wound and who gets his desserts when his "papers" are construed as toilet paper. Aside from pretense and sham, these characters also exhibit the abyss between language and reality, the comedy of making reality out of language alone.

I think that the most suggestive instance of this *décalage* appears in the proclamation against poets which Pablos reads to the old priest. Pablos proclaims that the bundles of songs and sonnets not good enough for wrapping paper should go straight to the lavatory (thereby reminding us that words are a step away from shit). He also evokes a kind of cosmic upheaval caused by confusing the realm of thought and reality, by literalizing metaphor:

> "*Article Two*
> "Considering that this infernal sect condemned to perpetual punning, chewers up of words and upsetters of phrases, have infected women with the said disease of poetry, we declare ourselves quit of any wrong we have done them in return for what they did to us at the Creation. And as the World is now poor and in need, we order that all verses be burned, like old rags, to remove the gold, silver and pearls, because most verses make their beloveds of all metals." (pp. 133-134)[14]

Along with the telling metaphor of poetry as venereal disease, we have a precise description of Quevedo's own style, a characteristic denigration (let the poets be silent) that is actually a magnificent homage (the poets have created their own world and have absconded with all the precious stones). There is a rampant confusion of realms here, an ironic recognition that language alone may be the source of beauty. There is something poignant, perhaps beyond irony, in the description of "our" impoverished world that is now "poor and in need." Quevedo seems to be depicting, through his images of venereal disease, rags, and toilets, the very world of the picaresque novel, one usually lacking in poetry and splendor. In *La Vida del Buscón* we have a sordid world that is *depicted* with magnificence (precisely what he says he is going to do in the preface), but we also have countless examples of how the world of language is a world of deception.

Magnificence in this world, somewhat like that of the *Quijote*, is to be found only in make-believe and illusion. Whereas Cervantes' character lives out his visions, those of Quevedo hawk theirs. Consider the case of one Magazo:

> he'd been a soldier, in a play, and fought the Moors, in a dance. When he spoke to men who had been in Flanders he said he'd been in China, and he told the China veterans he'd been in Flanders. He was trying to form a regiment, but spent most of the time killing his fleas. He let drop the names of several castles but he'd hardly seen one, even on coins. He made a big thing about honoring the memory of Don Juan, the victor of Lepanto, and I often heard him say that Luis Quijada was an honorable friend. He was always on about Turks, galleons and captains, but he got it all from a few songs about them. He didn't know a single thing about the sea; the only naval thing he knew was navel oranges. . . . (pp. 165-166)[15]

Here is the colonizing and counterfeiting imagination at work, vigorously substituting nominal achievements for real ones, using language to annex experience. The first line has the brilliance and symmetry of poetry, and its balance is a measure of Quevedo's dualism: "he'd been a soldier, *in a play*, and fought the Moors, *in a dance*." Navel oranges may be counterfeit naval battles, but they are surely the coin of the realm, accessible to commoners as well as to officers, earned by language alone. This is a sham, but it is also a kind of imaginative exploitation. We see, likewise, the insistent algebra of the novel: can the world of experience be duplicated or equated with the performance of the artist?

In addition to verbal gamesmanship, Quevedo delights in making strange, in taking the human element out of the spectacle. Occasionally Pablos views his fellows with the lenses,

not of a poet, but of a Martian, one who describes wholly alien antics; the suitors of the church are depicted *figurally*, and
their spectacle of love becomes a freak show:

> The place was crawling with worshippers. I used to edge in
> where I could and it was quite a sight to see the different
> postures adopted by the lovers. Some stared without blink-
> ing, others clutched their swords in one hand and their ro-
> saries in the other and stood like graveyard statues. Others
> said nothing but stood there with their mouths open like
> begging women, showing their guts to their beloved
> through their throats. Others held the wall up but pushed
> the bricks out of place as they did so. Some walked up and
> down like mustangs showing off their virile bearing. Oth-
> ers with their *billets-doux* in their hands looked like hunters
> luring on their falcons with pieces of meat. . . . But up
> above, where the nuns were, there was also a sight worth
> seeing, as their place was a little tower full of slits and a wall
> so full of holes that it looked like a sieve or a pomander-
> box. The holes were like eyelets through which to peep.
> Here was an arm or leg, there a hand and there a foot. Here
> there were extremities, heads, mouths. There weren't any
> brains, though. The other side was like a pedlar's pack, here
> a rosary, there a handkerchief, there a glove, here a green
> ribbon. Some of the nuns talked loudly, others coughed.
> Some made signs with their hats as if they were scaring
> away spiders with the whooshing sound. (p. 207)[16]

Like "angles" for eating, words stand alone in this passage,
derealizing the suitors. We are reminded, too, of the circus at
the uncle's feast: in both cases, we perceive fragmented, dis-
connected parts of bodies and grotesque operations, and all
sense of human integrity or control is absent.

The finest example of "people" relinquishing their human
shape to become something else occurs in the description of
the gentlemen thieves preparing for the day:

> . . . they all got needles and thread and put a few stitches
> into the tears in their clothes. One of them got himself into

an L shape to darn under his arm. Another on his knees looked like a figure 5: he was giving first aid to his stockings. Another stuck his head between his legs and doubled himself up to repair a hole in his crotch. Even Bosch's twisted postures don't compare with what I saw. (p. 159)[17]

Spitzer has eloquently described the implicit alienation in Quevedo's Baroque style, suggesting that wit and conceit in language always mirror a culture that has become problematic to itself. The vision of the thieves doing their morning routine is entirely *formal* and stylized. There is a kind of aesthetic tyranny at work here, born of distance and respectful of surfaces alone. Intentionality and consciousness and immediacy constitute the individual's own sense of his behavior (this is why mirrors and photographs are unsettling) but they are not visible; for the most part, observers grant that interiority, grant it without even realizing it, and thus the human form looks "natural" rather than grotesque. But Quevedo achieves a strictly aesthetic vision here, a hint already of the non-anthropocentrism which fully flourishes only in the 20th century with Sartre and later writers. Once the "naturalness" of objects and people has been seen through, reality becomes much more a *made*, rather than a *given*, thing. Quevedo's book is filled with image-spawners and reality-makers, and his non-anthropocentric vision functions as a stimulus for creativity. His characters remake the world; their artifice is their job.

The gentlemen thieves represent, I believe, a turning point in Pablos' education. Until his joining them, Pablos has customarily evoked his experience in terms of shame or derision. He has already begun to demonstrate his prowess as troublemaker, but only now does he find a proper setting. Along with their skills and their code, the thieves instill in him something we might call "professional pride." Thus far in this study I have been emphasizing the virtually schizophrenic split between mind and matter which Pablos confronts, a split that is intensified by the excesses in each camp. But what about Pablos himself? He has left home, he has left his master, in search of something. Spitzer suggests that he is the

"self-made man," while Parker argues that he seeks vengeance because of the social inferiority of his background.[6] What
is certain is that the gentlemen thieves are a group, and Pablos
finds among them a kind of home. They live together according to certain rules and even have a kind of morality. They
cut each other's hair and stitch each other's clothes. "Extras"
which are confiscated are donated to the public good. They
do not defecate on Pablos in bed, but rather "we were as close
together in bed as tools in a box" (p. 158);[18] when Pablos
grumbles for food, the answer may be ironic, but it also
smacks of belief: "You haven't much faith in our religion and
way of life. God provides for crows and ravens and even public notaries, so do you think He'll let skinny devils like us
down? You haven't got much guts" (p. 161).[19] God does provide for them, for a while at least, and partially because they
are part of a larger network of down-and-outers. This collective has both its code and its pride: one of the "brothers" who
tries to con them out of food is punished because "he was pretending to beg for others as if he were ashamed of doing it for
himself" (p. 166).[20]

This community is also one of artists, in the sense that they
have perfected their particular techniques to a fine point. We
are far from the clowns who want to soak up the sea in a
sponge; these are serious craftsmen with an equally serious
goal—to improve Nature:

> Our sworn enemy is the sun because it shows up all the
> darns, stitches and rags. So in the morning we stand in its
> full glare with our legs open and see the shadows of the
> tears and tatters between our legs and we give our breeches
> a trim with a pair of scissors. As it's always the crotch that

[6] A. A. Parker, *Literature and the Delinquent* (Edinburgh, 1967). Parker's
reading of the Spanish picaresque tradition, although much disputed by many
Hispanists because of its religious interpretation, is nonetheless a landmark
study for comparatists; it essentially calls the bluff of those who blithely assert that the "novel" began, say, with *La Princesse de Clèves* or with the work
of Defoe. Parker implies that the Spanish picaresque novel is the unacknowledged spiritual father of European fiction, and he does much to redress our
frequently lopsided sense of early fiction with its conventional emphasis on
England and France.

wears badly we take bits off the back to fill up the front and
sometimes our arses are so cut about that they're left bare:
our cloaks cover them but we have to watch ourselves carefully on windy days, or on a lighted staircase, or when riding. (p. 152)[21]

The clothes they wear have a genealogical history of their
own, and their dexterity in "alterations" is awesome. Their
religion is one of conventions, i.e., carefully maintained, artfully sustained appearances; to seem well fed and well heeled
while being destitute. Their code may be an empty one, but
it is refined rather than bestial: "We have to ride a horse once
a month, even if it's only a little donkey, and it's got to be in
full view of everybody in the street. And once a year we've
got to ride in a coach, even if it's only on the boot or the
back" (p. 153).[22] Their unavowed "article" of belief is to
cover the body, but there always seems to be a bit more body
present than clothing to cover it. Nature, like the sun, is stub-
born and persistent. This imbalance challenges their ingenuity, and we see elaborate, even brilliant, examples of sham
fashion parades: bare asses covered by cloaks, turned up col-
lars to hide neckbands, holes in coats covered by capes. If language is an alternative to matter, these itinerant artists intro-
duce the crucial metaphors of sewing and stitching as means
of transformation.

Transforming cloth is a small step from transforming people, and that too can be learned. These gentlemen have "bor-
rowed" the few items they dispose of, and are hence tracked
by people claiming payment; the solution: "In order not to be
recognized he undid his hair which he wore tied behind his
head and let it fall over his ears. That way he looked like a
Holy Week penitent, halfway between Jesus Christ and a
long-haired fop. He stuck a patch on his eye and started jab-
bering away at me in Italian. He had time to do all this before
we came up close to the other man" (p. 161).[23] Such wiles are
not to be dismissed lightly, for they make life an endless repertory and open up considerable maneuvering room for art-
ist-conmen. The counterfeiter has a dizzying array of choices,
ranging all through history and culture. To be "oneself" is to

be in debt: to become many and speak many tongues (rather than sincerely) is to acquire considerable estate. This freedom is, of course, countered by a loss of authenticity: Pablos realizes that "he was a gentleman who was all rented" (p. 161),[24] but he also sees that the rent need not be paid.

Pablos' final reaction in the community of gentlemen thieves is a complex and crucial one: he accepts their art and rejects their community. We will see that he also fails to acquire their pride. Ever the loner, Pablos abandons them in jail and goes on to better things. But, he leaves, changed. The artistic education is to bear fruit; the artist is the master of the disguises, the man who rivals Nature herself. Friendless now, Pablos the artist begins to exhibit some curious character traits. He tries twice to con his way into a profitable marriage, and the results are disastrous each time. In the first instance, Pablos uses his new skills to parade as a wealthy businessman; he also informs the girl's family that he knows magic spells, is a magician, and "could make the house appear to sink into the ground or burst into flames . . ." (p. 178).[25] The appeal to magic is a fascinating and telling one, for it leads us deviously but inexorably back to the life he has apparently abandoned. At the outset of his story, Pablos described his mother as a magician:

> She was rumored to be able to repair girls' lost virginities, bring back hair and make white hair turn black again. Some people said she could arrange any pleasure; others called her a satisfier of unsatisfied desires . . . (p. 86).[26]

The housekeeper at the University has the exact same talents ("she could overcome people's will and bring lovers together" [p. 114])[27] and when Pablos himself is later undone (literally), a final woman of magic, Something de la Guia, pops up beside his bed to put him back together again, even though "her real specialty was repairing virgins and patching up young girls" (p. 195).[28] These three women, all mother figures, have the same attributes: they can improve Nature and remake bodies. These women are vivacious and mysterious. Their magic is a way to halt time, to coerce others, to

erase experience (repairing virgins). Theirs is the potency for
which Pablos yearns, the true gift of transformation, rather
than the sham of disguise. But this is not to be. No less than
the Quijote's encounter with windmills, Pablos must, because
he is in a *novel*, confront contingency and time. The deliciously autonomous realms of madness, consciousness, art,
and language do not take over in this text. Pablos seeks to em-
ulate the ladies of magic, but Quevedo knows that life cannot
be stopped. That is why this book is anything but episodic (or
timeless): each adventure relentlessly follows the past one and
leads to the next one, usurping a little more of Pablos' life,
turning him a bit more into an article of clothing. It is as if
there were two hourglasses, containing his soul in one and his
life in the other, and Quevedo allows the soul to empty while
narrating the adventures. Magic belongs in romances, not in
novels.

Whereas it is suggested that Something de la Guia could fly,
Pablos cannot. He falls off the roof when pretending to be a
businessman, and he is thrashed and humiliated in front of the
girl's eyes while she confidently awaits the magical happy
ending. She thinks he is acting when he is being beaten, and,
given his profession as deceiver, that is one of the deepest
ironies of the novel. After failing once, Pablos decides to try
again, aiming still higher: he courts a young noble woman
and meets, this time, his true nemesis. If the claim to magic
takes us back to the mother, Pablos' adventure as Don Felipe
Tristan leads him to his childhood friend and early master, the
"genuine" aristocrat Don Diego. Some critics have com-
plained that this meeting is hopelessly coincidental and improbable, but I would argue that Pablos' meeting with Don
Diego constitutes the collision for which the whole novel has
been preparing: will Don Diego recognize his childhood servant? It is a big question, for all of Pablos' education has been
in the way of disguise, deceit, and repudiation of the past.
What happens, of course, is that the actor bungles his part,
even to the extent of falling off his horse, an unmistakable repeat of the childhood boy-king episode. Pablos is not only
recognized, he is deceived and tricked in turn. Having ever
stolen or "rented" bits and pieces of finery, Pablos is actually

permitted to don a "real" aristocratic cloak, and this vestmental triumph is the sign for his undoing: wearing "the real thing," he is beaten up and slashed from ear to ear, his face cut in half.

One expects the novel to end at this juncture. The message is clear: there is no magic; one cannot disguise oneself forever; one cannot escape childhood; one is, ultimately, recognizable. This would make a grim but coherent story.

Quevedo has gone beyond that, and, in so doing, has presented something still more disturbing. Pablos does not die. He does not stop practicing his trade. He is not brought back to his origins. The terrible thing in *La Vida del Buscón* is that he survives. He survives exactly as his experience has taught him to survive: a body and some clothes. His face is cut in half: well, it can be sewn back together. All you need is a barber, not a magician. It is not easy to destroy a body, and the characters in this story are wholly bodies. We have the young girl whom he woos, a person described entirely in terms of her hands (see Alpert, p. 178; *Buscón*, pp. 194-195); there is the fellow in prison called the Giant who is guilty of posterior crimes: "we hated and feared him so much that we all wore protectors around our arses like dog-collars, and nobody dared fart in case they reminded him where their backsides were" (p. 173);[29] he is accompanied by Robledo, who had "so many razor-slashes on his face that if you took the stitches away there wouldn't be anything left. He only had half his share of ears. His nose had been split and put together again, but it hadn't been made as well as the knife that had done the first job" (p. 173).[30] The gentlemen thieves crafted their clothes so as to cover their bodies, but Pablos has gone beyond their art and has found that skin can be sewn and resewn as easily as cloth. Not only can skin be sewn, it can be created; notice the beggars' king: "He had a huge false hernia and used to tie a rope tight around his upper arm so that it looked as though his hand was all swollen up, as well as paralysed and inflamed at the same time" (p. 199).[31] The finest flower among the flesh artists, however, is Mata, who has changed his name to Matorral and who enjoys changing the shape of those he meets, a kind of on-the-spot metamorphosis:

He dealt in men's lives and bought and sold knifings, which
suited him well. He had samples on his face and calculated
the length and depth of the slashes he gave from the ones
he received.

"There's nobody as skilled," he used to say, "as a well-
cut man."

And he was right as his face was as seamed as a leather
jacket and he was a walking leather wine-skin. (p. 211)[32]

This is Pablos' world, a wholly corporeal one without a trace
of inwardness. Pablos has already bought and sold (kidnapped) young bodies (children); he is now ready for the final
step. He joins up with Matorral and his more aggressive and
active craftsmen; he gets completely drunk, has a skirmish
with the police in this mindless state, and, as he says, releases
"two souls from their evil bodies" (p. 213).[33] Unthinking and
unfeeling murderer perhaps, but, according to what we have
seen, those two bodies were doubtless soulless as well.

As the novel comes to a close, we realize that the vestmental code, like the fecal one and the aesthetic one, is dehumanizing and lethal. To view human beings as would-be shit or
meat, or as the letter L or the figure 5, or as a shiny cape and
half a pair of boots, or finally as so much skin which is just so
much leather—all of these visions involve the disappearance
of the soul, for they do not give it a place to be. These are the
laws that inform the career of the *Buscón*. Ever making his
world and his appearance, Pablos has, almost unbeknownst to
the narrative, been hemorrhaging spiritually. At the end of
the novel, hunted by the police, Pablos senses his void and
describes it poignantly—for it is the only language he truly
knows—as nudity: "We had a good time in the Cathedral because, at the smell of criminals on the run came plenty of
whores who stripped to cover our nakedness. One called Gra-
jales took a fancy to me and dressed me in her new finery" (p.
213).[34] Pablos can change his clothes just as he can "move his
dwelling," but he cannot change "his life or his ways" because there is no longer any fixed self to alter.

Yet, we are forced to recognize that survival and self-re-

newal engage the energies of the individual, even when there
is no soul or identity left. Quevedo has depicted the life force
as a *carnaval*, an unending sequence of guise and disguise
which flaunts our notions of morality and integrity. Ingenuity
comes to mean elasticity, indefinite, monstrous malleability.

Pablos, who delighted from earliest childhood (boy-king)
in trying "to be somebody," has finished the parade. *La Vida
del Buscón* is existential in a way beyond even the "delinquent" thesis suggested by Parker. It depicts a radical insuffi-
ciency of self, a need to define and assert oneself solely
through the eyes of others; and yet, there is something irresistible as well as desperate in Pablos' itinerary as literal self-
made man. Although there is finally no discernible self underneath the clothes or the skin, a human life has nonetheless
been narrated. Lazarillo ends up trying to con his readers, but
Pablos is, oddly enough, reliable and sincere in this respect. It
is as narrating and fictionalizing voice that Pablos achieves the
magic power that elsewhere eluded him. His brief success as
playwright, especially the episode where his speech about the
bear frightened and convinced the maid so completely that
she dropped the plates and ran out screaming, bears witness
to a special kind of prowess, an art of deception that surpasses
even that of the gentlemen thieves. Yet it is most significant
that Pablos' stint as playwright is a short one. Pablos *demonstrates* throughout the text a need for power or magic: the
plot, episodic as it is, is an itinerary of possible vocations. But
the freedoms afforded by language—and the living space
which literature itself can generate—are only glimpsed, not
sounded or plumbed. Not until *Tristram Shandy* will the novel
depict a character who fully enters the imaginative realm,
who uses literature as a way of beating life. Pablos, in his repertory of roles, only toys with art, and then passes it by.

But Quevedo knew that literature itself is the greatest con
game of all, because something is always being created out of
nothing. He even foresaw that he would have "free readers,"
readers who "profit" and take advantage of his work, just as
Pablos "acquired" pages walking down the street as members
of his own retinue. Despite Quevedo's harping, it is a very

lovely image of how much in life is free and communal and available, if one is enough of the artist and has the resources to take it or make it. That act of appropriation beautifully mirrors the reader's entry into this book. Pablos' soul may have been lost between the occasional outcries of shame and piety, on the one hand and the enacted private odyssey toward skin-artist, on the other, but the magical disappearance act is narrated and on record.

The Unknown Soldier: *Simplicissimus*

If cunning and intelligence emerge as the cardinal virtues of *Lazarillo* and the *Buscón*, our next text, Grimmelshausen's *Der aberteuerliche Simplicissimus*, begins by stressing the very unpicaresque qualities of naïveté and innocence. Throughout this long and rich novel, beyond Simplicius' childhood ignorance and well into his education, the value of simplicity is stressed, and *simpliciter* is significantly used as an adverb to describe the right kind of belief and behavior, an adverb closely related to the word *Teutsch*, with its implications of directness and forthrightness, even authenticity. Critics frequently refer to Grimmelshausen's own simple vigor, his aloofness from the fancy and fanciful Baroque writing establishment of his age in Germany, his reliance on folktales and the Spanish picaresque influences, his earthiness. These features of Grimmelshausen's art and background are, indeed, essential, and there is probably no writer in Europe to be compared with him on those grounds, with the possible exception of Rabelais a century earlier. But the *simplicity* of the text is a richer, more complex, item than has been realized. Simplicity and innocence are, in fiction, a *point of view*, as well as a character trait; and, as point of view, they establish the dominant tone of the novel and herald in Grimmelshausen's magnificent, awful world as no other perspective could. What Dostoevsky has done in *The Idiot* and Faulkner in the Benjy section of *The Sound and the Fury* is already present in this 17th-century narrative: the way of the world, seen through the eyes of innocence, is madness.

The madman and the fool are hardly new to literature. We need merely think of Erasmus, Falstaff, Panurge, and, of course, Don Quixote.[1] But *Simplicissimus* is the account of a self-in-the-world during the Thirty Years' War, so that madness and innocence tell us more about what the world is, what it does to a person, than about Simplicius as a character himself. He is, in his own words, a blank slate, and the novel is essentially the record that is made on that slate. The radical vision of innocence is not sustained throughout the novel, and, as the boy matures and understands, the events are recounted with less strangeness and trauma, until, at the end, even the supernatural elements are described matter-of-factly. One could say that the style has been educated, that it has learned to accept everything as possible. There is nothing left but an exit. It is that education which I would like to chart.

To speak of education at all in this novel is to fly in the face of much critical opinion. At first seen as hurdy-gurdy and Baroque, *Simplicissimus* was later adopted into the *Entwicklungsroman* family, a genealogy that begins (in Germany, where most critics speak of the genre) with *Parisfal* and then goes on to Goethe's *Wilhelm Meister* and its prolific 19th-century progeny right up to Mann's *Zauberberg*. However, this view of *Simplicissimus*, with its emphasis on the development of the central character, is fiercely repudiated by many critics, who see it as a distortion caused by imposing a historicist-individualist grid on a text from a prior age which does not know such distinctions. Moreover, Simplicissimus often seems a function, a link between episodes rather than a growing character; there is little inwardness and perhaps still less education. The emphasis seems to be on what James called, in a different context, the scenic dimension. Many years ago Melitta Gerhard suggested that the element of self-knowledge was a very small component of the work: "Despite all the value of self-knowledge, despite all the occasional backward glances of the hero and hints of the author, *Simplicissimus* remains, nonethe-

---

[1] For a classic study of madness in three major Renaissance texts, see Walter Kaiser, *Praisers of Folly: Erasmus, Rabelais, Shakespeare* (Cambridge, Harvard University Press, 1963).

less, primarily a vivid depiction of visible events, and the
stage on which the author displays to us the development of
his hero is not essentially the closet of the soul but rather the
arena of the outside world" (my translation).[2] More recent
critical thinking about Grimmelshausen investigates the complex planetary symbolism of his work, showing a coherent
structural principle that has little to do with character or psychology. How, then, can one talk about self?

Günter Rohrbach helps us begin to answer that question
with his important distinction between "figure" and "character"; Simplicissimus not merely *is* a figure, he is forced into
being only a figure: "Where life is experienced so frighten-
ingly as doom, where man knows himself to be completely
powerless, then man can understand his situation only as a *figure* in the great universe, where he is manipulated by forces
which go beyond his control" (my translation).[3] With little
inwardness, episodic rather than sequential or developmental,
a kind of outward-directed, impersonal blank sheet that gets
written on by life, such is Simplicissimus, and such is the
story of a self in the Thirty Years' War. Development, and
possibly even education, are luxury items, hothouse products
simply unavailable during the war, where the seesaw of life
and death, of creation and destruction, is operative every minute, everywhere. The setting is too mobile, too energized, for
the self to be stable; the child sees, in his dream, a rigorous,
well-nigh mechanical annihilation of human assertion:

> For gluttony and drunkenness, hunger and thirst, whoring
> and sodomy, gambling and dicing, murdering and being
> murdered, slaying and being slain, torturing and being tor-
> tured, pursuing and being pursued, frightening and being
> frightened, robbing and being robbed, looting and being
> looted, terrorizing and being terrorized, mortifying and
> being mortified, beating and being beaten; in short, nothing

[2] Melitta Gerhard, *Der deutsche Entwicklungsroman bis zu Goethes "Wilhelm
Meister"* (Halle, 1926), p. 159.
[3] Günter Rohrbach, *Figur und Charakter: Strukturuntersuchungen an Grimmels-
hausens "Simplicissimus"* (Bonn, 1959), p. 257.

but hurting and harming and being, in their turn, hurt and harmed, this was their whole purpose and existence. (p. 27)[1,4]

Even the syntax announces an imperious leveling process, all things done being then undone, nothing being left at the end. It is hard to imagine an education here. The human species is caught in a powerful system of forces (forces residing within itself but beyond its control), and the entire plot of this book reflects such an order: ups followed by downs and then ups, money stolen, lost and regained and relost, innocence of childhood followed by the force of youth and then the corruption of the body. Readers have long felt that there is a basic pattern in Simplicius' life, resembling a classical drama with its beginning, rise, and fall, but surely such an overview does not do justice to the local disturbances that are everywhere enacted. Fortuna does not bother to be coherent in the short run. We will see, in *Manon Lescaut*, that what goes by the name of Fate may well be a precise economic or social principle; but, here, there is nothing so cogent. Simplicissimus will not be undone because of any specifics, but by the general rule that all which is done will also be undone. The book describes his life experience with that rule.

Obviously the Thirty Years' War is the appropriate and causative backdrop for such a view of life on earth. The scenes of carnage and destruction abound, and there is no respite from it. The book makes us realize how long thirty years is. It also suggests that our concepts of development and education are probably peacetime products, fruits of leisure, achievements of a world that stands still long enough for a man to stay standing up and do his particular developing and learning. Simplicius explicitly denies such a vantage point to his reader by forcing him to witness the carnage itself: "Although it was not my intention to invite the peaceable reader

---

[4] Grimmelshausen, Hans Jacob Christoffel von, *The Adventures of a Simpleton*, tr. Walter Wallich (New York: Ungar, 1963), p. 27. Subsequent translated quotations are drawn from Wallich (unless amended, as indicated) and will be noted in the text.

into my Dad's house and farm with these horsemen [because things will go badly indeed] there, yet the course of my story demands that I should leave to [dear] posterity a picture of the [horrors perpetrated back and forth] in this our German war . . ." (p. 7, amended),[2] and the torturing, raping, and killing follow forthwith.

But the agenda of this long novel, like the War itself, is so filled with these items that they become the norm. There is no place outside the War (the few seeming exceptions will be discussed later), and hence the War is environment itself, too big and invisible to be commented on because it is the ecosystem of which all living creatures are a part. And, strangely enough, this routinization of the War permits Grimmelshausen to transcend even its limits, to speak of men while describing men-at-war. The child Simplicius is perfectly suited to describe the chaotic world and its human actors. In a manner unavailable to subsequent writers, Simplicius will confront every aspect of his cosmos: the armies, the land, the country, the cities, a parade of people including whores, doctors and lawyers and students, realms normally closed to the "realist" writer such as dreams, witches' sabbaths, even an underwater kingdom with supernatural inhabitants. Grimmelshausen brings his character everywhere, makes him see and record; yet these events are ephemeral, like shifting scenes in a theatrical set, disappearing after Simplicius has left them, leaving his life unchanged. The meaning of this dialectic between wandering, displaced, self and infinitely varied spectacle is that life happens to you, that the events and people of your life are *there*, on the outside, but they do not cohere or penetrate into your own being. This is not overt psychology, but it is a powerful picture of the self-in-the-world, the self that goes through life additively, cumulatively, horizontally rather than vertically, starting at the beginning and stopping at the end, and achieving nothing but the trip. This is not an indifferent, neutral, external view; it is a tragic view. We are accustomed to considering alienation as a kind of mental, inner, notion, a conscious sense of being separated from the world; *Simplicissimus* renders, through plot and image alone, the story of a self completely sundered from his world and

continually in search of it. As in all great art, that story is enacted, rather than described, and for the remainder of this essay I shall seek to articulate the story of severance and ano-
nymity which Simplicius is compelled to live.

Let us begin with the story of the wolf. Even before the
War intrudes on the child's pastoral life, he knows that there
are dangers to his well-being. Simplicius' only weapon
against the wolf is his bagpipe, but there remains one big
problem: what is a wolf? His Knan tells him in no uncertain
terms that he better recognize it:

> "Lad," he would say, "watch out! Don't let the sheep stray
> too far, and play the bagpipe boldly, lest the wolf come and
> cause us loss; for he is a four-legged rogue and thief who
> eats man and beast. And if you are slack I will give you a
> hiding." To which I [answered with similar sweetness]:
> "Tell me what the wolf looks like, Dad, for I've never seen
> one in my life." "You jackass," he said, "[you must be life's
> biggest fool. God knows what is to become of you.] Big
> oaf that you are and don't know yet what kind of a four-
> legged rogue a wolf is!" (p. 4, amended)[3]

The child sings his protective song, but it attracts (rather than
repels) the enemy; the soldiers who appear appear as wolves:
" 'Aha,' I thought to myself, 'so here we are! These must be
the four-legged rogues and thieves my Dad told me of.' For
I mistook horse and rider (as the American natives did the
Spanish cavalry) for a single creature, and was convinced that
these must be wolves. I therefore sought to frighten these terrifying centaurs and to chase them away" (p. 6).[4] After the
wolf-soldiers have duly destroyed the child's home, he escapes into the forest and later comes upon another strange animal:

> What I saw was a tall man with long, greying hair which
> fell untidily about his shoulders. He had a tangled beard,
> almost round in shape like a Swiss cheese, and his face,
> though pale and thin, was quite kindly. His long gown was
> a patchwork of rags sewn roughly together. Round his
> neck and body he had wound a heavy chain like St William

of Aquitaine, and to my eyes he appeared so dreadful and frightening that I began to shiver like a wet dog. What greatly increased my terror was a huge crucifix, some six feet high, which he clasped to his breast. (pp. 11-12)[5]

The child's reaction to such a creature is immediate and perfectly logical: ". . . this must be the wolf of which my Dad had so recently told me. In my fear I whipped out my bagpipe—the only treasure I had saved from the soldiers—blew the bellows, tuned up, and began to play with all my might to drive away the fearful wolf" (p. 12).[6] It is in such passages that the *narrative* power of simplicity is demonstrated: the soldiers look like centaurs, the hermit seems monstrous, the wolves are everywhere; the child has only his bagpipe, as he will later, as a man, have only his story, his his-story. The song and the story do not tame or frighten the wolves, but rather they include them, yielding a picture of the world that is raw and bestial with most creatures being, in some way or another, wolves. Needless to say, there is irony here, particularly in the fact that the hermit will be revealed to be the child's true father later on; but later knowledge cannot erase the immediacy of the child's perceptions, because the world that is encountered in this novel fully bears out Simplicius' initial responses.

Chapter 25 of Book I is entitled "How the strange Simplicissimus found the world all strange, and the world found him strange likewise," and it aptly suggests the kind of estrangement inherent in Grimmelshausen's narrative situation. The boy, filled only with the Christian teachings of the hermit, is shocked by the lives and habits he sees: cursing, gluttony, drinking, and sex. The description of the dance will illustrate the unsettling power of such an optic: "I followed him to a large house where I saw men and women twirling and swirling around so fast that it made my head spin. I thought they must be demented, stamping and bawling as they did. . . . By the sweat that poured from them, and their stertorous breathing, I perceived that they had been working hard, but their cheerful faces indicated that their labours had not been disagreeable" (p. 49).[7] Simplicius is fearful that these raging bodies are trying to destroy the floor, and, with it, the foundations of the earth itself. For the untrained mind, free of preconceptions or knowledge, the spectacle of human beings dancing or eating or having their pleasure must seem grotesque.

Even stranger than the dancing scene is the event which Simplicius oversees while in the goose-shed. Unaware that the child is there, a man and a woman have made their way in:

> [Then I heard a whisper from the two of them], but I understood nothing of what they said [except that one party] complained of the evil smell of the place [while the other party gave comfort]: "Indeed, fair lady, I bitterly deplore the envious fate that denies us a better place to enjoy the fruits of love, but by my honour: your adorable presence makes this [despicable] hole more [charming] to me than paradise itself." Then I heard kisses and observed strange postures; not knowing their meaning I stayed as quiet as a mouse. But when the noises grew stranger, and the goose-shed—which was no more than some boards nailed together under the stairs—began to creak and groan, and the girl to moan as if in pain, I thought: these are two of those maniacs who helped stamp through the floor and have come here to do likewise and let you perish. (pp. 51-52, amended)[8]

Not until the famous scene of the *comice agricole* in *Madame Bovary* will literature display so acutely the chasm between elegant, civilized language on the one hand, and the bestial carnal uses which it serves. By now it should be clear what Grimmelshausen is achieving: the ubiquitous war motif is commonplace to the characters (albeit not to the *modern* reader), while those commonplace things such as food and sex are shown as strange and grotesque to Simplicius. *Simplicissimus* is more than the broad fresco that many see in it; it is, rather, in even more elemental terms, a jarring discovery of the antics and postures which human beings daily assume.

In times of war, those postures are more varied and numer-

ous than otherwise. It is understandable that this strange-
looking, strange-making, wild child, whose slant on things is
natural and Christian rather than secular and societal, should
be viewed with suspicion by the authorities. Uncertain
whether he is a fool or a spy, Captain Ramsay (later revealed
as his uncle, but of course too late) intends to test the boy by
trying to drive him truly mad. Simplicius' protector, the Parson, warns him of the coming trial and gives him a special
powder to counter the efforts of the Governor and his henchmen. The sequences that follow are rather dreadful in their relentless effort to destroy the boy's reason; he is transported
into a staged Heaven and Hell with accompanying entourage
of angels and witches. Finally, he moves into his first full-
length role: he is disguised as a calf. It is worth insisting on a
number of things here: (1) the child takes special medicine to
ward off madness, implying that chemicals and other agents
can alter or protect the vulnerable psyche; (2) there is a systematic effort to brainwash and alter the child, implying a
kind of malleability in human beings. We will see the medicine used again later, when Doctor Canard gives Simplicius
(then the beau Alman) medicated sausages as an aphrodisiac
so that he can be used as a stud for the Parisian high society
ladies. Simplicius' stint as a calf is but the beginning of a long
career of impersonation and disguise. As the novel progresses
and as the situation demands, he will be a woman (with disastrous consequences); the devil; the Huntsman of Soest; the
beau Alman an actor and gigolo in Paris; a quack doctor; a
pilgrim; a farmer; a nobleman actually the son of the hermit
and nephew of Governor Ramsay; an underwater visitor to
the Mummelsee kingdom; finally a hermit himself. The
book's deepest meaning resides precisely in this spectrum of
roles and careers played out by Simplicius. A life is a long affair, and most human beings enact more varied roles than our
monolithic sense of identity or profession acknowledges; yet,
we persist in believing that there is a connection (a development, if you will) between the offices we hold. That sense of
continuity, of being somehow the same within each of the
roles, of retaining something from each of them, of organic
growth, may be one of our fictions, but it is not one of Grim-

melshausen's. We have, in Grimmelshausen, a different, looser, more additive, sense of identity than in post-18th-century literature.

I would suggest that that looseness is a survival tactic. Life first, personality and commitment second. Most people in *Simplicissimus* play out numerous roles, fight on both sides, are endlessly lost and found again: Simplicius, Knan, Herzbruder and Olivier step in and out of each other's lives, always unpredictably, always changed in fortune if not inwardly. The need to lead a chameleon life makes such virtues as commitment, perseverance, and self-knowledge (the ones urged on the boy by the dying hermit) difficult, unattainable, perhaps unreal. Along with the mobile life, the treks in and out of forests, towns, countries and even the earth itself, there emerges a slackness, a *disponibilité*, a readiness to change character and sides, a precariousness of soul.

The Pastor warns the Governor early on, that it is dangerous and sinful to alter a man's identity, and he proceeds to recount a dazzling list of test cases, a history of neuroses and psychoses that he has read about. We hear of a man who thought he had become an earthenware jug and feared he would be broken; another who thought he was a rooster and crowed all night; another who thought he was dead and refused to eat or drink; another who thought he had barrels of water in his belly; another who thought his nose was so long that it trailed on the ground. This comic list is also fearful, because it reveals the fragility of the self, its bent toward metamorphosis or disguise, its lack of fixity. This list of madmen (to whom the splendidly insane Jupiter figure should be added), men without delimited selves, sheds a strange light on the many careers of Simplicius. The self is so easy to lose. The body goes through an unending repertory of disguises and is altered through time. Does the soul remain constant? The beau Alman sings French songs (without understanding French), and, just as the child attracted the wolves, the man excites the Parisian women who see him. The combination of fine language and bestial coupling in the goose-pen is repeated in more elegant surroundings, as the young stud services, in the dark, four rich women with whom the only exchange is

sexual and monetary. In short there is a pervasive imperson-
ality in *Simplicissimus*, wherein gestures that bodies do together—lovemaking and fighting—are wholly without intimacy; instead, life is on the move, as soldiers change camps,
mates, friends, and lives; the body moves on.

It is essential to recognize that the life of the body, in *Simplicissimus*, can be a good life. It is true that, in the end, the
world must be renounced and the flesh transcended, but the
bulk of the book depicts and even celebrates the appeal of material things. The final "Farewell, World" which closes and
circularizes the story of Simplicius, returning him to the hermit state of his childhood and his true father, does *not* set the
tone for the novel; the power of the story resides in its sensuous love of life. Simplicius is unable, as a child, to continue
the hermit life, "because, instead of considering divine and
heavenly things, I was overwhelmed by the desire to see the
world" (my translation, Grimmelshausen, p. 38). To see the
world is an appeal that the boy, and later the man, cannot resist. Sinful or not, deceiving or not, the world and the flesh
are, and being alive means being thrust into them. The earthy
fullness of the book, the loving details of *things*, the zest for
food and drink and sex, the goodness of being and staying
alive, occupy center-stage in *Simplicissimus*, and all the ethical
and spiritual controversy surrounding their meaning or ade-
quacy is somehow secondary.[5] The truest desire of Simplicius
is to make of this life a paradise. The convent Paradise, with
its pretty maids and rich beer and Westphalian hams, is a totally gratifying experience for the boy; he has no lingering
doubts or second thoughts about such hedonism. The only
problem is that such pleasures, given the radical instability
caused by the War, are of brief duration. Toward the end of
the story, Simplicius is powerfully attracted by the communal
values and life-style of the Hungarian Anabaptists, but his
Knan assures him that he could never establish such a com-

[5] It is open to question whether the story of the soul can be told. The mode
of literature itself is, for Grimmelshausen, creative rather than renunciatory;
words and images depict life, and it is a peripheral matter to determine
whether or not the results are good. The capacious inwardness of Diderot,
Sterne, and Rousseau does not appear to be *verbally* available here.

munity in Germany. The mad Jupiter proclaims a vision of a future Germany in peace and prosperity, and we see again a visible, earthly Utopia. Book V is filled with Simplicius' incredible journeys throughout the world, and even beyond the confines of the earth in the Mummelsee episode; his intrepidness and curiosity amaze the denizens of that underwater world: " 'Why have you undertaken, in such a belligerent way, to throw stones at us?' I answered, 'because, in our land each person has the right to knock on closed doors' " (my translation, Grimmelshausen, p. 442). "To knock on closed doors" is an apt summary for the vigorous and extensive itinerary of this earthbound pilgrim. How and why does this lead to renunciation?

For there is renunciation here. Despite the hurdy-gurdy shuffle of the world, Simplicius—unlike Lazarillo and Pablos—seeks more than survival. Here I would like to suggest that Simplicius pursues the "good" life in a broader sense than is often realized. Not just Westphalian hams and beer, but love and relationship, are also desired while on earth. There are very few instances of significant human relations in this novel, but those instances are illuminating. Let us return to the child's encounter with the hermit. We saw that the child took the strange old man to be the wolf. The hermit does not want to take in the child (to be revealed later as his own child); he wants to remain a hermit and make good on his salvation. The boy must plead and beg to attain the old man's consent. *Two people living together cannot be hermits.* Their life of two years together in the forest represents not only the boy's Christian education, but also his first intimate relation with another human being. There is love between the hermit and the child, and it contrasts vividly with the peasant family from which the boy comes, as well as with the future trials that await him. It is a troublesome love, troublesome for the hermit, who is pursuing his own path to God. To love another means to consider a soul other than one's own. The hermit foresees all too clearly the danger which will beset Simplicius in the world. He instructs him to be steadfast and to achieve self-knowledge. And then he dies, willingly, as the boy futilely tries to hold him back among the living. The hermit's importance for the boy is *not* the Christian doctrine he imparts; it is the love he (reluctantly) shares. It is fitting—because already experienced—that the man be revealed as his true flesh-and-blood father. It is as father, not as Christian, that the hermit shapes the life of the boy. Simplicius goes throughout the world seeking to replace the father, not as a guide so much as someone to love. The older Herzbruder fills the position for a time; his care for the young man is radically different from what Simplicius finds elsewhere in life: it is personal. He *knows* that Simplicius is not a fool:

> "My dear young friend, I am glad to be able to speak to you here alone, because I have your welfare at heart. I know you are no fool as you pretend, and that you have no wish to remain in the miserable and contemptible state in which you are. If [your own wellbeing matters to you,] and [you] will trust an honest man, tell me your story, and I will see if I can assist you, by word or deed, to rid yourself of your fool's clothing." (p. 83, amended)[9]

All the elements are here: the old man is gentle and caring; he is selfless; he sees that there is a person behind the mask, trapped in the disguise. Simplicius is overcome with joy at the man's offer, but this relationship, like that with his true father, is slated to be brief.

But the fullest, most complex relationship in the novel, is that between Simplicius and Herzbruder, the old man's son, Simplicius' heart's brother. Critics usually abstract Herzbruder and Olivier (the villain of the piece) into symbols of good and evil between whom Simplicius must choose. Although that dimension does exist, these two men are most important as men, as kinds of brothers to whom Simplicius is bound by both fate and feeling. These are the patterns of community and of human bonds which the hurdy-gurdy, leveling, fragmenting forces of the War cannot quite destroy. Critics say that the fortuitous encounters with Olivier and Herzbruder give structure to the novel; I would argue that these encounters give structure to Simplicius' life, that they remind him that the self exists relationally, that personal love and personal hate are still possible between isolated humans. Olivier, doubling as the Huntsman of Werl, presses Simplicius close as a person, makes him consider the resonance of his life; their stay together and Olivier's tale of his life constitute a strange kind of intimacy and sharing: a man, talking about his life, to another man. Here is the communal value of literature itself, that "free read" and bridge of language which connects lives that are apart. The theme of solitude may be the most important theme in this novel. Simplicius, even at his highest moments, is ever aware that he is not loved. Jupiter, enlightened by his madness, advises Simplicius to seek friends rather than riches. The love for Herzbruder is Simplicius' way of achieving the true good life, of asserting feeling and loyalty and pattern over the ups and downs of Fortune and the War: "With this young man, who, like his father, was called Ulrich Heartsbrother, I formed [such] a close friendship [that] we swore eternal brotherhood, never to forsake each other in good fortune or ill, in happiness or in sorrow" (p. 85, amended).[10] The language here is unmistakable: "eternal," "never to forsake"; this is commitment and permanency on earth for one's fellows. Amid the powerful forces which bandy about the characters, bringing them together, separating them, wreaking havoc with people and places, Simplicius nonetheless holds his end of the bargain. In the beautiful scene where the broken Herzbruder begs for food from Simplicius we see evidence that the soul indeed counts for a great deal in this novel:

> "Alas, good friend," he said, "for Heartsbrother's sake give me something to eat as well!" and when he spoke it pierced my heart, for I knew that this was Heartsbrother himself. I nearly fainted to see him in such misery, but recovered myself enough to embrace him and make him sit down beside me, whereupon we both fell to weeping—I with compassion, and he with joy. (pp. 207-208)[11]

Simplicius nurses his brother, and again the language is crucial: "So I tended Heartsbrother like my second self" (p. 383). Here we have the full gift of self, a generosity that has nothing to do with withdrawal from the world or cleansing one's own soul. In this light the pilgrimage with Herzbruder is distinctly

different from the other journeys of the text; quite *un*picaresque, it is undertaken wholly out of love. Yet, this bond between brothers cannot be sustained. The relationship reaches
a kind of comic sublimity, as Simplicius tries to walk on peas
and chastise his flesh because Herzbruder is doing it; unable
to carry out the self-punishment, Simplicius secretly boils the
peas to soften them; when Herzbruder discovers the fraud, he
severely chastises his friend, and the underlying conflict becomes poignantly clear: Simplicius is on a strictly human pilgrimage, he goes out of love for his brother, not out of salvation for his own soul. But, Herzbruder finds that his friend
is an obstacle between himself and God. This impasse is resolved by the maiming, castration, sickness, and eventual
death of Herzbruder. And Simplicius goes on. What we have,
ultimately, is a precise replay of the boy-hermit relationship.
There, too, love for one's kind impeded love for God: salvation of the soul is an exclusively private affair, admitting no
congress with others. Simplicius' entire life, until the end, is
a refusal of such self-serving privacy, but Grimmelshausen
shows that love is menaced from within and without, as an
impediment to God and as a fragile construct undone by
death and the war. Simplicius' finest impulse is to live in relation, to build a community, to seek an earthly paradise, to
share his soul with others rather than to deny it altogether
(Olivier) or to hoard it for his God (Herzbruder). The book
is, as I claimed at the outset, tragic because Simplicius cannot
enact this kind of communal humanism. In *Simplicissimus* the
self cannot sustain its bridges with others; and it cannot even
remove its masks. The older Herzbruder's concern that Simplicius remove his fool's mask is a prophetic indication of
both the necessity of disguise and the destruction of self
which results from disguise.

In an early scene the child watches people eating and then
retching, and he is fearful that the soul will exit from the body
along with the food. The question is a central one: is there
something inside of us that is not matter, that constitutes our
soul or our identity independently of our body and clothes?
To come to know that inner substance would be the kind of

self-knowledge which the hermit urges on the child; to maintain that substance would be the steadfastness which the hermit counsels; to share that substance would be the kind of brotherhood that Simplicius desires. Those are all failed courses. Simplicius' knowledge comes from knocking on closed doors, not self-scrutiny; his would-be steadfastness becomes a series of roles; his propensity for love yields little more than prostitution of the body. At the end, he retreats. He cannot retain his identity and survive. His finest trick, as the Huntsman of Soest, is the creation of shoes that point both ways, that leave no reliable tracks, that make a mockery of origins and ends; his goal must be to become invisible, untraceable, anonymous. He is doomed to be generic, the beau Alman, just a body, not the authentic Simplicissimus Teutsch. As Lazarillo becomes Town Crier and Pablos an arrangement of skin, so Simplicius tends to become a generality.

The most haunting image of his self-mutilation, his disappearance act, comes in the middle of the book when Simplicius discovers some buried treasure. It is a ghostly scene, and he discovers "true" riches, that is, money; to do so, he must first, as the legend later says, kill the spook who haunts the place. Simplicius does do just that, aimlessly, and is then miraculously led to the riches. He finds treasure, purely material value, the kind of lucre for which men are destroying each other and the country during thirty years. It is the ultimate quest or pilgrimage, as well as the Faustian exchange: one's courage and potency for shiny jewels. As he leaves the haunted house, the peasants say that they heard both a shot and a scream. With some poetic license I would submit that that scream, significantly unheard by Simplicius himself, hints at the dying soul. The treasure remains, but the soul has, as it were, given up the ghost. The final retreat to the forest, 250 pages later, is not so much renunciation of the world as a recognition of its dehumanizing power. Only in solitude and in death does the individual soul reassert itself and replace the buried treasure. But the life and the book are over: the soul is alone, and the final hermit existence, far from being a time of love and charity, is an exit.

Public Intimacy: *La Princesse de Clèves*

Up to now, this study has been on fairly safe ground, to compare *Lazarillo*, *El Buscón* and *Simplicissimus* is to do picaresque business as usual; to include *La Princesse de Clèves* in the discussion requires some explaining. There are substantial differences between Madame de Lafayette's courtly novel and the picaresque texts of Spain and Germany: the protagonist is not a down-and-outer, there is no depiction whatsoever of low life, nor even anything that might pass as "realism"; the development of events is rigorous and anything but episodic; the characters are taken exclusively from the court; the narrative is told in the third, rather than the first, person, yielding little immediacy; finally, the text has an avowed psychological interest, and French literary tradition generally views it as the first analytic novel. One might add, as well, that Mme. de Lafayette is trying to capitalize on a new genre, the *nouvelle*, which is a brief, fictionalized account of historical events, in this case, the court of Henry the 2nd. These features of the novel should not be minimized, and I include *La Princesse* in the picaresque company in order to interpret and assess these aspects in the light of our central concern: the retreat or even extinction of the self. The Princess has distinct advantages over the preceding heroes: she is never hungry nor in want of money; yet, her story is, more even than the picaresque tales, one of hunger, frustration, power, and riches. Unlike Lazarillo and Pablos, the Princess is from an illustrious family; unlike Simplicius, she does not have to contend with the Thirty Years' War. In short, she is protected from poverty and bloodshed, and she can thus devote herself more fully to selfhood; aristocratic, she has a rigorous and imperious sense of self, and the drama of the novel resides in her efforts to assert and defend that self. Because she is, in some sense, a luxury item, her story can be a love story—something which would be either hypocritical, frivolous, or peripheral in the other novels studied. We have seen how the materialist ethic of exchange and the pressures of survival impede selfhood in *Lazarillo* and the *Buscón*, how the hurdy-gurdy war makes a chameleon of Simplicius; the stage in *La Princesse de Clèves* is narrower but no less despotic and killing. Despite her social and material advantages, the Princess cannot survive. She can achieve neither a personal ethic nor a personal life; she does not have a place of her own.

Let us begin with her ethic. Into a court where *"la magnificence et la galanterie"* rule supreme comes the innocent princess, virtuous and well-nigh empty as well. Like a creature from another planet, she is gazed on with awe by those who meet her. The young lady's mother has seen to it that she has morals and a healthy fear of men to go along with them:

> Often she gave her daughter a description of love; she showed her its charms in order to convince her all the more easily of its dangers; she told her about the insincerity of men, their deceptions and infidelities, the family troubles brought about by liaisons; but then she showed her, on the other hand, how peaceful was the life of an honest woman, how virtue enhanced the beauty and refinement of a well-born person; but such virtue, she added, was hard to preserve and required both great self-distrust and a solid attachment to the only thing that can make a woman happy: to love her husband and to be loved in return.[1,1]

The girl has been taught suspicion and fear, both of men and of herself. But she does not yet know why. Her marriage with the Prince of Clèves is one of convenience and indifference: ". . . she would even marry him with less repugnance than another, but she had no particular liking for his person."[2] The marriage is planned, celebrated, and consummated, and still the young woman remains innocent, does not know that there is anything in men or in herself to fear. The Prince complains about this anaesthetized quality of his wife, and he also fears and suspects that she will emerge from this state of sensual and emotional inertia. This awakening does come about, and it constitutes the education of the Princess; passion makes her have a "particular liking" for a single person, and, in so doing, it gives substance to her empty shell and makes her a person.

---

[1] All translations from *La Princesse de Clèves* are my own.

In *La Princesse de Clèves*, feeling teaches; the senses instruct. Behind the moral precepts and the elegant diction lies an affective language of blushes and hot flushes and desire. This is a language that the body, if engaged, will instinctively speak, and the Princess' arduous education consists in interpreting, translating, the strage affective life that she rather "follows" than leads.[2] Madame de Lafayette endows her heroine with a keenness of instinct and desire that dwarfs her rational and moral precepts; like the work of Pascal whom she admired and La Rochefoucauld with whom she collaborated, *La Princesse de Clèves* depicts humans as shrewd but walled off from their shrewdness, as creatures seeking their self-interest with great subtlety while trying to use moral codes as elemental as the Morse Code.[3] There seems to be a kind of hiatus between

---

[2] For a penetrating discussion of the time lag between expression of feeling and self-knowledge, see Jean Rousset, "La Princesse de Clèves" in *Forme et signification* (Paris: José Corti, 1962), pp. 21-25; the best discussion of the role of *le regard* is to be found in Bernard Pingaud, *Mme. de La Fayette par elle-même* (Paris: Seuil, 1966), pp. 82-101.

[3] The authority granted to self-interest (*amour propre*) among the French 17th-century *moraliste* writers is well known. Lafayette's confidant and friend in later years, the Duc de la Rochefoucauld (to whom some even ascribe part of the writing of *La Princesse de Clèves*) reveals the workings of this force everywhere in his own depiction of the human heart: *Les Maximes*. Although most of the *maximes* are characterized by their brevity and wit, La Rochefoucauld achieved in some of his fragmentary prose renderings an almost hallucinatory sense of how blind our consciousness is, and how unerring our instincts are. One passage, in particular, demonstrates the nature of *amour propre* with such intensity that it is worth citing here:

L'amour-propre est l'amour de soi-même, et de toutes choses pour soi; il rend les hommes idolâtres d'eux-mêmes, et les rendrait les tyrans des autres si la fortune leur en donnait les moyens: il ne se repose jamais hors de soi, et ne s'arrête dans les sujets étrangers que comme les abeilles sur les fleurs, pour en tirer ce qui lui est propre. Rien de si impétueux que ses désirs, rien de si caché que ses desseins, rien de si habile que ses conduites: ses souplesses ne se peuvent représenter; ses transformations passent celles des metamorphoses, et ses raffinements ceux de la chimie. On ne peut sonder la profondeur ni percer les ténèbres de ses abîmes. Là, il est à couvert des yeux les plus pénétrants; il y fait mille insensibles tours et retours. Là, il est souvent invisible à lui-même; il y conçoit, il y nourrit et il y élève, sans le savoir, un grand nombre d'affections et de haines; il en forme de si monstrueuses que, lorsqu'il les a mises au jour, il les méconnaît ou il ne peut se résoudre à les avouer. De cette nuit qui le couvre, naissent les ridicules per-

our devious internal needs and the accounting that goes on in our heads. Thus, the Princess, hitherto an open book for her mother, begins—unbeknownst to herself—to close up after she has met Nemours: "She no longer felt the same inclination to tell her mother what she thought of this Prince's feelings, as she had with her former suitors; without intending to deceive her mother, she nonetheless said nothing."[3] As the affections begin to come to life, the Princess must recognize that the role of consciousness and intellect is to *report* rather than to control or initiate. Lucidity, the hallmark of French classical literature, is a tragically passive virtue. The Princess has not yet felt enough to achieve it. Yet, the awakening of the emotions brings with it an unfurling of the person; after meeting Nemours, the Princess finally becomes curious about the world around her, and about intrigue in particular. She feels a strange new life inside her, and the only expression it can take is a desire to hear of the affections of others.

It is in this light that we may interpret the "stories" of the Duchess of Valentinois and of the miserable Sancerre, as analogs, monstrous analogs "out there" of the emotive world

---

suasions qu'il a de lui-même; de là viennent ses erreurs, ses ignorances, ses grossièretés et ses niaiseries sur son sujet; de là vient qu'il croit que ses sentiments sont morts lorsqu'ils ne sont qu'endormis, qu'il s'imagine n'avoir plus envie de courir dès qu'il se repose, et qu'il pense avoir perdu tous les goûts qu'il a rassasiés: mais cette obscurité épaisse, qui le cache à lui-même, n'empêche pas qu'il ne voie parfaitement ce qui est hors de lui; en quoi il est semblable à nos yeux, qui découvrent tout, et sont aveugles seulement pour eux-mêmes. . . . Il est dans tous les états de la vie et dans toutes les conditions; il vit partout et il vit de tout; il vit de rien; il s'accommode des choses et de leur privation; il passe même dans le parti des gens qui lui font la guerre; il entre dans leurs desseins; et, ce qui est admirable, il se hait lui-même avec eux, il conjure sa perte, il travaille lui-même à sa ruine; enfin il ne se soucie que d'être et pourvu qu'il soit, il veut bien être son ennemi.
(La Rochefoucauld, *Maximes Choisies* [Paris: Classiques Larousse], pp. 18-20.)
Although the tone of this piece, with its connotations of a blind, mole-like creature, genially going about its business within us, seems very far from the decorous precincts of *La Princesse de Clèves*, the knowledge of the heart depicted in each writer is very much the same. Finally, La Rochefoucauld uncannily evokes that same Dedalean labyrinth (replete with monster) which haunts Racine and which even finds its echoes in Lafayette.

that is burgeoning in the young woman. The world of the
Duchess of Valentinois is ruthless and amoral; she, like most
of the court, uses her sex in raw political terms. If she is the
"world," then the Princess' education is hopelessly irrelevant;
on the other hand, if the Duchess acts out of jealousy and desire—and the Princess now begins to know what jealousy and
desire are—then perhaps she is a closer, more accurate role
model than the mother. As passion emerges in the young
woman, it ineluctably relates her to the monsters around her,
those "sisters" whom she dares not resemble. The story about
Sancerre's misadventures with Mme. de Tournon is still more
bristling. Sancerre grieves the death of his mistress, but he is
fated, the following day, to learn of her infidelity with his
friend Estouteville, an infidelity of such proportions as to
make a mockery of her relationship with him. Beyond his
pain, his world scheme is awry, for he cannot contain the
double knowledge:

> Mme. de Tournon was unfaithful to me, and I learn of her
> infidelity and betrayal the day after I learned of her death,
> at a time when my heart is filled with the sharpest pain and
> the most tender love ever felt; at a time when her image
> stands in my heart as the most perfect thing in existence,
> the most perfect for me, I find that I was wrong, that she is
> not worth my tears; yet her death is no less painful to me
> because she was not faithful; and her infidelity is no less
> painful because she is no longer alive. . . . I deliver the same
> tribute of pain to her false passion as I thought I was grant-
> ing to a real passion. I can neither hate nor love her mem-
> ory; I can neither torture nor console myself.[4,4]

In view of such a spectacle, the Prince makes his pregnant remarks about the control and restraint *he* would display, were
he in such a situation. But the novel is undercutting the
Prince: he will face a dilemma worse than Sancerre's, and he
will face it worse; the Princess may think she is merely hear-

---

[4] In this passage, as in so many others, one cannot avoid thinking of Racine,
not only in terms of his vision, but especially in the language itself, the elegant, perfectly polarized expressions, the syntactical balance that contains a
world coming apart.

ing a story about sexual politics, but she will find that she will
be as implicated in intrigue as the Duchess is. Passion is one.
In love or jealousy, the Prince and the Princess will tend to
become Sancerre or the Duchess; the league of passion is large
and egalitarian, and the only way to avoid such degradation
is death, an option which both of them will more or less
choose.

Hence, the purpose of the interpolated stories is to show us
what these heroes will become, what they are already becoming; the stories speak of the chaos of love in a direct brutal
way that they can feel but never say. In fact, the stories are
their language. It is essential to recognize that this novel, so
incredibly filled with details of plots and intrigues among innumerable minor characters, is nonetheless exclusively focussed on the Princess, the Prince, and Nemours. They only
seem to disappear while the novel speaks of the Vidame's
multiple and dangerous affairs with the Queen and others, or
the rise of the Guise family after the King's death and the subsequent dismissal of previous favorites: passion is one, and
Mme. de Lafayette is illuminating its amoral, shrewd authority in every nook and cranny of the book. She is showing, out
front, what is gradually being nurtured less visibly inside the
three protagonists. Especially the Princess is unaware of the
developments taking place within her and mirrored outside;
her itinerary is a blow-by-blow learning process, a coming to
know herself on the inside.

Although all the stories are fundamentally the same story
of passion, they go by different names. The Princess can remain cool to the Duchess and Sancerre, but the story of the
Vidame and his mistress comes to her with a terrible, mistaken label: the infidelity of Nemours. The letter, describing
a highly sophisticated vendetta caused by jealousy, is ascribed
to Nemours, and the Princess makes giant strides in her education: "Never was suffering so keen and sharp . . . this pain,
which she found so unbearable, was jealousy itself, along with
all the horror it brings."[5] Pain is the expert teacher, the prodigious interpreter who decodes and shrieks out the message;
pain is the sign of jealousy, and jealousy is the index of love.
The beauty of *La Princesse de Clèves* is that the letter is false,

but the pain is true. Nemours is innocent, but the princess can
never be innocent. She has been initiated into passion, and she
now *knows* the fear and suspicion which her mother tried to
teach her. Jealousy is the vulnerability of human emotions; it
is timeless and infinite, and it creates the very environment in
which specific cases of true and false, yes or no, faithful or
not, are played out.

Passion is everywhere, in one's own arteries, in others, in
the Court, in international politics. The specifics seem to
count for very little. In that light, it is important to reconsider
the false letter. The letter was written to the Vidame, but perhaps it may be taken for Nemours'. Names do not appear in
it, just the nature and operations of the animal itself. Passion,
like the bodies it animates, is generic; like the universal style
of this novel, passion knows no particularity. The Princess
will make the most intimate confession imaginable to her
husband, but it will be witnessed by another, retold by still
others, and it will become another "story," part of the public
record. Private lives do not exist. The most personal realm
that human beings have, their love life, is the most consistent
public item on the agenda: gossip. Secrets are never kept: the
Prince is even angry that Sancerre should have kept his affair
with Mme. Tournon to himself for so long. *La Princesse de
Clèves* depicts an inexorably public world where individual
lives and loves retain little integrity but are rather transformed
into official record. The three main characters hold center-
stage because they harbor the same forces everywhere visible.
To be sure, there are the spotlights and spectacle of the court,
the treaties and alliances, the rumors and intrigues, the tour-
naments and balls: this historical pageantry is no mere façade,
but, rather, it competes with personal lives and reveals, willy-nilly, how little privacy these people had (or retained). The
public world functions doubly in this novel: (1) it intrudes,
eavesdrops, spies, and gossips; (2) more insidiously, it con-
taminates the language and behavior of the self, beyond the
individual's own awareness.

The Court has eyes everywhere. The Queen, trying to test
the Vidame, tells him a half-truth that powerfully summarizes

the novel: "You are in love, she continued, and perhaps because you have confided in no one, you think that your love
is not known; but it is known, and known to interested parties. They observe you; they know the places where you see
your mistress; they intend to surprise you there."[6] Not until
Kafka will literature again show such a totalitarian sense of
"on," of the individual on trial. The Princess pleads with her
husband to remain at Coulommiers, so as to avoid both
Nemours and the eyes of the Court as well. Coulommiers, in
the country, with its charming pavilion, would seem the antithesis of the Court, but even in this rural setting, the princess
finds herself surrounded by servants; Nemours too steals into
this haven, and he witnesses, in pure voyeur fashion, the two
climactic scenes of the novel: the confession and the revery.
At the close of the novel, we learn that Nemours has rented
a room in Paris for the express purpose of looking at the Princess while she is in mourning. The novel is a massive assault
on privacy, a transformation of intimacy into public spectacle
ranging from anonymous love-letters ascribed hither and
thither to scenes of intimacy witnessed and chronicled. Can
we speak of individuals?

Perhaps that is the answer: individuals do not speak in *La
Princesse de Clèves*. Mme. de Lafayette uses the most abstract,
universalized classical language that she could devise; Nemours, the supposed paragon, seems to come from an assem-
bly line: "This prince was a masterpiece of nature; his least
admirable quality was to be the most comely and pleasing
man in the world."[7] This is stylization with a vengeance. The
characters themselves, constantly seen and heard, overseen
and overheard, speak a guarded language. Success lies in expressing one's individual needs through a public language; in
Saussure's terms, characters have only a *langue* to achieve their
parole. But that *parole* must be disguised and public, because
of all the eyes and ears. Nemours is the specialist in such matters. He is the master at love declarations in crowded rooms,
at conducting his personal business under the guise of respectful generalities. One of his finest performances occurs when
the King is speaking of astrology and fate:

"I, of all people," said M. de Nemours aloud, "should grant no credence to that"; and, turning to Mme. de Clèves who was next to him: "It was told to me," he whispered to her, "that I should be made happy by the kindness of a person for whom I would have the most violent and respectful passion. Judge for yourself, Madame, whether I should believe in such predictions."

Mme. the Dauphine, hearing what M. de Nemours said aloud, assumed that he was whispering some false prediction that he had received; she asked him what he was saying to Mme. de Clèves. If he had had less poise, he would have been caught off guard by the question. But he answered without faltering:

"I was telling her, Madame," he answered, "that it was predicted I would be raised to a position of fortune far beyond my merit."

"If that's the only prediction you received," answered the Dauphine, smiling, thinking about the business in England, "you might find grounds for upholding it."

Mme. de Clèves easily understood what Mme. la Dauphine implied; but she also knew that the good fortune of which M. de Nemours spoke, had nothing to do with being king of England.[8]

There is no embarrassment or hesitation. Nothing is lost in the translation from private whisper to public declaration. The transition between the two domains is effortless, with each person effecting his own special "reading." Nemours' love language displays an uncanny ability to get his message across even in public settings, thereby exposing the Princess at all moments; it also reflects the fact that only public places are available for personal use, that there is no private language or place. Nemours and the Princess can be alone and speak openly of love only at the end of the book, the end of their affair, and this direct encounter can take place precisely because the Princess is determined to refuse the Duke. It is strange, even a trifle ludicrous that after so much suffering and frustration, so much exposure and desire, the two lovers should be brought together in the same room only at the

close: "Words cannot express what M. de Nemours and
Mme. de Clèves felt when they were at last alone and able to
speak to one another."⁹ The book and, to some extent, the
Princess' life depend on keeping Nemours at bay. The Princess pleads for what the Court and her husband can hardly
grant: solitude. But exposure is enforced. If love threatens, let
it be starved.

Yet, the solitude is no less intolerable than the Court. Nowhere is the burden of loneliness better expressed than in the
Queen's words to the Vidame:

> One day, among others, the subject of trust was discussed.
> I said there was no one whom I trusted entirely; I added
> that one always paid a price for confiding in others, that I
> knew a good many things I had never divulged to anyone.
> The queen said that she respected me all the more, that she
> had not found in France anyone who could keep a secret;
> what pained her the most was that she could no longer take
> pleasure in speaking her heart; it was crucial, in life, to have
> someone to whom you can talk, especially for people in her
> position.¹⁰

What the Queen is stating as a need for friendship is actually
(as the Vidame recognizes, when he hears it) a declaration of
love. Friendship and love are the only alternatives to solitude,
on the one hand, and intrigue, on the other. Friendship clearly
seems the safer, preferable, bond to the Princess. Her love for
her mother and, later, her relationship with her husband ex-
emplify this need for trust, for someone else to care for her
and to whom she can speak. Neither bond can be maintained,
however. The mother, well before her death, deals deviously
with her daughter, trying to poison her sense of men in general and Nemours in particular; the mother's death speech to
the Princess is an act of blackmail:

> "We must part, my child," she told her, taking her hand;
> "the danger you are in and the need you have of me make
> our separation all the harder. You have a liking for M. de
> Nemours; I do not ask you to admit it; I am no longer able
> to use your sincerity to guide you. Long ago I perceived

this affection; but I said nothing about it, for fear of opening your own eyes to it. You know it only too well now:
you are on the edge of the precipice; great effort and discipline are needed to hold you back. Remember what you
owe your husband, what you owe yourself; remember that
you are going to lose that very reputation you have acquired and which meant so much to me. Be strong and
brave, my child, withdraw from the Court, make your husband take you away; have the strength to make hard
choices; no matter how awful they look at first, they will
be easier to live with than the consequences of a liaison. If,
to do what I ask, you need reasons in addition to virtue and
duty, I would merely add this: if any one thing could destroy the happiness I feel in leaving this world, it would be
to see you fall, like other women; if this misfortune is to
happen to you, I die joyously so as not to be a witness.[11]

The Princess' husband clearly replaces her mother now as a
friend, and the famous confession, as an act of total trust and
release, is hinted at several times before it actually occurs. The
confession itself, heralded with great fanfare ("All right, sir,"
she said to him, throwing herself at his knees, "I am going to
make a confession to you such as never before made by a wife
to her husband"), will fail for the same reasons that the
mother's relationship fails. In both cases, the love they bear
the Princess is not disinterested, but possessive and even despotic; rather than release or affection, they both offer pressure
and judgment, forcing the Princess still further into herself,
heightening rather than diminishing her solitude. Friendship
and trust, with their concomitant values of dignity and control, fare badly in this novel, because Mme. de Lafayette (like
Racine) knows that human relationships are always passional;
a true friend is one who loves, and how can one who loves
behave like a friend?

   "Make no mistake about it, Madame," replied M. de
Clèves, "you deceived yourself; you expected from me
things as impossible as what I expected from you. How
could you believe I would remain calm? Had you forgotten
that I am passionately in love with you, that I am your hus-

band? Either one of these reasons could drive one mad:
think what they are like together! And they do cause me
great harm," he continued; "I am swept by violent and
confused emotions which I cannot control. I find myself no
longer worthy of you; you seem no longer worthy of me.
I love you, I hate you, I insult you, I apologize to you; I
admire you, I blush to admire you. I have utterly lost my
peace of mind."[12]

All of the elements of passion are there: the contradictions, the
loss of control, the rage; the Prince has become Sancerre.

There is one more instance of friendship to be examined; a
liaison with Nemours that would be innocent and carefree.
For a moment, early in the book, such a meeting takes place,
and it represents a childlike, almost infantile, sense of happiness without ties, of love without sex. I am referring to the
letter-writing venture of the Princess and Nemours:

> They closed the doors in order to work; orders were given
> that no one bother them, and M. de Nemours' servants
> were sent home. This air of mystery and secret trust had
> considerable charm for the Prince and even for Mme. de
> Clèves. The presence of her husband and the affairs of the
> Vidame de Chartre lulled her conscience. All she felt was
> pleasure in seeing M. de Nemours, a pure and untroubled
> joy that she had never felt before: this pleasure gave her a
> directness and gaiety that M. de Nemours had never before
> seen; his love grew all the stronger. Since he had never yet
> enjoyed such moments with her, his own liveliness was in-
> creased; and whenever Mme. de Clèves tried to come back
> to the letter which they were to write, the Prince, instead of
> seriously helping her, constantly interrupted her with his
> wit. Mme. de Clèves became as foolish as he; so that even
> after they had been together so long that the Queen Dau-
> phine had twice sent word to hurry up, they still hadn't
> completed even half of the letter.[13]

This scene is a small masterpiece. It shines on the novel with
its joyousness and love dalliance, showing a laughing princess, untroubled and unthinking. It is a rare example of total

privacy: the two are closed up in a room together, and they do achieve great intimacy, an intimacy oddly sanctioned by authority. Their activity together in that room recalls the famous coach scene in *Madame Bovary*, where the lovemaking of Emma and Léon is mirrored in the movements of the coach, but here the joint work is exclusively literary: they are writing a letter (as well as laughing and flirting). It seems to be a moment of pure friendship, but, when it is over, the Princess will be struck all the harder with guilt and awareness, struck by the recognition that "friendship" always turns out to be passion in disguise. Finally, despite the lightness and gaiety of the scene, Mme. de Lafayette underscores its terrible consequences: not merely does the Princess realize her involvement with Nemours, but more crucially, in the public world, the Vidame will be ruined by the hackwork which the lovers turn in to the Queen. The young people go blithely about their way, but others are exiled and heads fall, as giddy love exacts its high price. Friendship, then, is a mirage; it beckons to the Princess as a refuge, but it turns out to be an ambush.

Love (as passion) alone remains as an alternative to solitude or the Court. *La Princesse de Clèves* shows, subtly and powerfully, that passion between two people either entails their death or is doomed to impotency. Within the elegant confines of this decorous society, passion is nonetheless a monster. When the Prince learns that his wife loves another, his initial noble response yields to a breathless onslaught of questions:

> And who is he, Madame, this lucky man who frightens you so? How long have you liked him? What did he do to make you care? What path did he take to reach your heart?[14]

In style, tone and even imagery, these words recall the impassioned jealousy of Racine's Phaedra when she learns that Hippolytus loves Aricia.[5] In both worlds, the heart is conceived

---

[5] Racine's play is, of course, an overt reworking of the minotaur story; like Lafayette, he knows that jealousy is wildly interrrogative:
Aricie a trouvé le chemin de son coeur.
. . . .

as a labyrinth with a road or a thread-lined path leading within, and at the heart of the heart is the legendary monster who devours human beings. In both works, that monster is rampant, acting in and through human beings, asserting the power of passion over against all forms of will and restraint. Racine magnificently redoes the myth itself, and both Phaedra and Hippolytus are slain by passion; Lafayette depicts a world that is more fearful, characters even less able than Theseus' son to kill or to assume their monsters. Passion in *La Princesse de Clèves* is quite simply the annihilation of the self, and the veterans are only able to skirt around it for a while before being eventually undone.

Passion removes control and alters identity. Nowhere is this lesson more economically and poignantly rendered than in Nemours' theft of the Princess' portrait. She is trapped by the characteristic public-private bind, as she catches sight of what Nemours is doing:

> Mme. de Clèves was quite discomfited. She should obviously ask for her portrait back; but, to ask for it openly would be to advertise to everyone the Prince's feelings for her, and to ask for it privately would more or less authorize him to tell her of his love. Ultimately, she decided it was better to leave him the portrait, and she was quite pleased to grant him a favor without him even knowing that she was doing it.[15]

Of course, Nemours sees everything and lets the Princess know that he knows. Beyond the psychological dialectic at play, however, the gesture of Nemours has profound symbolic overtones: to steal the portrait of the Princess is to vanquish the princess. Symbolically, it depicts a loss of self, but—and this is quintessential—it is only a symbol, only a portrait that Nemours possesses.

Lovemaking is confined, for the Princess, to portraits and

Ils s'aiment! Par quel charme ont-ils trompé mes yeux?
Comment se sont-ils vus? Depuis quand? Dans quels lieux?
                                        (*Phèdre*, IV, 5)

to letters; it can be enacted nowhere else. The most urgent, blatantly sexual, scene in the novel is significantly one of portraits and substitutes; Nemours, again in his voyeur role (one that seems very natural to him), is posted outside the pavilion at Coulommiers, and he gets an eyeful:

> He saw that she was alone; but his vision of her was so incredibly beautiful that he could barely master the emotion he felt. It was hot, and she had nothing on her head or breasts, except her hair, tumbling in disorder. She was on a divan, with a table in front of her, where there were several baskets filled with ribbons; she pulled out some of them, and M. de Nemours realized that they were his colors, such as he had worn at the tournament. He watched her tie the ribbons around an Indian cane, an unusual piece that had been his, and which he had given to his sister, from whom Mme. de Clèves had taken it without letting on that she knew it to be M. de Nemours'. After finishing this task with a charm and grace which the feelings of her heart shone forth on her face, she took a candle and went over to a large table, in front of the painting of the siege of Metz with its portrait of M. de Nemours; she sat down and gazed at this portrait with the kind of fascination and reverie that love alone can cause.[16]

This scene contains the entire novel, both its method and its meaning. All the symbols are present: the colors of Nemours,[6] his cane, and his portrait. The situation itself is highly erotic: the princess is virtually naked, and she is encircling the

[6] With a kind of grisly irony, Lafayette has stressed the chivalric character of the Princess' infatuation with Nemours. Most notable is the fine scene where she sees him triumphant at all the wedding activities:

Les jours suivants, elle le vit chez la reine dauphine, elle le vit jouer à la paume avec le roi, elle le vit courre la bague, elle l'entendit parler; mais elle le vit toujours surpasser de si loin tous les autres et se rendre tellement maître de la conversation dans tous les lieux où il était, par l'air de sa personne et par l'agrément de son esprit, qu'il fit, en peu de temps, une grande impression dans son coeur. (p. 263)

The fine breathless prose, articulated by the brief series of *passé simple* "*vit*," ushers into the novel something almost like pageantry and hero-worship. The scene in the pavilion is indeed a modern "climax" to the courtly gambit.

cane with ribbons in a manner that leaves little doubt about
the phallic status of the cane and the masturbatory nature of
her gesture. Above all, this scene will be their symbolic union:
the man watching the woman caress his cane; it will be their
only union; it will replace their union. In this scene we see the
full extent of the self's emasculation and fear: the sexual act
that the Princess and Nemours could perform (Lafayette hints
that the Princess half expects him to come to her) has been
transformed into a symbolic spectacle, with a solitary actress
and a solitary spectator. Her gesture is onanistic in the sense
that it gives her gratification without exposing her to her
lover.

It functions very much the same way for Nemours. This
time he has all the evidence he needs that she is enamored of
him; yet, Don Juan though he is, expectant though she is, seductive though the setting is, nothing happens other than talk.
Nemours talks to himself and thereby releases his passion.
The love is not consummated sexually, for internal reasons,
not because of some decorum or *bienséance* which Lafayette
might have felt she had to observe. Nemours, filled with desire to the point of bursting, speaks; he only speaks and he
speaks alone:

> Because, ultimately, she loves me, he said; she does love
> me, there is no doubt about it; there can be no greater signs
> of affection than those I have seen. And yet I am treated as
> sternly as if I were despised; I had trusted to time, but there
> is nothing left to expect from that quarter; I can see that she
> does not waver in her struggle against me and herself. If I
> were not loved, I would seek to win her affections; but I do
> appeal to her, she does love me, and nonetheless she con-
> ceals it. What can I hope for, what change of fate can I ex-
> pect? Really! The most lovable person in the world loves
> me, but that abundance of affection which comes from the
> certainty of being loved will only make me suffer all the
> more from her harsh treatment. Show me that you love
> me, beautiful Princess, he cried, let me see your feelings; tell
> me but once that you love me, and I will consent to all fu-
> ture harshness. At least look at me myself with those same

eyes that gazed upon my portrait tonight. Is it possible that
you looked at it with such tenderness, whereas you fled
from me so cruelly? What do you fear? Why is my love for
you so frightful? You do love me, it is useless to hide it;
you yourself have given me unmistakable and irrepressible
hints. I know my good fortune; let me be happy, and stop
torturing me.[17]

This is, in all senses, the most pathetic speech in the novel. It
is the full love declaration, overflowing with emotion, more
and more direct in its plea; it moves from "she loves me" to
"show me that you love me" on to the marvellous "what do
you fear," and the closing "let me be happy." Just words.
Words spoken in the near-by village, while the Princess sleeps
alone at Coulommiers. The words recreate the Princess, make
her present, effect the release of Nemours' passion, much the
same as the cane and ribbons did for the Princess.
   Passion is felt and sublimated but not assumed or shared in
this novel. Just as all places end up, by virtue of witnesses,
being public places, and all language becomes Court gossip,
so does the individual finally transfer his private needs and
desires onto the available public apparatus: portraits, ribbons,
colors, words. The self cannot thrive, because solitude is unbearable and relation is lethal. Especially the Princess cannot
attain selfhood. The public world has usurped all the space
available, and her private ethic cripples her. The education her
mother gives her is corroded by the education she experiences: the idealist code, with its dictates of will and mastery,
is crushed by the minotaur. All of her so-called advantages—
rank, wealth, leisure—have given her a moral elegance and
pretensions toward selfhood that are wholly annihilated.
Having tasted jealousy and pain, she denies Nemours and
chooses to remain experientially intact and virginal; the appeal of harmony and safety lead her to rebecome the empty
shell she was at the outset. The passional life betokens a
frightening community of sisters and brothers, a kind of generic miasmic affective matter, from which anonymous love
letters are drawn, to which the impersonal Court language alludes, out of which all the manic and doomed people are

LA PRINCESSE DE CLÈVES

formed: the Duchess, Sancerre, the Vidame, the Prince, Nemours, herself. Death is preferable and more exclusive. The
private life and the affective bonds between individuals cannot be hallowed in this book, and the Princess is obliged to
wither away, leaving no progeny other than "inimitable examples of virtue."

The parade of Lazarillo, Pablos, Simplicius, and the Princess is a special kind of *corrida*, a virtual ritual of public pressure and private eclipse: the coarser adapt and the finer succumb, but selfhood is extinguished in every case. It is
especially the algebra itself, the trade-offs demanded and consented, the exchanges desired and denied, which these novels
display with such acuteness. This is the arithmetic of self-enactment.

En un si grand revers que vous reste-t-il?—Moi;
Moi, dis-je, et c'est assez . . .
                                   —Corneille, *Médée*, I, v

ORPHANS

WITH VARYING EMPHASES, each of the texts studied in the last
chapter depicts the obstacles that beset selfhood. The protagonists of these stories either fade into the setting or disappear
altogether. Their own needs cannot be gratified within a social framework: Lazarillo goes wholly public; Pablos, now
just so much skin, departs for the New World; Simplicius
weathers the long war, but is emptied in the process; the Princess is overcome by the twin threat of anonymous passion
and despotic Court.

   Yet, some novelists were able to dramatize the individual's
development as an optimistic undertaking, the encounter between self and society as a mutually enriching education. In
the novels of Defoe, Marivaux, and, with some qualification,
Fielding, the self comes fully center-stage, as it never does in
earlier narrative; more marvelous yet, it flourishes, as it never
will in later narrative. The protagonist operates in an environment that is undisguisedly hostile or corrupt, but the self is
neither extinguished nor seriously challenged; rather, it finds
countless inner resources, and—despite the different optic of
each author—Defoe, Marivaux, and Fielding effect a celebration, a veritable coming of age of the individual. Problems
and struggles still linger, but they will function as steps toward fulfillment and success. The outside world—miraculously, it would seem today—nourishes as it contains, pro-
tects while it presses, and ultimately yields and recognizes the
merits of Crusoe, Moll, Marianne, Jacob, Joseph Andrews,
and Tom Jones. The fiction itself serves the cardinal function
of making known the protagonist. The process of *coming to*

know is therefore central, both in the text and by means of the
text, and it enlists all resources, those of the self and those of
narration. Moll and Marianne are both self-made women,
both "gentlewomen" in a world that appears to refuse them
that title. Unlike the fragmentation, dispersion, and anonym-
ity of the earlier fictions, the operative principles here are affirmation and integration. Joseph Andrews, device though he
is of a comic romance, nonetheless asserts his independence
and displays the special excellences of his body-nature.

The issue is not a simple one. The environment needs considerable taming. Crusoe must overcome solitude and an alien
setting; Moll is adrift, without family or fortune, in London
and the New World; Marianne is an orphan in class-obsessed
French society; Jacob is a lusty peasant on the make; Joseph
and Tom go through their adventure routines in a manifestly
corrupt English setting, and their comic struggles issue in a
power recognition of their innate legitimacy. But make it
they all do. Defoe, Marivaux, and Fielding share a common
reverence for the power of the individual, and that accounts
for my grouping them together. *Moll Flanders* will be studied
as a portrait of the self-in-time, whereas *La Vie de Marianne*
moves along psychological axes; *Joseph Andrews* stages the
comedy and the pathos of the self through the unique fortunes
of the body; these works stand as very special and—given
what is to come—very brief triumphs of the individual.

The Self-Made Woman, I: *Moll Flanders*

Defoe has not had an easy time with critics. The excellences
of his book seem too haphazard, the ironies too unintended.
The finer the critical nets, the more rewarding, but also the
more ambiguous, Defoe's novels appear. Surely, *Moll Flanders*
is the richest of his fictions. But, to claim, as I shall be doing,
that Moll is one of the most fully realized individuals in literature is to face the immediate charge: who is Moll Flanders?
Does the reader know? On the first page of her story, she
hedges radically:

> It is enough to tell you, that as some of my worst Com-
> rades, who are out of the Way of doing me Harm, having

gone out of the World by the Steps and the String, as I often
expected to go, knew me by the name of *Moll Flanders*; so
you may give me leave to speak of myself under that name
till I dare own who I have been, as well as who I am. (p. 7)[1]

Moll is, from the outset and definitively, for her world and
also for ours, incognito. With so much withheld, what can be
given? Even the appellation Moll Flanders seems to be grudg-
ingly meted out to the reader ("It is enough to tell you").
Moreover, names count in this novel. It is important to know
with whom one is dealing, to see clear; and Moll herself, as
narrator, takes considerable pains to orient the reader, to qualify words, to distinguish between apparent usage and reality.
"In plain English," "my Brother, *as I now call him*," and a host
of other qualifications indicate Moll's sharp awareness of reliable and unreliable language.[2]

Moll's initial statement may equally be construed as a
forthright offering to the reader: this much, and no further.
How much? At a crucial moment, Moll, in her fifties, at
Newgate at last, is reunited with her Lancashire husband, and
her poignant question rings throughout the novel: "*My dear*,
says I, do you not know *me*?" (p. 232.) Even, we may recall,
during their passionate youthful encounter, Moll still "re-
serv'd the grand Secret, and never broke my Resolution,
which was not to let him ever know my true Name, who I
was, or where to be found" (pp. 124–125). Again, can there be
knowledge or intimacy, where there is such holding back?

To sketch an answer to that question, let us consider the
double nature of disguise, what it hides and what it enables.
Moll has wanted, from childhood on, to be a gentlewoman.
At best, however, she can only appear to be one; hence those
carefully plotted marriages wherein Moll artfully parades as
a woman of means, thereby ensnaring a husband but remaining technically honest by avoiding outright verbal deception.
In these cases the feint is marginal, and Moll is easily forgiven

[1] Daniel Defoe, *Moll Flanders*, ed. Edward Kelly (New York: Norton,
1973). All subsequent citations will refer to this edition.
[2] I am indebted to Maximillian Novak for this point, "Defoe's 'Indifferent
Monitor': The Complexity of *Moll Flanders*," in the Norton edition of *Moll
Flanders*, p. 415.

by her husbands once they find out the truth. In other instances, however, the deceit is more fulsome. One of the most
radical deceptions occurs when Moll "transforms" her sex;
i.e., she steals as a man. Defoe offers us here a very concise
business vs. pleasure image, as Moll successfully keeps her affairs separate:

> And as we kept always together, so we grew very intimate,
> yet he never knew that I was not a Man; nay, tho' I several
> times went home with him to his lodgings, according as
> our business directed, and four or five times lay with him
> all Night: But our Design lay another way, and it was ab-
> solutely necessary to me to conceal my sex from him, as
> appear'd afterwards. (p. 168)

Here again we see the bewildering double claim: "we grew
very intimate," but "our Design lay another way." On the
surface, Moll reneges drastically. Yet, the book bears her out,
since, in this particular case, she escapes the gallows precisely
because a male accomplice is being sought. To be known,
either by one's true name, perhaps even in one's sex, is manifestly dangerous business. In light of these maneuvers and
disguises, how can one talk of authenticity or identity?

Although Moll did not invent the mercantile, barter code
of her time, she demonstrates a ready willingness to cope with
it. It is hard not to view both the marrying and the thieving
as dehumanized, impersonal exchanges, devoid of all ethical
content.[3] Much time is spent in the novel counting money
and describing the plate, cloth, and watches that Moll steals.
We seem to be close to the exclusively materialist world encountered in the *Lazarillo*. Even the vocabulary used for affective matters is a mercantile one: in describing her first, least
"seasoned" love affair, Moll consistently refers to lovemaking
as work (e.g., "he comes up again in half an Hour or therea-
bouts, and falls to Work with me again as before ... [p. 20]);

[3] For two of the most well-known interpretations of the novel along these
lines, see Mark Schorer, "A Study in Defoe: Moral Vision and Structural
Form," *Thought*, xxv (1950), 275-287; and Dorothy Van Ghent, "On *Moll
Flanders*," in *The English Novel: Form and Function* (New York: Rinehart,
1953).

equally telling is the ubiquitous word "offer" (e.g., "but he had no more to do with me, or offer'd anything to me other than embracing me . . ." [p. 91]). The most brazen, paradigmatic instance of sexual activity depicted as exchange-work-offer occurs in the anecdote that Moll recalls:

> I knew a Woman that was so dexterous with a Fellow, who indeed deserv'd no better usage, that while he was busie with her another way, convey'd his Purse with twenty Guineas in it out of his Fob Pocket, where he had put it for fear of her, and put another Purse with guilded Counters in it into the room of it: After he had done, he says to her, now han't you pick'd my Pocket? she jested with him, and told him she suppos'd he had not much to lose, he put his Hand to his Fob, and with his Fingers felt that his Purse was there, which fully satisfy'd him, and so she brought off his Money. (p. 178)

This scene epitomizes the business exchange, and it has the extra spice of being, in all senses, a counterfeit exchange.

Moll has been judged by many to be equally callous and mechanical, and that is the parallel I would now like to test. My thesis is that Moll's exchanges and deceptions—even the most blatant ones—usually become acts of communication and even commitment; enrichment there may be, but it is more than monetary. As Faulkner would say, there is nothing "fault nor false." One of the finest such sequences involves Moll's efforts to remain demure while accepting money from a wealthy suitor. Let us then keep in mind the episode of the whore and the false coin as we see how Moll gets hers. Asked to show her suitor all her money, Moll fetches "a little private Drawer" containing some six guineas and a little silver, and she throws it all on the bed:

> He look'd a little at it, but did not tell it, and Huddled it all into the Drawer again, and reaching his Pocket, pull'd out a Key, and then bade me open a little Walnut-tree box, he had upon the Table, and bring him such a Drawer, which I did, in which Drawer there was a great deal of Money in Gold, I believe near 200 Guineas, but I knew not how

much: He took the Drawer, and taking my Hand, made me put it in and take a whole handful; I was backward at that, but he held my Hand hard in his Hand, and put it into the Drawer, and made me take out as many Guineas almost as I could well take up at once.

When I had done so, he made me put them into my Lap, and took my little Drawer, and pour'd out all my own Money among his, and bade me get me gone, and carry it all Home into my own Chamber. (p. 88)

Parallels are not lacking between this scene and the whore's theft. But the insistence on hands being placed in and out of drawers, money in and out of laps, lends a powerful erotic interest to these gestures. Defoe has drawn this scene with considerable fineness, and it wholly merges the economic and the affective into a fusion of motives, a rather touching and surprising intimacy. In this light, it is a moment of tenderness, and the language of hands and coins achieves a delicacy rarely found orally in the novel. Above all, this is a felt, realized exchange between two human beings, not a fraudulent deception as in the whore's trick. And this leads me to the central argument in my reading of Defoe: Moll authenticates the exchange, just as she personalizes the masks and makes good on the deceptions. Herein she differs radically from Lazarillo and Pablos, because all that would be sham or dehumanizing in her conduct is ultimately *assumed* by Moll, yoked into the service of an integral self.

Let me now reconsider the question of Moll Flanders' identity. Her childhood ambition remains with her throughout: to be a Gentlewoman. When she first states this goal as a helpless orphan, she is roundly ridiculed; but her definition of the term is most illuminating: "all I understood by being a Gentlewoman, was to be able to Work for myself, and get enough to keep me without that terrible Bug-bear *going to Service*, whereas they meant to live Great, Rich and High, and I know not what" (pp. 11-12). This is really no less than a declaration of independence, a desire for being one's own person, which ultimately has little to do with societal codes. Two routes, taken sequentially, seem to be open to Moll: marriage and

then thieving. Many novelists would have doubtless abandoned Moll after her last erotic affair. Defoe somewhat
hugely stops her love(s) story midway in the book, so that
the second life (in the fullest sense of the term) of thieving
may begin. In so doing, he reminds us how far life exceeds
the boundaries of romance, how limited the erotic interest
must be in a life that goes from infancy to three score and ten.
Life does not stop with marriage (although literature often
does), and Defoe achieves something rather enormous in his
portrayal of a vigorous old lady bent on affirmation at all
costs. Thieving, we realize, is, like marrying, essentially an
arena for deploying talents and resources.[4] The body may no
longer seduce, but the fingers remain nimble, the eyes keen,
the feet agile. There is a powerful and lithe intelligence at play
in Moll's exploits. As she dons disguise after disguise, walking about the city, "peering, and peeping into every Door and
Window I came near" (p. 198), she becomes a veritable alle-
gory of urban intelligence and consciousness. Powers of intellect and perspicacity are needed for successful thieving:

> a Thief being a Creature that Watches the Advantages of
> other People's mistakes, 'tis impossible but to one that is
> vigilant and industrious many Opportunities must happen,
> and therefore she [Mother Midnight] thought that one so
> exquisitely keen in the Trade as I was, would scarce fail of
> something extraordinary where ever I went. (pp. 209-210)

Moll's prowess along these lines is so remarkable that she becomes, in words that will resonate throughout this study,
"the greatest artist of my time."

Moll's triumphs are those of cunning and creativity (disguise is, by definition, creative), but her goal is essentially that
of pleasure rather than material benefit, the pleasure of self-
assertion, the supremely human pleasure of technique. If she
cannot be a "gentlewoman" in the accepted social manner,
then she will be one à sa façon. In one of the most stunning

---

[4] This recognition that the deployment of energies is intrinsically "good"
calls to mind nothing so much as Keats's famous remark: "Though a quarrel
in the streets is a thing to be hated, the energies deployed in it are fine," in
Criticism: The Major Texts, ed. Walter J. Bate (New York, 1952), p. 348.

sequences of the novel, Moll splendidly demonstrates her
mastery over circumstances, her ability to make the two
gentlewoman-definitions merge: independence *and* social
stature. Falsely (!) accused of theft in a mercer's store, Moll
enacts an elaborate drama of offended dignity. She demands
and receives reparation, and the entire episode is a tribute to
the power of art over life, the orphan's resources over society's standards. Decked out in all her stolen finery, accompanied by an entourage of dignified impostors, Moll has her
day of victory. Even the Law proclaims Moll's legitimacy,
and we witness her imposing on the world her private show.
Here is a special victory of individualism, admittedly less ex-
otic than Crusoe's mastery over the elements, overtly immoral in its con-game dimension, but authoritative and
arresting for those who are concerned with avenues of self-
realization.

At times Moll's talent is so compelling as to be demonic,
and there is more than a little obsession in Defoe's novel.
Donning disguises at a frenetic pace, exponentially expanding
her "identity," Moll often appears overwound, addicted to
the challenge of thieving and deceiving. When she actually
steals a *horse*, essentially just to show that it can be done, her
behavior verges on the pathological. She clearly plies her art
far beyond the realm of need; her performances are strangely
disinterested. How does one assess this behavior ethically? To
be sure, there is talk about repentance, shame, and wicked-
ness, but Moll's technical prowess seems to belong to another
realm.[5] False to morality, she is true to her gifts. Many therefore see in her the consummate hypocrite, mouthing pieties

[5] Martin Price's reading of Defoe has been very helpful to me here; his succinct and humorous statement of what Defoe is about is addressed to the
same kind of amoralism that I am trying to interpret: "If there is any central
motive in Defoe's novels, it is the pleasure in technical mastery. . . . It is beside the point to complain that these operations are 'merely' technical and
practical; undoubtedly the man who invented the wheel had beside him a
high-minded friend who reproached him with profaning the mystery of the
circle by putting it to such menial uses." This essay is in Price's *To the Palace
of Wisdom: Studies in Order and Energy from Dryden to Blake* (Garden City:
Doubleday, 1964); in general, Price's reading of 18th-century literature in the
light of energies seems very useful to me.

and committing felonies. But I suggest that she affirms her particular brand of excellence over and above morality, because she cannot deny what is richest and fullest in her. And, in this regard, she is astonishingly honest. Moll *knows* what virtue is, and she knows it to be largely a tangential rather than a central truth, a reminder rather than a stimulus. After robbing a family in distress, Moll acknowledges brief pangs of conscience:

> I say I confess the inhumanity of this Action mov'd me very much, and made me relent exceedingly, and Tears stood in my Eyes upon that Subject: But with all my sense of its being cruel and Inhuman, I could never find it in my Heart to make any Restitution. The Reflection wore off, and I began quickly to forget the Circumstances that attended the taking them. (p. 161)

Morality and conscience exist, but not for very long at a time. One cannot imagine Richardson achieving such a truth. Perhaps her most impudent slap in the face to piety is her avowal, when Fortune is again smiling in America, that it might have been better not to bring her Lancashire husband with her. Those readers who are resurrecting a last-minute Romance will find such incorrigible egoism hard to take. Moll cannot be absolved of her self-interest.

In fact, Defoe seems to be demonstrating that only one with such a powerful sense of self truly has something to "offer." Moll's fleeting desire to be free of her husband—which only the reader is privy to—is followed by a second movement of conscience and commitment: "However, that wish was not hearty neither, for I lov'd my *Lancashire* Husband entirely, as indeed I had ever done from the beginning" (p. 262). Relationship is always beyond, rather than instead of, self-interest. You cannot exchange what you do not have, and Moll becomes a gentlewoman in just that sense: she is her own person.

That education began early. The first marriage with the younger brother, Robin, is unpalatable not only because she loves the elder brother, but also because *her* will is counted for nothing: "Ay! *said I,* does he think I can not Deny him? but he

shall find I can Deny him, for all that" (p. 29). A moment
later, she adds, "Yes, yes, *says I*, you shall see I can Oppose
him; I have learnt to say NO now, tho' I had not learnt it before; if the best Lord in the Land offer'd me Marriage now, I
could very chearfully say NO to him" (p. 30). The marriage
with Robin will take place, but the lesson, the first lesson of
selfhood, has been learned. To say NO means to recognize
one's own will, to go one's own way. Moll becomes a quasi-
spokesperson for women's right to deny: ". . . as the Market
run very Unhappily on the Mens side, I found the Women
had lost the Privilege of saying No" (p. 54). In remarkably
modern words, Moll exclaims that marriage need not be a
master-servant affair:

> I cannot but remind the Ladies here how much they place
> themselves below the common Station of a Wife, which if
> I may be allow'd not to be partial is low enough already; *I
> say* they place themselves below their common Station, and
> prepare their own Mortifications, by their submitting so as
> to be insulted by the Men before-hand, which I confess I
> see no Necessity of. (p. 59)

Yet, if Moll were merely a prefiguration of women's lib,
she would hardly be an enduring character in fiction. What is
most noteworthy about her is the inner strength and, even,
generosity which attend her ability to say NO. Because Moll
can say No, she can, more importantly, also say Yes, Yes to
herself, to others, to life in general. If Goethe's Mephisto is
"der Geist der stets verneint," then Moll is the spirit of affirmation. We see this writ both large and small. After the Lancashire fiasco, Moll finds that she is pregnant; once the child is
taken care of, she is ready to pick up with her banker-suitor
with whom she has been deviously corresponding all this
time. At last, fit to be seen again, she meets him in the country. He is prepared to do some "offering" of his own, and he
is equipped with ring, license, and still more:

> Why, *says I*, are you Distracted? Why you were fully sat-
> isfy'd that I would comply and yield at first word, or re-
> solved to take no denial; the last is certainly the Case, *said*

he; but you may be mistaken, *said I*; no, no, *says he*, how can you think so? I must not be denied, I can't be denied, and with that he fell to Kissing me so violently, I could not get rid of him.

There was a Bed in the Room, and we were walking to and again, eager in the Discourse, at last he takes me by Surprize in his Arms, and threw me on the Bed and himself with me, and holding me fast in his Arms, but without the least offer of any Undecency, Courted me to Consent with such repeated Entreaties and Arguments; protesting his Affection and vowing he would not let me go, till I had promised him, that at last I said, why you resolve not to be deny'd indeed, I think; No, no *says he*, I must not be deny'd, I won't be deny'd, I can't be deny'd: Well, well, *said I*, and giving him a slight Kiss, then you shan't be deny'd, *said I*, let me get up. (pp. 141-142)

This is one of the most charming scenes in the novel, and it is emblematic of Moll's gift for assent. It matters little that she never considered denying him; what counts is the poetic truth of the passage, the graceful and gracious Yes which Moll can say to life and chance.

Moll savors happiness, is able to say, and to mean, in the midst of a turbulent topsy-turvy life, "I never liv'd four pleasanter Days together in my life" (p. 146). The reader may have some difficulty keeping track of Moll's husbands, but each one is indeed genuine as long as he lasts. Above all, Moll keeps her own books straight. When married to her banker, she cannot simply dismiss her past. The entire picture is recalled:

Then it occurr'd to me what an abominable Creature am I! and how is this innocent Gentleman going to be abus'd by me! How little does he think, that having Divorc'd a Whore, he is throwing himself into the Arms of another! that he is going to Marry one that has lain with two Brothers, and has had three Children by her own Brother, one that was born in *Newgate*, whose Mother was a Whore, and is now a transported Thief; one that has lain with thirteen Men, and has had a Child since he saw me! poor Gentleman! *said I*, What is he going to do? After this reproaching myself was over, it followed thus: Well, if I must be his Wife, if it please God to give me Grace, I'll be a true Wife to him, and love him suitably to the strange Excess of his Passion for me; I will make him amends, if possible, by what he shall see, for the Cheats and Abuses I put upon him, which he does not see. (p. 142)

Here is both the maturity and the novelty of *Moll Flanders*. Moll goes a quantum leap beyond picaresque fictions and asserts the priority of character in literature: after all the adventures, the masks and disguises, husbands and thefts, the self is left to take inventory. The episodic plot, the role-playing, the hurly-burly past which is conveniently invisible, all those things belong to a person, and Moll is, in our terms as well as hers, "taking stock" in this passage, recognizing and assuming her estate. Fiction is indeed the only literary form for depicting Moll's fundamental doubleness, her recorded adventures and liaisons, on the one hand, and her insistent homing instinct on the other hand, her possessive sense that this grocery list is *hers*, that she must not be dispossessed of it, that she alone safeguards it. Defoe is adumbrating a code of humanism and responsibility here that transcends any moral dicta. Moll is the person to whom her adventures have happened. One's past is not visible, and that has its immediate advantages: "O! What a felicity is it to Mankind, *said I*, to myself, that they cannot see into the Hearts of one another!" (p. 142). Yet, one can, and must, at least sporadically, see into one's own heart. Despite all the hustling, beehive activity, Moll Flanders does carry her full life with her. Often, she focuses exclusively on that measurable, stealable, marriable world before her; often she is opaque to herself: "it was all Fear without, and Dark within" (p. 151). But, there are moments (and moments are the only conceivable unit for such activity) of recognition and sounding, a kind of roll call when all the past avatars are acknowledged as parts of the self. Time makes life episodic, but Moll reclaims her episodes.

Doubtless the most poignant effort to fix the episodic life, to wring stability and value from transience and accident, can be seen in the passionate encounter with the Lancashire husband. Each has deceived the other into marriage, and they part, as they must, each to ply his trade alone. It is the picaresque. But Moll is shattered, and her need cannot be denied: "I eat but little, and after Dinner I fell into a vehement Fit of crying, every now and then, calling him by his Name, which was *James. O Jemy!* said I, *come back, come back*, I'll give you all I have; I'll beg, I'll starve with you" (p. 120). He does come back, drawn irresistibly, responding to Moll's voice which he heard some twelve miles away. It is a moment of transcendence; Moll is "amaz'd and Surpriz'd, and indeed frighted" at the power of passion over matter. But matter cannot be ignored; their situation is untenable; each is without funds, and Jemy is wanted by the law as well. All the logic of Moll's education dictates that she go her own way, but, instead, she pleads for permanence and union: "I told him, I was so compleatly miserable in parting with him, that I could not be worse; and that now he was come again, I would not go from him, if he would take me with him, let him go whither he would, or do what he would" (p. 121). Such lines, coming from Moll, are nothing less than revolutionary; far from being measured or looking out for number one, Moll throws caution to the winds and accepts her lover *totally*, without reservation or limit ("whither he would or what he would"). There is courage and integrity in this utterance. To be sure, Moll will separate, bear her child, and remarry; but the sincerity of her desire is not undercut simply because life leads her in another direction. Here we are at the heart of Defoe's disturbing achievement: Moll is *willing* to pledge her life to Jemy, to redeem the episodic structure of the novel; later, she will be equally willing to assume *this* event too as part of her past, and she will then try to make amends to her new husband for the invisible experience she carries within her. She accepts her present and incorporates her past; she refuses to deny.

Defoe is disturbing, because Moll's life continues to unfurl, relentlessly, making each of these pacts a mere episode. In so doing, he tempts us to make easy judgments, to view all as ironic, to count the husbands and to discount Moll's sincerity.

We seem to place a special value on permanence and stability
in novels. Books themselves are such brief affairs, that the
shifts and infidelities of a fictional life are glaringly evident to
us. The fiction of fiction authorizes a miraculous shorthand
whereby a few years are condensed into a few pages, a life
into a book. It is possible for readers to be most exacting, des-
pying and decrying change at every turn. Defoe's book is
quite vulnerable to such a critique: Moll's marriage to the
banker is, *for us*, some twenty pages after her union with her
Lancashire Jemy; a year has passed for Moll. Five or six husbands over a seventy-year life seems less crowded than it may
in a medium-length novel. I am arguing that Moll is neither
a hypocrite nor a passive floater; she engages vigorously in
life, but she cannot stop it. Life changes her projects, gives her
husbands and careers. She brings integrity to each venture,
but life brings her new ventures, brutally. Defoe's novel has
the lack of economy, lack of rigor that each of us experiences,
over a lifetime. Most human principles and standards are
short-lived things. If life makes liars of men, it is essentially
because they continue living. Rigor and pattern are particularly desirable and at home in art, because they rarely survive
time. And it is time that Defoe has miraculously put into his
fiction; Moll's is the fullness of a life-in-time, and that is why
it is hard to judge her. Her great strength is that she lives in
the present. In this light Defoe's book is the precise opposite
of Flaubert's *Education sentimentale*: Frédéric Moreau's life is
frittered away and dissolved in front of our eyes, whereas
Moll is achieving four days of happiness here and there for a
full seventy years.

Again, who is Moll Flanders? It took Defoe a whole book
to answer. We cannot provide apt one-line appellations for
people who have lived seventy years. It is particularly hard to
specify their *character*. Assigning a character is one of the central motifs of *Moll Flanders*. For a suitable marriage, and, indeed for general social success, an unblemished, researchable
character is a prerequisite; but, as Moll finds out, "the lives of
very few Men now-a-days will bear a Character" (p. 60). Social deterrent though it may be, lack of 'character" is the *sine
qua non*, in Defoe, for having character. Defoe's deepest inter-

est goes invariably to those who have led chameleon lives, who have lived out each moment with conviction, who have traveled many routes, who have transgressed but not forgotten consistency. The Lancashire husband is a specimen of such lifemanship, and he appeals to Moll both emotionally and aesthetically: "In this time he let me into the whole Story of his own Life, which was indeed surprizing, and full of an infinite Variety sufficient to fill up a much brighter History for its Adventures and Incidents, than any I ever saw in Print" (p. 124). Mother Midnight, too, has been tested by time and found not wanting. When visiting her later in life, Moll

> found that she drove something of the old Trade still, but that she was not in such flourishing Circumstances as before; for she had been Sued by a certain Gentleman who had had his Daughter stolen from him, and who it seems she had helped to convey away; and it was very narrowly that she escap'd the Gallows; the Expence also had ravag'd her, and she was become very poor; her House was but meanly Furnish'd, and she was not in such repute for her Practice as before; however she stood upon her Legs, as they say, and as she was a stirring bustling Woman, and had some Stock left, she was turn'd a *Pawn Broker*, and *liv'd pretty well*. (p. 154)

There is undisguised admiration in this paragraph for the sheer pluck and resiliency evidenced by this old lady still on her legs. Defoe's heart is in these survivors. Life is a marathon, but the best are those who embrace every phase of it. This novel shows the deep cleft between measuring tools, on the one hand (morality, etc.), and the unchartable, unpredictable and, finally, undeniable goodness of life itself.

Eschewing pattern in favor of fullness, Moll exhibits qualities of resourcefulness, suppleness, and energy that amount to a kind of homely wisdom. In reading Defoe's story, we are reminded how long life is and how static our categories are. The answer to Moll's identity is concisely expressed in the title page; like a series of *dramatis personae*, all the stages of Moll's career receive their due, superficially discrediting her "character," but flaunting her ultimate success as a "gentlewoman," i.e., an independent self:

The Fortunes and Misfortunes of the Famous Moll Flanders, etc. Who was Born in Newgate, and during a Life of
continu'd Variety for Threescore Years, besides her Childhood, was Twelve Year a *Whore*, five times a *Wife* (whereof
once to her own Brother) Twelve Year a *Thief*, Eight Year
a Transported *Felon* in Virginia, at last grew *Rich*, and liv'd
Honest, and died a *Penitent*.

Moll is the entire package, an itinerary that needed husbands,
old and new worlds and much time. Defoe's accomplishment
is to have depicted the span and variety of her life as that of an
integral self. Moll may seek husbands and steal plate, but her
truest possession, the one she is most committed to, is her
own experience. And that experience is shared. For, beneath
and undergirding the motif of disguise and concealment, runs
a still deeper vein: confession. Confession equals narration of
her authentic life, even when it shames her. Moll is authentic.
She refuses to counterfeit money, and she refuses to fake feelings. Her disguises are expressive; concealment for other purposes is distasteful to her. When urged by the elder brother to
yield to a relationship that smacks of incest, she desperately
tries to fight it; pressed by her mother to accept the incestuous
union with her brother, she bolts.

Finally, Moll is a woman who wants to communicate. Her
marriages take on a different meaning when seen as the acts
of a woman who cannot abide being friendless and alone.
Men and women, as Moll well knows, are not always "able
to bear the weight of a secret Joy, or of a secret sorrow" (p.
254). There must be expression. Hence, the magnificent repentance scene at Newgate is actually a confession, a secular
rather than a religious confession. It is the gesture of a person
who sees the shape of a life-in-time. Abhorrence is what Moll
claims to feel, but what she in fact "offers" the Minister is the
narration of her life:

> This honest friendly way of treating me unlock'd all the
> Sluices of my Passions: He broke into my very Soul by it;
> and I unravell'd all the Wickedness of my Life to him: In a
> word, I gave him an Abridgement of this whole History; I
> gave him the Picture of my Conduct for 50 Years in Mini-
> ature. (p. 226)

All the motifs are powerfully fused here, in what is the poetic climax of the novel: passion, opening up to another, time and narration. What Moll has to confess is not so much her sins as her life. To grasp and then to share the fullness of one's life; this is at once the particular excellence of Moll Flanders and of fiction, and Defoe has "offered" it to his readers.

The Self-Made Woman, II: *La Vie de Marianne*

Marivaux's heroine Marianne—seemingly so different, yet ultimately so like Moll Flanders—pursues a dazzling course of self-assertion in her itinerary from orphanhood to aristocracy, a pilgrimage perfectly reflected in the title itself: *La Vie de Marianne ou les Aventures de Madame La Comtesse de ★★★*. Marianne, like Defoe's protagonist, is bent on becoming a gentlewoman, and, although their definitions of the terms are at some variance (Moll seeks independence, whereas Marianne desires social recognition), the struggle against an apparently hostile setting is splendidly victorious in both cases.

Marianne is an orphan, and the entire novel is in the service of demonstrating, more precisely of generating, that excellence and superiority for which she has no papers or prior evidence. Without family or background, Marianne is only herself, a fact which constitutes her major weakness and her major strength in the novel. The notion of the orphan is, in itself, a fertile one, and, ever since Oedipus, myth and literature have made much of obscure births. We have seen, in *Simplicissimus*, that the concealed noble birth of the protagonist confers, late in the game, a kind of legitimacy on the superiority which Simplicius has already evidenced. Closer to Marivaux is, of course, Fielding, whose two major protagonists, Tom Jones and Joseph Andrews, find their love lives and their social lives confounded by the mystery of their origins. Fielding is concerned most with the dramatic potential of the situation, the taboos of incest that he plays with, the social pretensions that he satirizes, the promise of equilibrium and happy endings that he reserves. Although Marivaux is equally effective in illuminating the importance that society places on name and birth, his attitude toward the prestige of rank is ambiguous, especially in Marianne's case, since she herself wants, above all, to achieve the status she feels entitled to. There is no war against society here. Marivaux's great accomplishment, however, is to exploit—narratively and morally—the remarkable, unsensed potential of the orphan model. Fielding is interested in, but hardly limited to, the fates of his characters Tom Jones and Joseph Andrews; as characters we may indeed find them wanting, subordinated to larger machinery, overshadowed by creations such as Parson Adams or even Squire Allworthy, eclipsed by the wise, immensely personal, narrative voice that organizes both texts and does the real communicating with the reader. Marivaux, however, has taken the full measure of the orphan figure. *La Vie de Marianne* answers, over and over, the public question that faces all orphans: who are you? We hear, repeated so often that it verges on litany, the details of Marianne's birth and upbringing. Many critics admonish us that we must accept Marianne's own inner certainty that she is, indeed, of noble birth; and, of course, the title-page confirms any lingering doubts on that score. But, the beauty and deeper significance of Marivaux's novel lies in its unarticulated, but fully dramatized, questions: what is superiority? what is aristocracy? what is authority? how does a person demonstrate them?

The entire novel[1] depicts the activities of a person who must *prove* she is a gentlewoman, an orphan who has no papers to rely on. What Marivaux succeeds in doing—and this feat is not a little subversive—is to prove that excellence is a matter of heart and mind, not of documentation. The novel form turns out to be a most useful tool for such a demonstration. Marianne *achieves* her aristocracy; she does not inherit a noble mother, but, instead, she forges, before our very eyes, ties of kinship with Mme. de Miran that dwarf the woman's feelings for her own son. Despite its fanciful plot built on coincidences, *La Vie de Marianne* is not *romanesque* in the traditional sense. There are no significant surprises or revelations. In this light, the story of Tervire (the last three books) diverges considerably from that of Marianne; Tervire

---

[1] The first eight books, those dealing with Marianne.

will discover, replete with *guignol* trappings, that the down-and-out Mme. Darneul is, in reality, her own mother. It is crucial to recognize that no such rabbit-in-the-hat tricks are played in the story of Marianne. Admittedly, Valville turns out to be Mme. de Miran's son, Climal is Valville's uncle, etc., but this is just so much icing on Marianne's cake, opportunities for her to demonstrate that relationships are ultimately forged and chosen, rather than undergone. In short, there is no *a priori* in this novel. Hence, to *assume* that Marianne is a gentlewoman is to miss the point: Marivaux wants to set forth the process of recognition itself, to make us see how and why society accepts Marianne; his means for doing that is the creation of a book that flaunts Marianne's particular excellence, an excellence of heart, mind, and style which will oblige *us* to recognize Marianne as well.

Thus, we really have to choose between the two titles: *La Vie de Marianne ou Les Aventures de Madame la Comtesse de* ★★★. This is not essentially a book of adventures, for that would be plot-bound and *romanesque*; rather, it is the story of a life, and the superiority of the life is intricately related to the telling of the story. Here, in fact, is Marivaux's *gageure*. The literature of his time abounded with adventures of countesses; he wants to narrate the reflections of Marianne. He therefore insists, for reasons that are serious as well as coquettish, that the result is not a "novel" (thereby legitimizing the many reflections):

> Her friend asks her the story of her life, and she writes it in her own way. Marianne is in no way conscious of literary form. She is not a writing woman, but a thinking woman, one who has experienced many things and seen a great deal, whose entire life is a mix of events that has given her considerable knowledge of human character.[2,1]

The greatness of the novel is inseparably wedded to the form of Marianne's reflections. Her knowledge is one with her manner of expression. As orphan, Marianne is dependent en-

---

[2] Pierre Carlet de Chamblain de Marivaux, *La Vie de Marianne, ou Les Aventures de Madame La Comtesse De* ★★★, ed. Frédéric Deloffre (Paris: Garnier Frères, 1957). All translations from *La Vie de Marianne* are my own.

tirely on her natural resources: charm, beauty, wit, and, especially, style. Her style, we shall see, is everywhere triumphant. At her first encounter with the bustling city that she
must conquer, we read: "And I effortlessly understood the
thoughts of all these people; my instincts saw nothing they
did not already know."[2] It is a remarkable utterance, and it
demonstrates the essentialist view that Marivaux holds, the
view that excellence and knowledge are innate rather than acquired qualities; but the poise and nonchalance of the statement, the easy verbal take-over—these qualities are in and of
the phrase itself. Language does not merely translate the refinement of Marianne's thoughts; it conveys that refinement
and therefore seduces wherever it goes. Unlike Tom Jones
and Joseph Andrews, whose superiority is moral and natural,
Marianne's greatest "virtue" will turn out to be her language.
Let us consider one of the most pert examples of her style;
these are her reflections upon deciding to return the fine dress
to Climal, whose intentions are now unmistakable: "So I got
up to go and fetch it; but in moving only these couple of feet,
this proud heart softened, and somehow my eyes watered,
and I heaved a great sigh: perhaps for me, perhaps for Valville, perhaps for the lovely dress: I couldn't say which of the
three."[3] This little reflection, with its loving attention micro-
scopically focussed on the seam between gesture and motive,
is exquisitely useless; in its wise ambiguity, all clear notions
of virtue and motivation recede. But, beyond clarity, there
emerges the fineness of a mind that can probe so nicely and
articulate with such delicacy. Narrative action slows to a
standstill, and there is a kind of psychological zoom effect,
wherein the close-up gently removes the bottom from the
picture. Only the reader is present to be seduced here, but
Marianne's reflections are aimed largely at him (are not readers the well-known final arbiters of excellence and rank?). Of
course, the same style is on show with others too, and Madame de Miran states quite vividly the composite nature of
Marianne's appeal: "She has a heart, a soul, a way of thinking
that would amaze you" (p. 323). Heart, soul, and way of
thinking are indistinguishable in Marianne, and that is the
charge of Marivaux's language.

Marianne's reflections, her *babil*, the *marivaudage* that the contemporaries often found excessive, this is the texture and the tissue of the whole novel; this is the ongoing evidence of Marianne's *"façon de penser,"* i.e., her sole claim to aristocracy. We read Marivaux today precisely for his style, and in *La Vie de Marianne* that style heralds onto the scene—the stage which Marianne occupies, but also the stage of fiction itself—the enormous reaches and recesses of the self-probing intellect. In Marivaux we see the endless, static, reflexive play of the mind itself, producing and creating itself as spectacle, pirouetting gaily, and yet bequeathing the stunning record of its own play. Marianne will succeed in her claim, because she speaks and writes as she does. The idle, narcissistic inner life, the one that, as Voltaire accused Marivaux, *"pèse des oeufs de mouche dans des toiles d'araignée,"* the nuance and gratuitous delicacy of sensations and distinctions which rarely go beyond the realm of *bagatelles*, these are the accouterments of Marivaux's orphan, who has nothing else. By writing a different kind of book, not a novel but rather a spoken account of one's inner thoughts, Marivaux has created a dazzling *mise en scène* of Marianne's mind. Plot virtually disappears. Whole pages are devoted to digressions on motive. The novel actually abandons Marianne well before she has become Madame la Comtesse, because Marivaux really cannot abide such tedium and, after all, the real work has been done: demonstrate Marianne's excellence and power of seduction. Any fool can supply the events; only genius can provide the mind that transcends them.

The optic of the novel is thus resolutely on the inner workings of the mind. The ethical underside of this aesthetic is a philosophy of individualism and *amour propre* of staggering proportions. The nameless orphan is, by definition, the archetypal individual, the person with no past or luggage who must chart her own course. On reading *La Vie de Marianne*, one is inevitably reminded of the *moraliste* literature, with its emphasis on vanity and *amour propre*.[3] But, where Pascal

---

[3] I have already touched on this issue in my reading of *La Princesse de Clèves*. Marianne's entire *modus operandi* recalls the La Rochefoucauld description of the antics of *amour propre*.

warns and La Rochefoucauld exposes, Marivaux goes on to
create a new ethic, a code of apparent abnegation which is actually shameless self-interest. Although there is much talk of
coeur, esprit, and *âme,* the power that animates, integrates, and,
in some sense, subsidizes these niceties, is vanity: "But don't
you know that our soul is more proud than virtuous, and
hence more sensitive to the needs of its vanity than those of
its true honor."[4, 4] Pride becomes synonymous with self; beyond all moods and qualities, all the attitudes which we may
and do assume and reject, there remains a faithful, unchanging
core of consciousness and vanity: "for, our pride and us are
only one, whereas our virtue and us make two" (p. 86). Pride
is the undiscovered country, the limitless resource even of orphans, the stable hub, the nameless egoism behind the names,
the center, but, also, because it recuperates all, the circumference:

> Respect my qualities as much as you wish, you will hear
> from all men, for, in so doing, I am pleased, provided that
> you revere me who contain the qualities but am not one
> with them; because, if you drop me, if you neglect me, I am
> not happy, you're off the mark; it is as if you gave me lux-
> uries while denying me necessities; keep me alive first, and
> entertain me afterwards.[5]

This is the language of an organism with an acute set of priorities, a refined awareness that the self both precedes and surpasses its repertory of masks. This type of activity, the day-
to-day, minute-to-minute, psychological negotiations of the
individual count more than any tally of debits and credits. As
long as the machine functions properly, it is always in the
black, because its chief prowess resides in its demonstration,
not in its results.

Marianne has only one possession: "I was nothing, I had

---

[4] Here is an instance where Marivaux's French has a range of nuance and
discrimination which I am unable to match. Where I translate "more proud
than virtuous," Marivaux has offered a double series: *"plus superbe que vertueuse, plus glorieuse qu'honnête"*; the relative poverty of English in the area of
psychological niceties says something as well about the kinds of fictions produced in England and in France during the 18th century.

nothing that could make me respected; but even those who have neither rank nor imposing wealth have nonetheless a soul, and that is a great deal; it is sometimes more than rank and riches; it can take on everything."[6] Marianne's strategy is elemental: if an orphan has enough spiritual clout, she is ennobled. The mind (or soul) has distinct advantages as an arena for combat, because one cannot lose. The self is able to convert loss into gain merely by assuming or willing it. Marivaux even goes so far as to assert that living itself is a mere appendage of self:

> . . . our life, in some sense, is less precious to us than our self, our passion. If you look at the workings of our instinct in that regard, it would seem that, to be, it is not necessary to be living, that it is only by chance that we are alive, but it is through nature that we exist. In this light, for example, when a man takes his life, he leaves life only to save himself, to be rid of a hindrance; it is not himself that he is tired of, but rather the burden he carries.[7]

Marivaux's essentialism, his code of *amour propre*, reaches sublimity in this passage. An entire new playground for the self has been opened up, one conveniently without perimeter. Action and gesture become radically devalued, as the self flexes its muscles. Death, the classic bug-bear, is handsomely tamed, transformed from traumatizing pressure to means of affirmation. Marianne never approaches suicide, but she is quite ready to give up Valville, to renounce all goals, as long as the decision is hers. Marianne's truest game is, after all, not possession but recognition.

And herein lies the central paradox of the novel: each renunciation is a secret acquisition. *Qui perd gagne.* To abdicate all worldly gain, to do so in full spectacle, irresistibly confers worldly success. *La Vie de Marianne* is profoundly secular; the convent figures prominently in it, but as a place where renunciation is wasted rather than appreciated. Marianne can give up her lover, because she gains on the exchange:

> . . . for I loved a man whom I must give up; and that was a painful item; but, on the other hand, I was tenderly be-

loved by this man, and this is a great pleasure. That way one is at least certain of one's value; you win on the basics, and you can afford to wait on the rest.[8]

Marianne must be recognized and desired by Valville; union itself is less urgent, a corollary rather than a prerequisite. We are very far from Romeo and Juliette, or even Des Grieux and Manon. Recognition, *reconnaissance*, plays a preponderant role in a novel whose central passion is vanity. *Reconnaissance* also means "gratitude," and Marianne dutifully expresses it to her benefactors, especially to Mme. de Miran. The orphan seems in infinite debt to the *grande dame* who champions her, but, if we look closely, we cannot fail to recognize that recognition itself is the issue at hand (not gratitude): recognition of Marianne's grandeur, not her would-be mother's. Marianne is effectively a female Don Juan, an avenging angel who fells men and women indiscriminately, forcing people from all walks of life to recognize her excellence. Valville can be renounced, because his mother and Mme. de Dorsin are, ultimately, bigger game, more able to appreciate her *générosité*, more worthy of her worthiness.

The most infallible sign of the desired recognition is tears, and there is much weeping in Marivaux, torrents of tears which crown moments of pathos. The other sign of recognition is desire, the desire of a mother or of a lover. The story of the orphan Marianne manages to keep these sources of pathos refined, to mute the melodrama by infusing it with nuance and psychological nicety. Marianne displays her mind to the reader at such length and depth that we run little risk of crude responses. But, the story of Tervire is like a warning, an almost farcical, unintended replay of Marianne's life. Tervire's narrative is one-third the length of Marianne's, but it is packed with *romanesque* reversals and pathos. Decent characters become evil; mothers and sons appear and disappear; above all, there is incessant weeping. Tervire's predilection for scenes of tearful recognition reaches its macabre climax when the dying Dursan is reconciled with her mother; Tervire successfully stages her coup, but both parties (the reunited) more or less die from it. Likewise, the reconciliation with her own mother, appropriately attended by sordid material details and Kafkaesque suspense, leaves the mother paralyzed. These excesses are not present in Marianne's own narrative, largely because the "plot" is dwarfed by the reflections and digressions of the protagonist.

In dealing with Marianne, Marivaux's fable consists essentially of occasions for Marianne to present the spectacle of herself. She goes to church to be seen. She is taken to Mme. de Dorsin's to be seen. Her enemies try to bury her in a convent precisely so that she will not be seen. M. de Climal wants to put her up at a friend's, so that others will not see her. Yet, as orphan, she is nothing but her performance, a display of her visual and verbal wares. To see Marianne is to be seduced by her. Why?

Marivaux's novels abound in portraits, and some literary historians delight in comparing other sources with the image that the novelist draws. More interesting than "factual" correspondance between Mme. de Miran and Mme. de Lambert, or Mme. de Dorsin and Mme. de Tencin, is the rationale of the portrait itself, the project of painting a person in words. Marivaux undertakes these evocations with surprising humility: "When I say that I shall give you the portrait of these two ladies, I mean that I shall give you some of their features. No one can render human beings."[9] In these portraits Marivaux gives precious little physical detail, but instead he evokes a mental picture, a cluster of character traits. (We know that Marianne herself wants very much to have a portrait of Mme. de Miran.) Faces are revelatory in Marivaux, and words can grasp their secret. But what do they reveal? Does the soul show? This is the central project, not only of Marianne but also of Marivaux: to display the soul, to reveal it through its physical envelope (for only the envelope is visible), to discern everywhere the interface between body and spirit. This is no easy matter, because a well-trained body invites overreading. Marianne alerts us to this danger by means of a strange warning at the outset of her story:

> I saw a pretty woman whose way of speaking was considered a delight, no one talked the way she did; one would

have said vivaciousness and refinement themselves in speech: it was a field day for the *connaisseurs*. She got small-pox and was disfigured; from then on, the poor woman was only a bothersome chatterer.[10]

Marivaux (and Defoe as well) seems to be testing the notion that nothing helps a woman so much as her body. In gauging the resources of the self, we must give the body its full due; bodies are powerful agents of seduction, and they are obviously a prime factor in any discussion of the self-made woman. For the woman may be treated as primarily a body, an object of exchange in which considerations of soul and identity are superfluous. Prostitution on the one hand (*Moll Flanders* and *Manon Lescaut*) and rape on the other (*Clarissa*) demonstrate the peculiar trumps and peculiar liabilities of attractive female protagonists. The most enduring fictions register both the physical attractions of their women and also their need for selfhood and independence. Finally, the body possesses its own language and creates its own discourse; *Les Liaisons dangereuses* exhibits the full spectacular realm of body language, a realm of creative activity that verges on the demiurgic. Yet, the discourse of the body is radically limited in time and often tragically beyond the control of its inhabitant; death and destruction visit the body, and they are grim reminders that the soul cannot afford to rely exclusively on its physical envelope, that other modes of expression and enactment must be found and explored. In *La Vie de Marianne* Marivaux runs the gamut, thereby giving us a panoramic sense of the self's devices for expression, recognition, and seduction.

What seduces in Marianne? The scene where she first appears in church is a veritable striptease, emphasizing the orphan's aristocratic body. The men, "kept breathless," witness a sequence of charms ranging from Marianne's "most beautiful eye in the world," to her "bare hand" bringing with it "necessarily" "a round arm, which you could see at least half of, in the position I was then holding it" (p. 62). Soul is not very evident in this initial display of wares, and Marianne is understandably concerned that Valville not mistake her for a strumpet. Marivaux must plot his book in such a way that

Marianne's more spiritual inner resources are rendered visible
to an ever greater public. This need is met, with great flourish, in Marianne's trial scene. It is, in many ways, a test case,
an inevitable, even longed-for, trial of Marianne's merit. The
spectacle of the orphan before the minister and assorted dig-
nitaries is a replay of her striptease in church, but the stakes
are higher. She is already a bit seasoned, moreover, and there
will be more soul and less flesh to exhibit this time. This scene
clearly recalls, for us, Moll Flanders' brilliant courtroom appearance, her "public" victory over the mercer; let us recall
how Moll plays out a veritable paroxysm of disguise, doing
the gentlewoman to the hilt, even to the extent of furnishing
a sham aristocratic entourage for back-up. For a brief moment, Moll changes reality by imposing her art. Yet, Defoe
places Moll's triumph just before her capture, hinting that her
feat smacks of hubris, and that masquerade can carry the day
only so long. Marianne, however, is not disguised. Her entire
strategy consists in being seen as she is, in being recognized.
Each time she attempts disguise she is foiled, and, surely,
Mme. Dutour is intentionally used by Marivaux to keep Marianne honest, to remind all parties, even at the most inoppor-
tune moments, that this is a foundling, someone who started
from scratch. Marianne must win openly, not by deception.
Gossips, such as Mme. de la Fare, will do their best to stop
her: it merely adds zest to her victory.
    Still another turn of the screw is provided. Marianne is kid-
napped before being brought to trial, and only by "chance"
do Mme. de Miran and Valville appear on the scene in time.
The whole apparatus reeks of *romanesque* proceedings, but the
abduction of the girl is a powerful reminder of the orphan's
(especially the female orphan) vulnerability. As Marianne is
tricked and whisked out of her convent, we are indeed not
very far from Sade. The girl has no protection, no authority
other than her soul, and Marivaux enjoys emphasizing the
ambivalence of that dilemma. Her person is anyone's to take,
and this helplessness brings about innumerable situations
where she must excell the only way she can.
    In front of the minister, in front of the power structure it-
self, Marianne does her number again: the litany of her mis-

fortunes and, to top it off, her willingness to give up Valville, on her own terms:

> . . . I have something to announce to you that will reassure all the relatives about the marriage they fear between M. de Valville and me; namely, it will never happen; I guarantee it, I give you my word, and you can trust me. And if I did not give you these reassurances before Mme. de Miran arrived, you will be good enough to pardon me, Monseigneur; what prevented me from doing so was the feeling that would be inappropriate and unseemly for me to give up M. de Valville as long as threats were made to coerce me.[11]

Exuding greatness of soul, Marianne tearfully but exultantly renounces everything once more, and once more renunciation is the key to recognition and—ultimately—possession. The minister is overwhelmed by such grandeur, and he succinctly identifies the nature of Marianne's victory: "Can we make virtue unlovely?" The question is more rhetorical than real, because Marianne's power of seduction is stronger than their ability to resist it. Marianne can go further in renunciation than they can in prevention. Her performance is totally self-contained, since vanity and pride are more and more gratified, the more she gives up. Marianne has achieved the ultimate economy as well as the supreme protection. Impregnable, like a kind of moral porcupine, she cannot be attacked, and, within the closed arena of her *orgueil*, she can renounce indefinitely. She wins the day, showing that her power is the greatest. The minister bestows total recognition: "Now, Mademoiselle, forget all that has taken place here, as if it never happened; and do not grieve over not knowing who you are. The nobility of your parents is uncertain, but the nobility of your heart is undeniable, and I would prefer it if I had to choose."[12]

The orphan's only course turns out to be the only right one. Whatever else people may have, even the poorest have themselves. The self is small against the world, but it has its own resources, and Marivaux's novel is—in its style, conception, structure, and meaning—a tribute to those resources. Marianne displays herself. If she cannot have, well, she can reject. The outside world need not be coveted or stolen, because it can be seduced. Others are, for Marianne, only sources of recognition, and consequently there is little passion, urgency, or collision in this novel. All Marianne's bridges are to herself, and that way lie both her grandeur and her safety. At her public victory at the minister's, only one relative is unconverted by the miracle, and she makes a shrewd prophecy: "Goodby, Miss fortune-hunter; we are told that you have made it only up to a child of rank; but you won't stop there, and we shall be quite lucky if one fine day you don't find yourself a princess."[13] Why not? It could happen, given the extraordinary confidence that Marivaux has in the power of the self to come out on top (not to change Reality, merely to come out on top). At the beginning of her story, Marianne enters Paris, and she envisages the city that will be a jungle for Balzac, an auction for Flaubert, and a virtual Bedlam for Rilke; for Marianne, the city is little more than an outgrowth of her own body, a comforting, nourishing cocoon in which to live, grow, and flourish: "There was a sweet affinity between my imagination and the things I saw" (p. 17). Here is the social contract, and inspiring it is a serene belief in the self. Life is a spectacle, not so much to be looked at, as an opportunity for one's own merit to be—infallibly—discovered and recognized.

Thus we have, from beginning to end, the display of Marianne. She begins as an abandoned two-year-old infant; then she seduces Climal and Valville (and Marivaux stages them with perfect symmetry: the old man intrudes while the young one is declaring his love, and the precise reversal happens a few pages later); let us add to this list Mme. de Miran and Mme. de Dorsin; nor should we forget Mlle. de la Fare and Tervire; and there are more suitors as well; the bourgeois Villot genuinely falls under her spell; the understated yet marvellous finale appears as her story closes with the tantalizing marriage proposal made by the elderly officer. If we examine this sequence of seductions, we note a significant evolution: it begins with Climal, who wants Marianne's flesh alone and ends with the officer who loves her solely for her character.

His declaration marks the supreme victory for the orphan, conferring legitimacy on her by virtue of her soul:

> But I had no need of love to fall under your charm; I needed only to know the quality of your soul. What do I care about your family? Even if we knew it, even were it royal, would it add anything to your personal merit? Moreover, do souls have parents? Aren't they all of equal rank? Well! it is only your soul that I desire.[14]

It is the ultimate success story, the final striptease. The soldier's last line almost palpitates with hunger and covetousness. The naked soul shines through the flesh, and it is almost pornographic. Marivaux wisely avoided pursuing this story, because his character is virtually canonized at this point: her body, even her wit, have become unnecessary, redundant: it is her story, her *histoire*, that has seduced the old man:

> "Monsieur," I said to him, "do you know my story?"
> "Yes, Mademoiselle," he answered, "I do know it, and that is why you see me here. It is your story that taught me that you are worth more than anything in the world; it is your story that has drawn me to you."[15]

Her story is the guarantee of her value. *Histoire* as story, not as history; not the past of her family, but the account of her own life. These are the new credentials. The soldier is, like the others, awed by Marianne's deeds, but, in speaking of her *histoire*, he acknowledges the rest as well, the style, even the *bagatelles* and banal reflections, the entire package that is called *La Vie de Marianne*. Her story has ennobled her. One could even say that it has, as all literature does, replaced her.

The soldier is a stunning surrogate for the reader, a man who has heard Marianne's story and is seduced by it. This final suitor focusses exclusively on her inner qualities, and he thereby ratifies Marivaux's literary achievement. The flesh does not tempt him, just as it cannot seduce the reader. The body cannot get onto the page. Nor can the crests and lists of quarters. Language can show the workings of the mind, and Marianne's excellence must be realized through words, if the reader is to assent to her success. I have tried to show that

Marianne's supremacy lies precisely in the area of Marivaux's supremacy: a style, a manner of thinking and speaking, that is so *refined* that it establishes its own aristocracy and dispenses with the rest. This project comes at a moment in history and literature when the notion of merit has become problematic, and when the novel form is both opening up and closing in, opening up to reflection and closing in on the life of the individual. Much like Faulkner, who *needed* an idiot in *The Sound and the Fury* so as to present those affective, non-rational truths as the core of the Compson story, so Marivaux needed a character whose only resources would be inner, whose medium would be his: language. For the novel, unlike history, knows and celebrates inner lives, and, in that light, all great characters in novels—despite their crests or backgrounds—have to make it on their own as orphans. Marivaux's orphan has outlived herself at the close: like the second part of the *Quijote*, her life is now public domain, and she need not continue living. Her manner will be a fertile one for later novelists, and her form of striptease will become one of literature's chief delights. Finally, she may claim nobility, but she displays the virtues of making it on one's own, and that old man's love declaration is a figure for the strange legitimacy which confessional literature ever seeks. It is a nobility based on the intrinsic value and irresistible seduction of a narrated life, the result of a disturbing, ineluctable connivance between reader and text. Such a claim as Marianne's can be made good only when the individual's inner life takes center-stage and exercises its own rights. Moral and social codes yield before the exhibitionist power of narrative art.

The Body Beautiful: *Joseph Andrews*

Can we legitimately discuss selfhood in *Joseph Andrews*? Unlike Moll and Marianne, Joseph appears to have little autonomy or even aesthetic integrity. He is only in a narrow, provisional sense an orphan, and his orphanhood seems more technical (even pyrotechnical) and surely less cathartic than that of the two women protagonists. Moreover, although he gives the novel its name and the gist of a fable, many readers

and critics find him virtually eclipsed by his *vedette* compan-
ion-in-arms, Parson Adams, Fielding's answer to Don Quijote. Finally, he negotiates his fortune in a fiction that frequently backstages him in favor of its truest luminary, the
genial *raconteur* "Fielding" so beloved of critics and so splendidly present as narrative voice; "Fielding's" rich perspective
on events, his hearty appeal to the reader to while away the
hours with him, his delightful theatrics, mock heroics, and
stagecraft, all contrive to posit in the mind of the public one
fleshed-out human being ("Fielding") and a host of figures,
devices, puppets, and caricatures being marshalled in and out
of the fiction's precincts; his characters are so patently doing
authorial business that it seems most willful to claim that Joseph Andrews achieves selfhood in the fiction bearing his
name.

   As critics have noted, *Joseph Andrews* is characterized by the
comic, non-developmental cure of self-exposure, rather than
the progressive, tragic one of self-discovery.[1] However, it is
largely Parson Adams who is the enabling (although unsee-
ing) instrument for the incessant revelations that Fielding arranges. Adams, naive and trusting, and himself unchanging,
functions as a catalyst who brings out into the open the wide
spectrum of affectation and hypocrisy which Fielding aims to
expose. But Joseph is another matter. His is the life-story, the
romance project, that lends pattern and urgency to the episodic structure. Unlike Adams, he will complete the novel
quite differently from the way he began it, and, to an extent
that we are now going to measure, all the hurdy-gurdy inter-
vening material of the novel may be envisioned as the education of Joseph Andrews.

   The central conceptual planet around which Adams and
Andrews orbit is, of course, Nature. For Nature is the luminous source to which Fielding wishes to return. In this light
we may regard the famous preface to *Joseph Andrews* as both
a narrative strategy of exposure, of decrying affectation wherever it appears, and also as an ethical nostalgia for Eden, a pro-

[1] See Maynard Mack, "*Joseph Andrews* and *Pamela*," reprinted in *Fielding: A Collection of Critical Essays*, ed. Ronald Paulsen (Englewood Cliffs: Prentice Hall, 1962), pp. 52-58.

gram that would enable deceived and chastened characters
(consider Wilson in this light) to attain a second innocence.
Thus, there is a crucial twin thrust to Fielding's novel: an
often hilarious exposé, on the one hand, of foibles, vanity, and
hypocrisy, of the discrepancy between image and substance,
resulting in a panoramic indictment of a godless England: "he
[Adams] returned as pennyless as he went, groaning and la-
menting that it was possible, in a country professing Christi-
anity, for a wretch to starve in the midst of his fellow-crea-
tures who abounded" (p. 148).[2] But, the complementary, less
comic, business of the novel is the business of response, of determining a rationale for conduct in a corrupt setting, of set-
tling the question of *living*, once the job of *exposure* is completed. Joseph is central here, for he alone acts as well as
triggers: whereas Adams exposes the gulf between Nature
and codes, Joseph erects a code of Nature. Now Nature, as
philosophers and aestheticians know, is a Pandora's box, an
infinitely fertile and ambivalent concept that is called on to
support virtually every creed known to man. Hence, it is re-
freshing to note that Nature, for Fielding, is well-nigh synonymous with the human body.
    The body looms large in Fielding. A wise and genial anat-
omist, Fielding knows the role that stomachs and genitals
play in human behavior; he understands appetite, and he delights in depicting it in all its guises: innocent, illicit, authorized, repressed, grotesque, beautiful. No viable code of conduct can fail to do justice to the body's needs; yet, *Joseph
Andrews* is no epicurean tract: Fielding understands raw appetite (indeed, he thrives on it as novelist), but he integrates it
into a harmonious code of rectitude and freedom. When
Betty, Mrs. Tow-wouse's chambermaid, succumbs to Joseph's beauty and presses herself on him, is repulsed, and then
yields to Mr. Tow-wouse's advances, she is rebuked for being
bestial: her response is surely as serious as it is comic: " 'I have
done nothing that's unnatural; and I will go out of your house
this moment, for I will never be called she-dog by any mis-

    [2] Henry Fielding, *The History of the Adventures of Joseph Andrews and his
friend Mr. Abraham Adams* (New York: Norton, 1958). All subsequent citations will refer to this edition.

tress in England' " (p. 66). Betty's longing for Joseph mirrors that of Lady Booby (although the noblewoman is tortured by *her* desire): each is irresistibly attracted by Joseph, by Joseph's body, and Fielding does not find such attraction either strange or aberrant.

If lovely bodies attract, unlovely bodies repel. Fielding clearly relishes ugliness, and, like Hogarth, he is drawn to the expressiveness of the body, an expressiveness as well served by hideousness as beauty. If need be, even deformity will do:[3]

> She was not at this time remarkably handsome; being very short, and rather too corpulent in body, and somewhat red, with the addiction of pimples in the face. Her nose was likewise rather too large, and her eyes too little; nor did she resemble a cow so much in her breath as in two brown globes which she carried before her; one of her legs was also a little shorter than the other, which occasioned her to limp as she walked. (p. 16)

The incomparable Slipslop signals the primacy of the body, the crucial body-Nature equation, just as authoritatively as does the chaste Joseph.[4]

The irresistible body is quite enough to energize the most complex plot. There is nothing subtle or sublimated about the

[3] Here we see, I think, a rather flagrant violation of Fielding's claim in his Preface that only moral (as opposed to physical) deformity will be exposed and ridiculed: "Now, from affectation only, the misfortunes and calamities of life, or the imperfections of nature, may become the objects of ridicule. Surely he hath a very ill-framed mind who can look on ugliness, infirmity, or poverty, as ridiculous in themselves . . ." (xxv). To be sure, Fielding never does ridicule infirmity or poverty, but how can we exclude "ugliness"? It will not do, to insist that Slipslop is "chastised" exclusively for *moral* defects (although she is well stocked in that category too); man of the theater that he is, Fielding brings in the entire physical luggage of Slipslop to abet her moral misdemeanors.

[4] Deformity may be, in fact, far more widespread than we assume it to be. In articulating his general view of the satirist's goals, Fielding bequeaths us a vision of almost epic distortion: the evil-doers in *Joseph Andrews* are drawn and thereby exposed, "not to expose one pitiful wretch to the small and contemptible circle of his acquaintance; but to hold the glass to thousands in their closets, that they may contemplate their deformity, and endeavor to reduce it, and thus by suffering private mortification may avoid public shame" (p. 167).

motivation in *Joseph Andrews*: virtually every character in the novel wants to possess the two beautiful bodies: Joseph and Fanny. Thus we have multiple comic and not-so-comic scenes of near rape and sequestration, as Slipslop and Lady Booby and Betty lay their hands on Joseph, as almost every male in the novel tries his hand with Fanny. The cutting edge of Fielding's story lies in the fact that his seductive bodies are quasi-orphans, that those bodies which others are bent on enjoying and appropriating are, in fact, the only possession their "owners" have. Unlike Richardson's Pamela and Clarissa, or Laclos' Tourvel, Fanny harbors no sublime inner world, no realm of emotional or moral complexity: her excellence is one with her person:

> Fanny was now in the nineteenth year of her age; she was tall and delicately shaped; but not one of those slender young women who seem rather intended to hang up in the hall of an anatomist than for any other purpose. On the contrary, she was so plump that she seemed bursting through her tight stays, especially in the part which confined her swelling breasts. Nor did her hips want the assistance of a hoop to extend them. The exact shape of her arms denoted the form of those limbs which she concealed. . . . Her hair was of a chestnut brown. . . . Her forehead was high, her eyebrows arched, and rather full than otherwise. Her eyes black and sparkling; her nose just inclining to the Roman; her lips red and moist, and her under lip, according to the opinion of the ladies, too pouting. . . . To conclude all, she had a natural gentility superior to the acquisition of art, and which surprized all who beheld her. (p. 132)[5]

Fielding's novel dramatizes the nature of the "surprize" experienced by those who "behold" Fanny: inevitably, it tends toward rape. Joseph and Fanny have only to be seen, and they

---

[5] Joseph is also described in similar terms (see p. 23). Although this attribution of "gentility" and, in some cases, nobility to a character's physical appearance is a stock-in-trade in 18th-century fiction, it is nonetheless problematic for all that. Fielding will take the body very seriously as an index of excellence; Prévost will go still further in developing the erotic implications of such a view.

will be desired. Marivaux carefully arranged scenes enabling Marianne to demonstrate her wares, both physical and mental; Fielding's young couple are every bit as much on display (although they have no vanity or self-awareness in the matter), and his plot hinges, like Marivaux's, on the eventual kind of recognition or legitimacy they will receive. Fanny's beauty and Joseph's are the only stock they have, and, by portraying them as exploitable orphans or helpless servants, he says a good deal about the power structure of his time.

He also says a good deal about selfhood: precisely because their body is their supreme possession, Fanny and Joseph refuse to negotiate with it. Crucial to my argument is the notion that Joseph's "virtue" is more than comic, more than a parody of Richardson's Pamela: his virtue is quite simply his own body, and his own use of it constitutes no less than the orphan's declaration of independence:

> "Madam," said Joseph, "I can't see why her [a lady's] having no virtue should be a reason against my having any; or why, because I am a man, or because I am poor, my virtue must be subservient to her pleasures." (p. 25)

Joseph, like Moll, seeks independence and freedom to live as he pleases. The freedom he claims is largely, as it is to be in the case of Clarissa, a physical, a sexual, freedom. There is little to laugh at, in Joseph's desire to reserve himself for Fanny; in the youthful escapades of Mr. Wilson, who reports on no less than three visits to the surgeon, Fielding has etched an unforgettable picture of sexual excess and sexual penalty.

In short, there reigns a distorted, idealized image of Fielding's novels and Fielding's world, an image of roughhousing and gruff good humor, warm taverns, tankards of ale, foxhunts and yarns spun out amidst the fumes of pipe-smoking, lusty, people. "Fielding," the humane, generous, congenial narrator has understandably bequeathed this image, because he himself warms up and brightens—through his very telling—a narrative that is colder and darker than is usually allowed. Corruption and excess are everywhere prevalent, and only the pyrotechnics of a *deus-ex-machina* ending can save Joseph and Fanny from the clutches of the powerful predators.

The aura of tobacco smoke and tale-telling is identified with Fielding's work, because a large part of his novels takes place in taverns and inns; and it does so because it is dark and stormy and dangerous on the road. Cervantes' Don meets with bizarre folk in his epic of the road, but Joseph and Adams and Fanny meet primarily with thieves, muggers, and henchmen.

The novel of the open road, to which Fielding prophetically invites us as fellow-travellers, contains large stretches of darkness and violence. Bearing in mind Fielding's professed aim to espy Nature behind affectation, keeping equally before us the overlap between Nature and the body, and, finally, remembering that the body's sanctity constitutes, for Fielding, the literal integrity of the self (especially of the orphan), now let us consider three of the central dark and violent scenes to which I have alluded.[6] The first occurs early on, when Joseph is accosted on the road, robbed, stripped of his clothing, and beaten unconscious. Fielding then stages a grisly version of the Good Samaritan story, tinged with peculiarly modern echoes of fearful bystanders, unwilling to be involved. The situation is elemental: how to respond to Joseph's naked body, the very envelope of his Nature and his Self? The gentlemen in the coach respond by ribald jokes, while the lady's decorum absolutely forbids commerce with male nudity, preferring to let the body bleed or freeze to death, rather than taking it in. Only the generosity of the postilion and, later, of Betty, save Joseph through their concern for his vulnerability.

If the body is scorned here, it is attended to more energetically in the next scene that I want to mention. Adams and a gentleman are discoursing in the woods at night about the vagaries of courage and cowardice, when "on a sudden, they heard the most violent shrieks imaginable in a female voice" (p. 117). The gentleman flees, but, "the shrieks now increasing," Adams, "on coming up to the place whence the noise proceeded, found a woman struggling with a man, who had

---

[6] I am indebted here to Mark Spilka's work on *Joseph Andrews*, especially his article on comic irony where the body-nature paradigm is discussed at length: "A Comic Resolution in Fielding's *Joseph Andrews*," reprinted in *Fielding: A Collection of Critical Essays, op. cit.*, pp. 59–68.

thrown her on the ground, and had almost overpowered her"
(p. 117). What ensues is a fierce struggle in the dark, filled
with the blood that flows so freely in Fielding's novels, at the
end of which Adams subdues the would-be rapist and seeks
to console his near-victim: " 'Be of good cheer, damsel,' said
he, 'you are no longer in danger of your ravisher, who, I am
terribly afraid, lies dead at my feet; but God forgive me what
I have done in defence of innocence!' " (p. 119). But, it is dark,
and the young woman is "not without apprehensions even of
her deliverer" (p. 119). As Adams muses over his potential
manslaughter, the young woman fears another potential rape:
"The silence of Adams, added to the darkness of the night and
the loneliness of the place, struck dreadful apprehension into
the poor woman's mind; she began to fear as great an enemy
in her deliverer as he had delivered her from" (p. 120).

What is happening here is stark: we do not know who is
who in the dark. Joseph's naked body in the ditch is scorned;
Fanny is attacked in the sheltering night; Adams, at night, is
only another violent male, one who may complete what the
other started. There is nothing very cosy about these two
scenes, and they vividly illustrate the appeal and safety of taverns and inns. The question of "who is who in the dark?" is
arguably Fielding's most brilliant insight, and the magnificent
mistaken-rooms and musical-beds scenes in both *Joseph Andrews* and *Tom Jones* amply testify to the comic potential of
such a query. But, "who is who in the dark?" ineluctably
hints at the larger, now echoing, enigma: quite simply, "who
is who?" at all. Here is the affectation-chase, taken to its ultimate existential parameters, and *Joseph Andrews* presents considerable evidence that the world and the self are more multiple and mobile than convention allows. Multiplicity and
mobility are the very touchstones of the magnificent bed-
swapping crescendo of *Joseph Andrews*. All sexual identities,
just as the bodies of their owners, are up for grabs. Beau Di-
dapper, thinking he is bedding with Fanny, is instead abetted
by the lusting Slipslop. To this misplaced pair comes the naked Adams, and he is drastically abused by Nature's signs:

He made directly to the bed in the dark, where, laying hold
of the beau's skin (for Slipslop had torn his shirt almost

off), and finding his skin extremely soft, and hearing him
in a low voice begging Slipslop to let him go, he no longer
doubted but that this was the young woman in danger of
ravishing, and immediately falling on the bed, and laying
hold on Slipslop's chin, where he found a rough beard, his
belief was confirmed. . . . (p. 307)

The baroque round-robin achieves its finale when Adams un-
knowingly slips between the sheets with the sleeping Fanny.
Awakened, both, by Joseph, Adams proclaims his innocence
in absolute terms: "As I a Christian, I know not whether she
is a man or a woman" (p. 310). Joseph must lead the innocent
and ignorant Adams to his place. The comic exuberance of
this final scene is made possible by the same ignorance and
mobility which occasioned the scorn toward Joseph in the
ditch and the dread felt by Fanny in the dark. To honor Nature may be Fielding's creed, but his book is filled with characters who either transgress or deny it. In a topsy-turvy, met-
amorphosing world, to find one's own bed and proper mate
may be a feat of considerable navigation.

Beneath the sharp unitary veneer of Fielding's grotesques
lies a view of conduct that is anything but stable. The worthy
Adams explains to the bravery-obsessed gentleman that "a
man might be a coward at one time, and brave at another" (p.
116); the story of Leonora reveals, among other things, the
fission in personality and explosion of selves which the individual may experience: "As this vast profusion of ecstasy had
confounded her understanding, so there was nothing so foolish as her behavior: she played a thousand childish tricks, distorted her person into several shapes, and face into several
laughs, without any reason" (pp. 89-90); even Lady Booby's
changing emotional states may be ascribed to the hidden repertory which convention denies: "her mind was distracted
and her soul tossed up and down by many turbulent and opposite passions. She loved, hated, pitied, scorned, admired,
despised, the same person by fits, which changed in a very
short interval" (p. 261). More emphatic, even, than this discontinuity of self is the extraordinary mobility of the setting.
Joseph Andrews depicts a world where picaresque haphazard-
ness reigns, where babies may be kidnapped and exchanged at

birth, where orphans are even more peculiarly manipulated and exploited, at the will and pleasure of others. Finally, "Fielding" himself is drawn to mobility, an astonishing verbal mobility that plays out its tricks by shifting modes of narrative discourse,[7] interweaving dramatic and mock heroic description: surely the most enduring creation of verbal mobility is the divine Slipslop, a creature whose every utterance says more than she intends, opens up areas of discourse beyond what her monovalent exterior and corresponding heart could imagine: " 'Barbarous monster! how have I deserved that my passion should be resulted and treated with ironing?' " (p. 17), or " 'I assume your ladyship, I have no more to do with Common Garden than other folks. Really, your ladyship talks of servants as if they were not born of the Christian specious' " (pp. 272-273).

Fielding, as consummate dramatist, creates a stage-set rife with metamorphosis: bodies, sexual identity, and fixed meanings are liberated, set adrift from their moorings. Here is the fruitful New World that Diderot and Sterne will explore. In *Joseph Andrews*, however, darkness and mobility, episodic plot and corrupt codes, coalesce to create a kind of *ancien régime* fun-house, replete with *droit de seigneur*, freaks, rugs pulled out from under you, snares and traps at every turn: and it is against that circus-setting that Joseph's constancy and education must be measured.

[7] In addition to the well-known passages of mock-epic descriptions, Fielding is everywhere highlighting and utilizing his rhetorical tricks. Much like Joyce is to do in the "Cyclops" chapter of *Ulysses*, Fielding pits one style against another, juxtaposes cynical realism with flowery lyricism:

The wench soon got Joseph to bed, and promised to use her interest to borrow him a shirt; but imagining, as she afterwards said, by his being so bloody, that he must be a dead man, she ran with all speed to hasten the surgeon, who was more than half drest, apprehending that the coach had been overturned, and some gentleman or lady hurt. As soon as the wench had informed him at his window that it was a poor foot-passenger who had been stripped of all he had, and almost murdered, he chid her for disturbing him so early, slipped off his clothes again, and very quietly returned to bed and to sleep.

Aurora now began to show her blooming cheeks over the hills, whilst ten millions of feathered songsters, in jocund chorus, repeated odes a thousand times sweeter than those of our laureat, and sung both the day and the song. (p. 39)

Joseph coerces the episodic plot into a life-story. He asserts his love against every piety, convention, and law which counters him. He is lucid, where Adams is blind, and the young man leading the parson to his proper bed is emblematic of Joseph's developing selfhood. Whereas Adams causes hypocrisy to be visible, Joseph's role is to *assert* the legitimacy of Nature over and against all other claims. Unlike Adams, Joseph is not taken in by the deceit of appearances. In one of his earliest displays of lucidity, he reveals something of his own generosity as well; Joseph lessons Adams about hypocrisy:

> . . . for, whenever a man of fashion doth not care to fulfil his promises, the custom is to order his servants that he will never be at home to the person so promised. In London they call it denying him. I have myself denied Sir Thomas Booby above a hundred times. . . . (p. 155)

Joseph does not deny. He is animated by the body (Lady Booby's body does tempt him), but he is decorous and controlled in his pledge to Nature.[8] Joseph matures on the road; he debates with Adams on the relative merits of educational systems and the underlying causes of moral behavior. His constancy—to Adams as well as to Fanny—is fierce and absolute, defended with cudgel where necessary, articulated by passion everywhere in the latter part of the novel. Joseph Andrews is assailed by all the high-jinks that Fielding can throw at him: his new social status (now that his sister is married to Mr. Booby), the Christian code of acceptance if Fanny be permanently lost, and the ultimate barrier of incest if Fanny be his sister. It is on the strength of his rejecting these codes that my case for Joseph's selfhood is made.

Joseph's love ethos is every bit as absolute as Des Grieux's is to be, in *Manon Lescaut*. When Adams chides him for too much fondness, Joseph explodes in a dithyramb of certainty and assertion:

[8] Joseph does respond to others' flesh. He resists Lady Booby's advances, but effort was required: "But I am glad she turned me out of the chamber as she did: for I had once almost forgotten every word parson Adams had ever said to me" (p. 31).

"Well, sir," cries Joseph, "and if I love a mistress as well as you your child, surely her loss would grieve me equally."—"Yes, but such love is foolishness and wrong in itself, and ought to be conquered," answered Adams; "it savors too much of the flesh."—"Sure, sir," says Joseph, "it is not sinful to love my wife, no, not even to doat on her to distraction!"—"Indeed but it is," says Adams. "Every man ought to love his wife, no doubt; we are commanded so to do; but we ought to love her with moderation and discretion."—"I am afraid I shall be guilty of some sin in spite of all my endeavors," says Joseph; "for I shall love without any moderation, I am sure." (p. 286)

In defending the claims of his passion, Joseph Andrews is arguing for the rights of the self. Every code that is operative in this novel is transcended by Joseph's love ethic. He stands on his own, and refuses the authority of family and caste:

"I know not," replied Joseph, "that my parents have any power over my inclinations: nor am I obliged to sacrifice my happiness to their whim or ambition. . . . I am resolved on no account to quit my dear Fanny; no, though I could raise her as high above her present station as you [Mr. Booby] have my sister." (p. 277)

Mr. Booby hotly replies that his fortune authorizes his own marriage with Pamela, but that such action would be ridiculous on the part of Joseph. Joseph responds in kind, and his words are a tribute to the shaping, stabilizing powers of the self: " 'My fortune enables me to please myself likewise' " (p. 277). Let us give full weight to the word "fortune," for Joseph is claiming authority over all its possible meanings: financial wealth, cosmic chance, even narrational manipulation. Joseph is doing something crucial in these scenes: he is *establishing* a family. At one point, he is described as carrying off Fanny, "swearing he would own no relation to any one who was an enemy to her he loved more than all the world" (p. 297). Even the threat of incest can be braved, because relationship can be hallowed where the flesh cannot: "if they found themselves to be really brother and sister, they vowed a perpetual celibacy, and to live together all their days, and indulge a Platonic friendship for each other" (p. 311).

To make a family, to "own" a relation to a person of one's choice, is to assert a staggering human freedom. In the face of Fielding's mobility, Joseph shapes his own life. He is to discover himself the son of the Wilsons, but—unlike Oedipus or even Simplicius, for whom the knowledge of their origin is the key to their life—such retrospective, technical, legitimacy merely paves the way for a turn of the plot: it in no way determines or explains Joseph Andrews, for he is manifestly his own creation. Joseph's legitimacy, like Moll's and Marianne's, does not depend on mothers and fathers, but derives from the independent authority of the self.

Joseph's marriage with Fanny returns us and them to the essential Nature-body equation. No longer *Mr.* Joseph,[9] Joseph weds Fanny virtually without ceremony. The two beautiful bodies are to be united, and we are told that Joseph "refused all finery" and Fanny is equally unadorned. Fielding views their consummation as the ultimate fusion of natures, and he permits himself to "describe" her preparing for her wedding night: "Undressing to her was properly discovering, not putting off, ornaments, for, as all her charms were the gifts of nature, she could divest herself of none" (p. 319). Here is the final victory over affectation; the body, no longer exposed or violated, can be seen, savored, and can at last enjoy its special bliss. The two orphans have been "outfitted" with parents, but they have more truly discarded all possible externals—the clothing of society and culture, all forms of possible affectation—and they are celebrating uniquely their selves themselves.

That they should do so in an exclusively physical way cannot surprise us, for the body is the locus of the self in *Joseph Andrews*. In achieving union with Fanny, Joseph has made his individual way, and the road-epic of self-realization is terminated. Yet, Fielding knew that other avenues for self-fulfillment were possible, even if the romance must close with the

[9] By decking Joseph out in finery and giving him great expectations, Fielding is doing more than mimicking Richardson's *Pamela*; he is equating social rank and appearance with façade, indeed, with affection itself.

embrace. In one of the strangest exchanges of the novel, Adams argues for the enabling virtues of literature, as against experience; the dominant metaphor is precisely that of the voyage. The host, a former seagoing man, insists that travel imparts life experience: " 'Ah, master! master!' says the host, 'if you had travelled as far as I have, and conversed with the many nations where I have traded, you would not give any credit to a man's countenance' " (p. 160). To which assertion, Adams invokes a different type of locomotion:

> "Master of mine, perhaps I have travelled a great deal farther than you without the assistance of a ship. Do you imagine sailing by different cities or countries is travelling? No.
> 'Caelum non animum mutant qui trans mare currunt.'
> I can go futher in an afternoon than you in a twelvemonth."
> (p. 160)

As the discussion continues, it becomes clear that Fielding is measuring two kinds of trips: the contingent one of flesh and the imaginative one of thought and reading. Parson Adams, modeled as he is on Don Quijote, doubtless approaches the world through the lens of literature, and he frequently misreads appearances drastically for just that reason. Yet, Fielding is not Cervantes, and there is belief and admiration in the vicarious experience offered through literature. If Fielding is unlike Cervantes, and seeing the world through books may not be as foolish as we think, Fielding is nonetheless not yet Sterne, for whom the hobbyhorse replaces the horse, for whom imaginative and imaginary voyages become man's most powerful means of locomotion. The appeal of the literary journey, the growth of self in and through language, is not unfelt by Fielding, but it appears largely in the creation of that verbal jack-of-all-trades, "Fielding," rather than in the constant, unplayful Joseph Andrews. Verbal play, yes, but as the prerogative of the narrator, not yet as the instrumentality of the protagonist within the text.

Joseph Andrew's strength and weakness are to be found in his body. Unimaginative and uninventive, Joseph is at home entirely in his flesh; his configuration stops with his body.

But, in his body, there is both Nature and Grace. Neither a repertory of masks nor a biological prison, Joseph's body is an excellent thing, fully coextensive with his self, fully preserved and possessed as the inalienable property of the orphan who has nothing else. Joseph's body will take him and Fanny through life, and, as Fielding tells us, there is an important lesson in such prowess:

> Joseph and Fanny halted some time, considering what to do; at last they advanced a few paces, where the declivity seemed least steep; and then Joseph, taking his Fanny in his arms, walked firmly down the hill, without making a false step, and at length landed her at the bottom, where Adams soon came to them.
>
> Learn hence, my fair countrywomen, to consider your own weakness, and the many occasions on which the strength of a man may be useful to you; and, duly weighing this, take care that you match not yourselves with the spindle-shanked beaux and *petit-maîtres* of the age, who, instead of being able, like Joseph Andrews, to carry you in lusty arms through the rugged ways and downhill steeps of life, will rather want to support their feeble limbs with your strength and assistance. (p. 171)

Joseph is the *embodied* self, and he offers a kind of integrity and fixity which will come to seem Edenic, as the metamorphoses and imaginative extensions of his successors arrive on the scene.

What clashes here of wills gen wonts, ostrygods gaggin fishygods!
Brékkek kékkek kékkek! Kóax Kóax Kóax! Ualu Ualu Ualu!
Quaouauh!—James Joyce, *Finnegans Wake*

COLLISION

WITHIN THE TRAJECTORY of this study, the three novels analyzed in the last chapter constitute a brief interlude of equilibrium and happiness. The three orphans—Moll, Marianne, and
Joseph—are finally taken in by society in a mutual process of
recognition. The protagonists variously assert their independence and achieve their special legitimacy. In the picaresque
and Baroque models, such assertion was either impossible or
lethal: Lazarillo sells out, Pablos moves on, Simplicius retreats, and the Princess disappears. Defoe and Marivaux tap
the survival resources of the self, and Fielding shows that natural goodness must prevail. In no case do we find anything
that might be called genuine antagonism or incompatibility.

That is no longer the case in *Manon Lescaut, Clarissa,
Werther,* and *Les Liaisons dangereuses.* These are fictions of ir-
remediable conflict. The resourceful self of Defoe and Marivaux has now discovered, both within and without, needs
that cannot be assuaged and forces that cannot be absorbed.
The subjective fullness of Marivaux is no longer serenely self-
contained, but checked by its inner stresses: Des Grieux, Clarissa, and Werther have none of the charm and resilience that
we saw in Marianne; their exacerbated consciousness is focussed exclusively on loss and pain, rather than on seduction
and ascension. The economic and social constraints which
Moll could take in stride now work their will on the protagonists of Prévost, Richardson, and Goethe; rather than stimulating a splendid show of energies, money and caste are
causes of desperation and degradation for Des Grieux, of im-

prisonment and dispossession for Clarissa, of alienation and bitterness for Werther.

The environmental, contextual cocoon has burst: Des Grieux, Werther, and Clarissa experience a radical sense of limits, of aloneness and powerlessness. Yet, in some troubling way, literature benefits, as it always does, from such misery and enclosure. In short, the self has come into its own, and Des Grieux, Werther, and Clarissa have a hunger for self-ful-fillment and gratification unlike anything seen up to now. Whereas Lazarillo and Pablos were starving for food, these characters have capacious egos to nourish. Swollen, almost bursting with their inner wants, they usurp the attention of the novelist and maniacally display their wares on the printed page. Filled with longings and great expectations, they are bent on achieving selfhood. Their consciousness and their passion have become the authority of the novel.

The novel moves toward a tragic impasse, a perfect double-bind, in these works. The discovery of one's inner fullness and need is concomitant with the realization that the world outside the self—Society and the Other—must either disap-point or destroy. We are now far from beggars and orphans. Des Grieux, Clarissa and Werther are the children of privi-lege, the chosen few, the elite who are to inherit the earth: but the persistent motif of *Manon Lescaut*, *Clarissa*, and *Werther* is that inheritances are not forthcoming.

Inheritance betokens the legacy of the past and the where-withal to cope with the future. These three characters are fig-uratively and literally disinherited: each asserts an intolerable kind of pure individualism that expels them from parental protection and Old World values. Finally, the unswerving fo-cus on the self highlights and valorizes human emotion in a way unheard of before. Feeling displaces and discredits all else in these fictions; *Manon Lescaut*, *Clarissa*, and *Werther* function as paradigmatic love guests, both for their contemporary cul-ture and for the future of the novel. Fullness is inseparable from need, and self-fulfillment is inextricably blended with the promise and threat of relationship. Again the double-bind: not only does society hurt, but the love quest itself is doomed. Hence, collision signifies failure and confrontation at every level: the self collides with the other and with its setting. The individual's deepest need may be for relationship, but the novel of individualism, energized exclusively by the spiraling wants of the self, is rife with blindness and narcissism.

Finally, in *Les Liaisons dangereuses* we see the full spectacular drama of self-fulfillment and relationship. It is a kind of promontory, and final point in the journey of self-affirmation. The art and science of Valmont and Merteuil derive precisely from the centrality of affective wants. No novel has, before or since, better charted the parameters of knowledge and need. It would seem that the swollen self cannot shrink, that its range and repertory, once appropriated by language and literature, cannot be denied. But after *Les Liaisons*, relationship will no longer be a mode of enactment. New freedoms must be sought, and a new kind of literature must evolve, totally open-ended and dangerless.

Old Worlds and New Worlds: *Manon Lescaut*

At a particularly dramatic moment in Prévost's novel *Manon Lescaut*, the young protagonist Des Grieux has just rescued his mistress from the grim Hôpital; as they are about to make their getaway, the coachman asks what the destination is to be, and Des Grieux replies: "Go to the ends of the earth and take me to a place where I need never be separated from Manon."[1] The novel will finally take them both to the end of the world, to the New World, but even that may not be far enough. At the core of this novel is the need to find or to make a new place; it is the central preoccupation of the character Des Grieux and also the literary problem of the Abbé Prévost.

At one point, while imprisoned in his home, Des Grieux visualizes the good life in the following terms:

> I imagined an isolated house, with small woods and a soft brook at the end of the garden, a library of chosen books, a select number of virtuous and practical friends, a clean table with modest and frugal board. I then added a corre-

[1] The translations from *Manon Lescaut* are my own.

spondence with a friend residing in Paris who would keep
me abreast of public events, not so much to satisfy my curiosity as to entertain me with the madcap behavior of
men.[2]

This calm, bucolic setting, Des Grieux realizes, would be perfect in all respects except one: Manon should be there to share
it with him. Idyllic, a bit literary, certainly unreal, Des
Grieux's pastoral longings are wholly out of place in this fast-
moving urban novel, filled with con-men and thieves. And,
rather than completing the rustic picture of contentment, the
presence of Manon annihilates it, for she ushers Des Grieux
into a world unlike any he has ever seen or dreamed of. When
she comes to reclaim him at Saint Sulpice after he has made
his speech at the Sorbonne, he falls, in his words, back into
the precipice of an absolute passion; stunned by the rush of
his senses and emotions, Des Grieux can hardly respond to
her caresses, because he is passing into another world:

> What a shift from the tranquillity I had enjoyed to the tu-
> multuous emotions I now felt again! I was horrified! I trem-
> bled, as you would in the middle of the night in a deserted
> countryside: you feel carried off into a new order of things;
> you are gripped by a secret terror which wears off gradu-
> ally only when you carefully study the surroundings.[3]

This passage contains virtually the entire novel. Let us not
make light of the preromantic language of sensibility: "tu-
multuous emotions," "horrified," "trembled," "secret terror." Des Grieux is to learn a new order of things, a passional
order which will govern the remainder of his life. And to enter that realm of passion is to leave both the teeming world of
Paris and the desired idyllic landscape far behind for a new
setting that strikes terror in the eyes of its beholder, a setting
that is reminiscent of the title of a collection of stories by John
Hawkes, *Lunar Landscapes*. We note, especially, the passivity
of the victim who finds himself suddenly in a nocturnal
world, filled with a secret horror, seeking orientation. This
bleak landscape is the new affective world that Des Grieux is
to explore and which Prévost intends to set forth in his novel.

It is a setting of the soul and it may seem at variance with the streets and casinos of Paris, but the two lovers will eventually come upon a New Orleans that looks strangely like the land-scape we have just examined:

> There were barren, empty plains, where all that could be seen were some weeds and a few wind-swept trees.[4]

The New Orleans adventure turns out badly, but where can they go? "Where to flee? in an unknown desert land, inhabited only by wild animals and still wilder Indians?"[5] Their final joint effort is a pilgrimage across the American wasteland: "To get to their colonies we needed to walk for several days across barren plains and mountains so high and steep that the path discouraged even the crudest and strongest men."[6] The delicate Manon will not make it. Those sterile and barren reaches, populated only by animals and Indians, ushered into the story's plot only at the close, are experientially encoun-tered and charted at the outset by Des Grieux; it is the land of the heart, no longer a 17th-century parlor game version of the Carte du Tendre, but a reality so compelling as a realm of feeling that it is actualized as a place of dirt and rock and, fi-nally, death.

Manon Lescaut virtually opens with the expulsion of Des Grieux and Manon from France. From the outset the reader knows that the two lovers cannot be tolerated in the Old World. It is, on all accounts, a corrupt world. When Des Grieux's father lambastes him for immoral and dishonorable conduct, the young man gives us an impressive list of counts, dukes, princes, marquis, and bishops for whom cheating and whoring are routine matters. It is a world marked by hypoc-risy and exchange. Hypocrisy is everywhere, in that lip serv-ice is still paid to traditional concepts of morality and honor. The family still stands as a viable institution, but it functions as a prison; the father claims love and tenderness, but we see tyranny and cynicism; the older generation (Des Grieux's father, M. de B., the old G.M. the voluptuary) makes noises about respectability and loyalty, but is in fact in rampant de-cay and engaged in desperate sexual warfare with its own sons; the Church is a refuge for the underendowed, such as

Tiberge, and it conceals murders if the murderer is of noble birth; above all, it too functions as a prison. Prévost knows that this world of tradition is crumbling, and a new breed is on the rise and on the make. Whereas Lesage gives us an elegant picture of cheating and one-upmanship in *Turcaret*, Prévost introduces unforgettable creatures such as *frère* Lescaut, who knows the ins and outs of all gambling houses and swindler associations. When Des Grieux is without funds, *frère* Lescaut does not hesitate with his advice: "A girl like her should take care of all of us, you, her and me" (p. 55); if that is not acceptable, he can put Des Grieux "in touch with some old and rich woman" (p. 56). Parasites are everywhere, and Des Grieux is literally in good company when he becomes one. If hypocrisy masks the illness, I would be tempted to call the malady exchange. Everything and, it would seem, everybody in Paris has its price. Manon, somewhat like Zola's Nana a century and a half later, is the fine flower of an entire society's corruption. One's body, like other capital goods, is a commodity to be bought and sold; Manon knows this, and so do those who press her. M. de B. "had declared his love as a true *fermier général*, that is, by indicating in a letter that payment would be in proportion to services rendered."[7] When Des Grieux tries to accompany Manon before she is deported, the guards indignantly refuse him that privilege if he cannot pay the current Parisian rate for such favors. The finest example of exchange in the novel is of course the young courtesan whom Manon sends to Des Grieux as a replacement when she decides to stay with the younger G.M. In such a context, human and sexual relations are reduced to a barter state. It is against this backdrop that Des Grieux's passion must be measured and assessed. He asserts the primacy of love over all else; he does not want his father to buy him a girl, and he cannot abide Manon's inconstancy. He wants to establish a love ethic which cuts across all the rules of this dying Old World.

He has problems, not just those he runs into, but also those he carries around inside himself. For Des Grieux is an enormously flawed hero. It is well known that Montesquieu considered Des Grieux and his paramour to be among the first

instances of *"un fripon et une catin"* in literature.[2] Des Grieux
does continue to claim moral superiority over all those he encounters, even while he is a cheat and a murderer. He lies
whenever it suits his purpose, and it suits his purpose more
and more as the book progresses. When he has something to
gain from someone, especially money, he waxes absolutely
lyrical. Tiberge functions largely in this manner in the story,
and he triggers hypocritical effusions such as the following:

> Nothing is more admirable, or does more honor to virtue,
> than the confidence with which we approach those people
> whom we know to have great integrity. We sense that there
> is no risk involved. If they are not always in a position to
> offer assistance, we are at least certain to receive kindness
> and compasson. One's heart, which remains so carefully
> closed to other people, opens naturally in their presence, as
> a flower opens in the light of the sun, sensing that only
> good things are to come.[8]

At another point, when Des Grieux is putting the finger on
Tiberge, we read:

> Our conversation was most friendly. He wished to know
> of my intentions. I opened my heart to him without hold-
> ing back, except for my plan to escape. It is not in your
> eyes, dear friend, I told him, that I should want to appear
> other than I am.[9]

When it is time to touch the father, we hear the following:
"A father's heart is the masterpiece of Nature, who establishes
her rule there with ease and who controls all its workings."[10]
In short, Des Grieux is blatantly and lyrically unreliable about
his own motives, and the story he would tell us diverges considerably from the one we see in front of us.

[2] In our day, Erich Auerbach has come down still harder on Prévost's
characters: "As for its moral aspects, we hear a great deal about honor and
virtue, and although the Chevalier becomes a sharper, a cheat, and almost a
pander, he yet never gives up his habit of expressing noble feelings and of
allowing himself the pleasure of making moralizing observations which, to
be sure, are extremely trite and sometimes rather curious but which the author evidently takes quite seriously." *Mimesis: The Representation of Reality in
Western Literature*, tr. Willard Trask (New York: Doubleday, 1957), p. 351.

There is another problem with Des Grieux, and that is what
Poulet has called his discontinuity, or, more mildly, his oscil-
lations. The young man is accurate when he says, "I was destined for brief joys and long suffering" (p. 75). Des Grieux
shifts back and forth, almost pathologically, between states of
mind and feeling. Poulet has pointed out that the classic notion of a stable identity collapses here. What may have been
"*ondoyant*" in Montaigne is almost manic in Des Grieux.
Moreover, the structure of the novel is such as to heighten
and illuminate the crisis nature of the protagonist; the story
consists of a series of *coups de théâtre*, each involving the loss
of money or Manon, either by fire or theft or outright betrayal; and, in each case, Des Grieux responds in a most fulsome manner, through tears, swooning, changes of mood,
and a good deal of rhetoric. For Prévost is vitally interested in
those changing mental and affective states of Des Grieux. Des
Grieux lovingly deals with each of his crises so that the reader
will not miss the point. That world of passion which Des
Grieux enters at the outset of the story, metaphorized as a lunar landscape, a new world, is the chief business of the Abbé
Prévost. This slender book is sensuous and lush in its language and style; Prévost is interested in evoking the sensations of pleasure and pain. When Des Grieux has his first *tête-
à-tête* with Manon, he is astonished by his physical response:
"My heart was flooded by countless feelings of bliss such I
had never imagined. A sweet warmth spread through my
veins."[11] The young man is having a sensual education, and
the author succeeds in evoking the rush and flush and tingle
of pleasure that he feels. Even though they are seen as children, the couple cannot keep their hands off each other and
are lovers before they know it. Des Grieux discovers the
power of sex, and it is abundantly clear that their erotic relationship is mutually satisfying; Manon takes on other lovers,
but only Des Grieux can fully gratify her sexually: he is the
only one "who could make her perfectly savor the pleasures
of love."[12]

Along with the erotic power of their union, Prévost also
wishes to emphasize the multitude of emotive states which
Des Grieux experiences because of Manon. When he learns,

for example, that Manon has been thrust into the Hôpital, he is overcome with fury and madly attacks old G.M.:

> He was freed from my hands. I myself had almost lost all strength and breath. God, I cried, sighing mightily; heavenly justice! Must I live on, even a minute, after such infamy? I wanted to throw myself on the beast who had just undone me. I was stopped. My misery, my cries and my tears were beyond belief. I did such extraordinary things that all who were there, and who did not understand my reasons, looked at one another with as much fear as surprise.[13]

Prévost wants us to perceive the spectacular dimension of Des Grieux's reaction, because he is intent on heralding into literature, through this novel, a world of pathological, disruptive, inchoate emotional states left relatively unexplored by earlier literature. Des Grieux's finest hour is probably the multiple affective reaction to the ersatz courtesan whom Manon sends him to pass the time away with. He speaks first of a "dark and ominous calm," which suddenly becomes "a terrible onslaught of fury"; then tears come as "the feeling of rage that I just felt changed into deep pain" (p. 136). Shakespeare and Racine had dramatized passion before, but one is tempted to say that Prévost is among the first to be in the enemy camp, sometimes celebrating, sometimes clinically observing, always attentive to the outbreak of the emotions as the most authentic expression of the self. We are accustomed to the label "the age of sensibility," but it is important to realize how new it all is in this novel, how Des Grieux is a hero in the name of and because of his passion. The young man quite simply redefines nobility as the faculty to feel:

> Ordinary people are sensitive to only five or six passions, around which their life revolves, and to which all their emotions can be traced. Take away from them love and hate, pleasure and pain, hope and fear, and they will no longer feel anything. But those of a more noble cast can be moved in countless different ways; it would seem that they have more than five senses, that they can experience ideas

and sensations which go beyond the ordinary limits of nature.[14]

To be "*commun*" is to be alive merely to five or six passions;
but those who experience the gamut, the extremes and the
nuances of the affective life, those people are the truly "noble"
ones. The political language of Des Grieux's assertion is borne
out by the transgressions he enacts throughout the novel; his
love is innocent, and he is not only justified, but somehow superior, in his passional exploits. This is a dangerous doctrine
to proclaim. The young man's father is quite willing to buy
him a courtesan, and Manon herself, wise in the arts of ex-
changing bodies, offers him a replacement as well. But what
is anonymous lust or pleasure is converted by Des Grieux into
a private ethos, a new code of ecstasy and fidelity which
supersedes and, if necessary, abolishes all previous standards
and values. The individual's affective life has been discovered
in all its fullness by Des Grieux, and everything else must be
swept aside.

To be sure, Des Grieux has no political consciousness
whatsoever, and the more corrupt the society is, the easier it
is for him to prey on it. But the novel shows vividly that
Manon, and the passional world she leads him to, are totally
incompatible with the Old World's conventions and expectations. Des Grieux's career is a kind of civic-societal descent
into hell: Des Grieux is transformed, willy-nilly, into a flawed,
fraudulent, but nonetheless outspoken existentialist hero:
Manon becomes his religion, his honor, his creed: "What is
there to match her? Up to now I have given up nothing. For
me, she replaces glory, happiness and fortune."[15] The ethic of
passion is a threat to this dying world, and Des Grieux will be
resisted by any and all means available. At the very core of
Des Grieux's affective revolution is his sexual prowess; society will strike back in just that area.

We have said that the plot is a series of disasters, of *coups
de théâtre*, each eliciting a flow of tears and powerful emotions. But, if we look closer, we will see another pattern as
well; let us begin with the famous passage that Auerbach has
analyzed and that he calls the interrupted supper. It is an inti-

mate scene which is building up to a kind of emotional release
as both the lovers are softly weeping; there is a knock on the
door, Manon gives Des Grieux a kiss, disappears, and in come
three servants who hold Des Grieux and take away his knife.
The next scene I would mention finds the couple, not at supper, but in bed; they have deceived G.M., but their reward is
not to be enjoyed: "We were still in bed when a police officer
came into our room with half a dozen guards."[16] They are
again separated. A more elaborate replay of this same scene
again finds them in bed, this time in the bed which the young
G.M. had intended to use with Manon; we read, "We were
lost in ecstasy, and the sword was hanging over our heads."[17]
By this time, we begin to wonder whether that blade is sus-
pended over Des Grieux's head, or over another part of his
body. It is their nemesis, old G.M. who comes into the room,
and the description is telling:

> We were ready to get in bed. He opens the door, and my
> blood curdles at the sight of him. O God, it is old G.M., I
> told Manon. I jump for my sword; it was unfortunately
> caught up in my belt. The guards, who saw my attempt,
> closed in quickly to take it from me. A man in his nightshirt
> is powerless.[18]

All of these scenes are, with varying emphases, a form of coi-
tus interruptus, and I think one can say straight-out that the
forces of order want not only to separate Des Grieux and
Manon, but, more specifically, want to prevent him from
making love to her, want to emasculate, even to castrate, Des
Grieux as the most effective way of dealing with the threat he
poses. In this light, a number of bizarre scenes open up rather
interestingly. For example, the plan for rescuing Manon from
the Hôpital involves disguising her in a man's clothes; they
have gotten into her room, she is putting on the clothes, but
there is one hitch: no pants.

> Nothing was missing for her outfit, except the pants that I
> had unfortunately forgotten. Forgetting that necessary ar-
> ticle would have doubtless made us laugh, had the trouble
> it caused us been less serious. I was frantic that such a *bag-*

atelle might cause us to be arrested. So I made up my mind and decided to walk out without pants myself. I took off my own and gave them to Manon. My cape was long, and with the help of several pins, I made myself decent enough to go to the door.[19]

It is a marvelous, uncanny little vignette, and it adds nothing to the narrative business at hand. Why is it there? We must assume that Prévost, a century and a half before Freud, was depicting fear of castration, or impotency, or exposure, in the form of a man in public without his pants on, trying to cover up with a cape. In like manner, the door to Manon's room at the Hôpital can only be opened or penetrated by means of "a frightfully large key" (*"une clef d'une grandeur effroyable"*). Again, there is no reason for this key to be of a *"grandeur effroyable,"* other than to suggest some kind of sexual apprehension. The last instance I would mention is perhaps the most classical: is Des Grieux's gun loaded or not? He asks *frère* Lescaut to give him an unloaded gun, but, in trouble, he pulls the trigger and it turns out to be potent after all; when he then sees Lescaut, he first blames him for the murder, but then thanks him for having loaded the weapon nonetheless. It is a richly symbolic scene: Des Grieux, in and out of numerous social institutions which all act as prisons, is carrying a gun: is it loaded? Is he potent enough to overturn that society? Or will he lose Manon, and be disarmed and unmanned?

Up to now, I have argued as if Des Grieux's only problem were society, but it is Manon herself who deceives him, who seems to share but cannot live by his individualized love ethic. She protests, sincerely I think, that her love for him never wavers, even though her body changes camps and partners rather frequently. Manon is perhaps society's most insidious weapon, the epitome of the Old World's exchange ethic: her beauty and her body are her only assets, and she will trade with them when necessary; love, she implies, is beyond the body, and the fidelity she both grants and requests is that of the *heart.* Material circumstances alter body conditions:

> I swear to you, dear Chevalier, that you are my heart's idol, and you are the only person in the world whom I could

love as I do; but, don't you see, my dear sweet friend, that
in our current situation, fidelity would be a most stupid virtue? Do you think we could be very tender, if we were hungry?[20]

Is the fidelity of the heart just a convenient myth, an escape
clause for utter promiscuousness? Or is it a mature, almost
sublime, recognition that the heart can remain intact and pure
even in a contingent, materialist, barter-world?

Much has been written (usually by men) about the mystery
and elusiveness of Manon as character. Seen almost exclusively through the eyes of her lover, the young woman herself
is both embellished and, strangely, intact. We do not know
her from the inside, as we do Des Grieux; she is, in many
ways indeed, an object, an object of Des Grieux's perception
and desire, an object of sexual exchange in the Parisian market. Raymond Picard has pointed out how irrelevant any
moral code is,[3] when discussing Manon's "natural" behavior;
this is obviously not just the reader's problem, but it is quin-
tessentially Des Grieux's quandary as well. Manon's mystery
may account for her seductiveness, but it must be added that
she is unknowable because Des Grieux wants to possess—not
to know—her. *His* wants and sensations are so compelling, so
delicious, that we (and he) may miss the extraordinary narcissism of his pose. These two young people, who love each
other so arduously, are consistently baffled by the other's position. Des Grieux finds it crude and inconceivable that
Manon can give her body to others while claiming constancy
to him, and he never attempts to deal with what she actually
says; Manon is confused each time Des Grieux lectures her on

[3] Picard describes Manon as essentially a natural creature, for whom con-
structs or principles are distinctly peripheral affairs.

Manon est *donnée* au lecteur comme un absolu: incompréhensible et im-
muable. Le problème de la volonté avait encore un sens pour des Grieux;
il n'en a pas pour elle. Manon est posée là, sans justification, sans recul à
l'égard d'elle-même, presque sans pensée. Elle *est*. On ne peut parler d'elle
qu'en termes de *nature*: relever ses illogismes ou ses immoralités serait vain
et même un peu ridicule. Dans cet univers de faiblesse humaine, elle est
pure faiblesse et pure gratuité. (Introduction to Garnier edition of *Manon
Lescaut*, p. cxx).

morality; she is genuinely distressed by his distress, but she will offend again because she does not really fathom what he is talking about. Yet, if the two people are at a stand-off, their positions undercut and illuminate each other, and the *reader* may well begin to sense that Manon's odd kind of constancy illuminates the intensely rhetorical, inflated, hyperbolic love language of Des Grieux, that he may love *love* more than Manon; likewise, Des Grieux's ethic of monogamous passion as sole fulfillment reveals the crass materialism of Manon, her dependency on pleasure and entertainment. Only when France itself is left, when the Old World is literally abandoned, will the impasse between the lovers disappear. I would like to insist on their impasse, because it allows us to see what we ordinarily would not see: the enormous ego-mania of each character. Des Grieux rants and raves as a love-advocate, but the states of pain and ecstasy he describes are strictly his own; likewise, Manon brings him, almost routinely, great pain, and yet she insists that she loves him. Each is faithful, not to the other, but to his or her own code; they are actually blind to each other.

The change that occurs is a subtle but profound one. Manon changes: her behavior in New Orleans is described as "*réglé.*" And she begins to speak in a first person plural which indicates an opening of the self of some magnitude. When the final crisis with Synnelet and the governor arises, Manon, well-versed in the art of going her own way and patching up things for herself, says something revolutionary: "Let us escape together; we mustn't lose a moment" (p. 196). Perhaps the finest indication that the materialist bind is broken, that one *can* be both tender and without bread, can be seen when Des Grieux says that the crudeness of their New Orleans situation is offset by the richness of their love:

> Moreover, you are an extraordinary chemist, I added, giving her a kiss, you change everything into gold.
> Then you will be the richest man in the world, she answered me, not only has there never been a love such as yours, it is also impossible for anyone to be as beloved as you are.[21]

What follows is a genuine *mea culpa*, a recognition that loving is not enough, unless it can move from possession to generosity, to an awareness of the other. That is the kind of love they have in New Orleans: it is mutual and even, and it does not require a materialist back-up, because it alone confers riches.

As we know, the story does not end here. The cottage in the woods is not to be. New Orleans may be composed of barracks and hovels, but it is ultimately modeled on Paris, and when Des Grieux and Manon confess they are not married and request permission to become so, they again confront the Old World. Perhaps Prévost is also saying that the slightest move in the direction of society, such as the wish for the public sanction of marriage, is fraught with dangers and may boomerang. Having finally resolved their own conflicts, the two lovers have yet to find an adequate new world. Their eyes may be opened to each other, but little else has been learned.

One is obliged to say that Des Grieux may have *left* the Old World but he has never adequately measured or recognized it. Critics have often noticed the mixture of styles in *Manon Lescaut*, the stylized passional language of Racine in a world of lackeys and thieves. Des Grieux, in his underwear, can exclaim *"Je suis d'un sang plus noble que le tien."* Imprisoned in the Hôpital, their love transforms it into Versailles. We have seen, in our discussion of the role of language in Quevedo's *Buscón*, that verbal resources may be the only resources we have, that Pablos is able to "breakfast" on words when nothing else is available. In *Manon Lescaut* the elevated courtly language of passion may give dignity to Des Grieux's love threat, but, even more powerfully, it blinds the young man to the real world he inhabits. Each time there is theft or betrayal, Des Grieux dutifully accuses the Gods and Fate itself; but, unlike the worlds of Sophocles and even Racine, where such language is appropriate, Prévost's world is utterly desacralized, and we may confidently substitute the concept of *money* when Des Grieux speaks of destiny. Money is the only inheritance Des Grieux seeks from his father; the rest he rejects. This, in itself, may be the most modern feature of the novel, and it ap-

pears fully a century before Balzac exploits it as his major
theme. Money is indeed the supreme ersatz; Des Grieux re-
counts his ardent quest for Manon, but we see that the true
goddess he pursues—found in gambling halls, in the purses of
friends and family—is money itself. But he does not know it.
He sees only his motive, whereas we see the contours of his
acts. This is a novel of cyclopic passion. Its parody seems to
be only for its readers.

One of the most telling scenes in the novel occurs when
Des Grieux masquerades as a young country priest parading
as Manon's brother in the house of M. de G . . . M . . . The
scene is worthy of Molière, as the young man slyly alludes to
his passion for Manon ("You see, Monsieur, our flesh is very
related")[22] while painting a satiric picture of the old voluptuary right to his face. Yet, the enduring irony in this passage is
surely self-directed: the naive young priest whom Des Grieux
impersonates is precisely the person he has ceased to be, the
person his natural virtues and his social rank intended him to
be. He is mimicking his own ghost. Des Grieux sees only his
own passion, but he is ignorant of Manon and of his world.
He does achieve relation with Manon, but he never does com-
prehend the sociological nature of the world he confronts or
the moral degradation of his own acts. Those larger codes of
reference are visible only to the reader. Here we may perceive,
I think, the critical corollary of individualist fiction: the centrality and authority of the self may emerge in the narrative
strategy, but the World and the Other do not conveniently
disappear. Hence the reader must assess these narratives with
care, in order to achieve that fuller picture, in which the self's
hunger is put into perspective and the dialectic between individual and setting is properly realized.

Yet, Des Grieux's myopia is the index of his passion as well
as of his ignorance. In New Orleans, he again confronts the
recognizable social machinery, but he is running out of room.
They leave New Orleans and head into the desert with nothing but their passion. There are no social accouterments left.
Early on, Tiberge had warned them: "May your luck and
your money disappear beyond recall, and you remain naked
and alone, so that you feel the vanity of those worldly goods

that have so inebriated you."[23] It has come about. Des Grieux,
without pants, has already suffered exposure once in Paris.
This second exposure is addressed, not to the genitals, but to
the entire person, and they are without shelter, without resources: "We sat down in the middle of a vast plain, without
even a tree for shelter."[24] There is *only Old World*, and it has
expulsed them, twice now. The phallic imagery pitifully reap-
pears as Des Grieux breaks his sword to dig a hole for
Manon's burial. The broken sword, an eloquent image of the
collapse of a chivalric code, will not even open up the earth.
Des Grieux is again naked to the elements, as he wraps
Manon's dead body in his clothes. Manon dies in this wasteland setting; it is that lunar landscape of the heart, and although Prévost suggests that our most authentic experiences
emanate from there, he shows with considerable power that
we cannot live there.

In *Manon Lescaut* Prévost announces the dilemma that will
haunt 19th-century French realism, and it delineates in paradigmatic form the plight of the problematic hero in a degraded world. By stressing the affective, pathological development of his protagonist, Prévost adumbrates a new kind of
writing and a new ethic of living. The swollen figure of Des
Grieux and the voluminous emotional life he discovers within
himself dominate the novel, making the narrative frame a
mere ornament rather than a refraction, making the discrep-
ancies of the tale visible and significant only for the reader.
Des Grieux's singleness of vision and of commitment are the
abiding authority within the text; the individual's psychology
reigns supreme, and the appetites of the self claim their due.
There is nothing within the text to brook or curb such hunger, and Prévost's loving, mimetic language weds us to Des
Grieux, grants him and us no escape routes of fantasy or
dream. The result is a collision course, as the young man
founders on a world he has ever misconstrued. That world,
present but misinterpreted throughout the novel, is resistant
to passion and hostile to the self. Ultimately, then, Des
Grieux is doubly doomed: the affective universe he discovers
is one of great pain as well as of ecstasy, and the social world
to which he brings his tidings of love will fight back. The

lame ending of the novel cannot palliate its stark truths: passion betokens an awakening of the self and a threat to society;
gratification is brief; reconciliation with this world, unconvincing; transcendence to another, impossible.

The Failure of Feeling: *Die Leiden des jungen Werthers*

In Goethe's *Leiden des jungen Werthers* we meet the test case,
or better, the problem child of individualism in early fiction.
The book was infamous in its time, eliciting not only admiration but even imitation in the form of real suicides committed in blue frock coat and yellow vest. Yet, posterity has been
less kind to *Werther*. Goethe himself gave the cue with his
quasi-repudiation in *Dichtung und Wahrheit*, his condescending, ironic reference to the "Werther" years; Goethe's attitude
toward the text is much more nuanced than is sometimes assumed, but the view of *Werther* as an adolescent case study, a
kind of exorcism through art of the pressures and desires
which beset the young writer himself, this is indeed the view
which most critics have adopted, relying inevitably—in extremis—on the disclaimers of the author himself. Hence,
Werther has come to symbolize almost all that is unhealthy in
Romanticism, even in modern culture: his cult of feeling, his
sense of inadequacy, his fascination with death, his passion-
sickness, his lack of restraint and reason, his yearning for the
infinite, his social double-talk, his fears, his cruelty; in short,
every quality he reveals or even adumbrates has been enlisted
in the massive accusational portrait of modern neurotic man
which he has become. Above all, he is dwarfed and condemned by his survivor, the man who did not commit suicide
or succumb to passion, the man who *lived* as artist-courtier-
scientist-sage for three quarters of a century.[1]

[1] Although there is considerable literature on the "Werther phenomenon,"
and Goethe's own changing moods have been documented, we still do not
have (and are not likely to have) some definitive judgment of the author on
the text. In 1824, the already old writer was asked to write a preface for a 50th
anniversary, de luxe reprint of *Werther*; we know that he again experienced
dislike for his notorious progeny, but the result was a moving poem "To

I have delineated this critical context, because it seems essential to place the text itself against it, to assess the words and
power of Goethe's novel rather than using Goethe's hindsight
as a corrective lens. Much of the criticism is doubtless justified: Werther is often depicted as excessive, even pathological.
But, let us not forget that he is the first to note such weaknesses. When he confesses to pampering his heart like a sick
child, he adds "Don't tell this to anyone; there are people who
would resent it" (p. 4).[2,1] How right he is! Likewise, well before Lotte accuses him of desiring her only because she is unattainable, he senses that his desire may be rooted in a permanent character flaw: "And, my dear friend, is my longing
for a change of condition perhaps only an irritating inner im-
patience which will pursue me everywhere?" (p. 39).[2] Not
only is Werther aware of his failings (thus leading his very
critics by the hand), but he is even capable of laughing at his
own excesses. When Lotte first calls him *"Lieber Werther,"* he
is so enthralled that he repeats it hundreds of times to himself,
"and last night, as I was about to retire and was chattering
away to myself, I suddenly said: 'Good night, dear Werther,'
and then had to laugh at myself" (p. 67).[3] Perhaps the most
charming and healthiest instance of self-humor comes in his
request that Lotte not put sand in the letter seals: "Today I
swiftly raised your letter to my lips and the sand gritted on
my teeth" (p. 29).[4] In short, this young man has more pres-

Werther," in which the purity and cleanness of Werther's suffering and exit
are juxtaposed against the survival choice of the author:

Noch einmal wagst du, vielbeweinter Schatten,
Hervor dich an das Tageslicht,
Begegnest mir auf neu beblümten Matten,
Und meinen Anblick scheust du nicht.
Es ist, als ob du lebtest in der Frühe,
Wo uns der Tau auf einem Feld erquickt
Und nach des Tages unwillkommner Mühe
Der Scheidesonne letzter Strahl entzückt;
Zum Bleiben ich, zum Scheiden du erkoren,
Gingst du voran—und hast nicht viel verloren.
                              (First stanza).

[2] Johann Wolfgang Goethe, *The Sufferings of Young Werther*, tr. Harry
Steinhauer (New York: Norton, 1970).

ence and perspicacity, more "grittiness" than many of his dogged critics allow.

That is not all. This novel is as sharp a critique of critics as has ever been written. How can people possibly make judgments? Werther repeatedly mocks the pristine virtues of coolness and objectivity. We see, in Albert, a virtual embodiment of the detached critical observer, and the text proves—no matter how we read it—that Albert errs disastrously in his reading of the situation. The reasonable, principled man of logic is demonstrably unable to cope with the Werther-phenomenon, and surely all the critics of the text should pay heed to his failure. Lucidity itself, the critic's primary article of belief, is derided as a sterile, helpless condition:

> My diary, which I have neglected for some time, fell into my hands again today, and I am astonished to note how deliberately I have walked into the whole situation step by step. How clearly I have always seen my condition, and yet I have acted like a child; even now I see it very clearly and yet there is no sign of a turn for the better. (p. 31)[5]

Knowledge of one's condition is idle twaddle. Werther *knows* he is headed for the void, and that knowledge is worth nothing. There is a reverence for inner motivation and impulse in *Werther*, for *Beweggründe* which dictate the course of our lives with or without our consent. Ultimately, the text reveals the nullity of knowledge and the irrelevance of all judgment. All we can do in the presence of human beings, this story seems to be saying, is to sense what animates them, to take their behavior as a given and to recognize its necessity. "Criticism" (both moral and, ultimately, literary) is little more than name-calling, a kind of after-the-fact philistinism. Again Albert takes the honors, as he righteously condemns suicide in an *a priori* fashion. Werther's reaction is strong:

> "Why must you people," I exclaimed, "when you speak about anything, say at once, this is foolish, this is wise, this is good, this is bad? And what does all this mean? [Does that give you a sense of] the hidden [reasons] behind an action? Can you reveal with certainty . . . why it happened,

why it had to happen? [If you could], you wouldn't be so
hasty with your judgments." (p. 33, amended)[6]

Here we see the cleft between the moral label-world and the
necessary unfurling of life, passion, and death. Choice and
control are bourgeois illusions, just as rules are little more
than girdles. Life proceeds rigorously and organically, a belief
that Goethe espoused throughout his life, and in *Werther* we
perceive the most elemental, tragic enactment of such a law.
Our response to the human drama can only be to accede to its
inner necessity. And feeling may take us further into that
realm than lucidity.

Finally, Werther has often been branded a failed artist.
When he acknowledges weaknesses such as the following, "I
couldn't draw now, not a line, and yet I have never been a
greater painter than I am in these moments" (p. 2),[7] the figure
of Goethe himself inevitably comes to mind, the man who experienced the passion and also molded it into artist form; likewise, Werther's later refusal to bend his written style to suit
the demands of his pedantic superior has prompted some critics to point out that Goethe himself was capable of writing
Werther and legal briefs during the same period. (Whether
such a feat is something to be proud of is never explored.)
Goethe's ability to achieve distance and irony, to compromise
when necessary, to convey his experiences into art, to go
through this stormy love affair on to other affairs, other re-
gions, above all, his sovereign ability to survive, to cultivate
his life and marshall his energies: these constitute an eloquent
and overpowering indictment of Werther as rash, neurotic,
and self-indulgent. Yet, despite all this, one fact does remain:
Goethe wrote *Werther*; and, to some extent, whatever he said
about the text, whatever his intentions may have been, all this
comes afterwards and, as it were, at the periphery. Above all,
the novel commands our attention as an integral creation itself, as the ultimate survivor through art that even the living
Goethe could not be. Art can never be the mere by-product
of a life, and the biography—even one as rich and many-fac-
eted as Goethe's—can never be used as a corrective for the art.
If anything, art is a secret arena of freedom and truth, an area

where desire and expression and, hence, realization merge, a place untouched by the manifold restrictions and choices which social and biological reality impose. Goethe, perhaps more than any comparable figure of his time, knew that responsible selfhood demands a heavy dose of renunciation, that human desire must be integrated to social need. Yet, he never stopped producing works of art during his long, active life; i.e., he never outgrew the almost vertiginous appeal of art's creation *ex nihilo*, a place unto itself, a powerful inner world that haunts his early poetry and stamps the figures of Werther, Tasso and Faust. Renunciation may be his later theme, but the art which embodies it mocks it as well, since the work of art is always an assertion, a way of "doing" things *quand même*, a privileged form of enactment when no other action is possible. Regardless of aesthetic demands, the artistic realm is uncensored; in it, all is true and authentic, perhaps all the truer and more authentic if the "facts" of the life give it the lie. For, if we take our sample of life at an adequate depth, we quickly leave the realm of achieved data in order to confront the unrealized, but all the more precious, projects and events of the psyche. The biography is brutally contingent and limited, whereas consciousness, thought, sensation, and dream may house our immense creations of desire. Because artists have given permanent expression and form to those deepest, richest, often antisocial and unavowable needs, they leave us a rare legacy, a kind of internal history that is often at odds with the public record. This is not to say that a man is primarily the sum of his urges and feelings, and that the enacted life is secondary; but we do need to see the art in itself, to view it without the blinders of intentionality, retrospect, and convention. Werther must be freed from Goethe, just as children must outgrow their parents; for Werther *is* Goethe's legacy, his progeny, his still living creation. And the starkness of his wants has as much to teach us as the renunciations of the author's life. Too long, critics have chided Werther's excesses and ironized his pathos; I propose to consider him, not as the aberration which Goethe avoided, but the truth which Goethe could not live, the uncompromised pure passion unto death which Goethe could neither live out nor deny, which could be enacted only through art.

In the figure of Werther, Goethe has expressed human longings and a magnificent tribute to human potential. He perceives and celebrates Nature in tones utterly new in European literature:

> When the lovely valley around me is shrouded in mist, and the high sun rests on the impenetrable darkness of my forest, and only single rays steal into the inner sanctuary, I then lie in the tall grass beside the cascading brook, and close to the ground a thousand varieties of tiny grasses fill me with wonder; when I feel this teeming little world among the stalks closer to my heart—the countless, unfathomable forms of tiny worms and gnats—and feel the presence of the Almighty, who created us in His image, the breath of the All-loving One who, floating in eternal bliss, bears and sustains us; my friend, when my eyes then grow misty and the world about me and the sky dwell wholly within me like the form of a beloved woman—then I often think with longing: oh if you [somehow] could express this . . . , if you could breathe onto the paper what lives so fully, so warmly within you, so that it might become the mirror of your soul, as your soul is the mirror of infinite God! (pp. 2-3, amended)[8]

There is something enormous at work in this passage, a titanic yet delicate sense of natural life and natural rhythms, a blend of person and setting that enriches and transforms both. We are far from the stylized, far more self-directed, reveries of a Rousseau, for there is an extraordinary kind of expansion going on here, a keen, precise awareness of other forms of life that feeds and increases the self as it takes in and celebrates the outside world. Werther lies in the grass, and his own being is so harmoniously linked to Nature that the divine presence itself is unobtrusively invoked as the final extension and secret source of the chain of being. There is gentle irony in his lament that he cannot bring such splendor to expression, for the entire performance eloquently belies his skepticism, and the whole is beautifully infused ("*eingehaucht*") into language. Werther has wonder; he is everywhere alive to power and beauty, and, through his sensations, the world becomes a magic, throbbing thing, and the individual is endlessly nourished and expanded by his perceptions and responses. Symbiotically, coextensive with the world, the self thrives as a privileged, open being.

This novel, a full century before Nietzsche, is a lyrical celebration of human potential. To say that is part of the *Sturm und Drang* protest against reason is to accept a slogan; unlike much of the heavy rhetoric of the period, Goethe's prose is actually able to convey a rare sense of power and promise. Spring is the season when the young man discovers Wallheim and Lotte, and Werther praises the very life principle itself:

> . . . when I then heard the birds about me enliven the woods and saw the millions of insects dancing gaily in the last red [rays of] sun, whose last quivering glance freed the humming beetle from the grass, and the buzzing and stirring about me made me conscious of the ground and the moss which wrests its nourishment from my hard rock, and the shrubbery which grows down the arid sand hill opened up to me the inner, glowing, sacred life of nature—how I gathered all this into my warm heart, felt myself like a god in [the] overflowing abundance, and the glorious forms of the infinite world stirred in my soul, giving life to everything. (p. 37, amended)[9]

The transposition from external spectacle to Werther's soul is signaled by an almost demonic expansion and, simultaneously, a vision into the depths:

> Enormous mountains surrounded me, abysses lay before me, and cataracts rushed down; the rivers flowed by below me, and the forests and mountains resounded from the echo; and I saw them, all those unfathomable forces, creatively at work on each other in the depths of the earth . . . (p. 37)[10]

Let us then see the full picture: enormous vistas in all directions, both within Werther and without, both harmonious and chaotic. Initiated into such grandeur, alive to such raw energy, Werther is understandably impatient with the *kleinbürger* mentality around him: "and the humans then seek security close together in little houses, put down roots and rule the great world in their own way! Poor fool, in whose opinion everything is so insignificant because you are so small!" (p. 37.)[11] We are far from the modern neurotic that many critics have made of Werther. It is the Voltairean play-it-safe type, the one that cultivates its garden and obeys reason, that seems the egoist, in comparison with Werther's grasp and generosity. I have been quoting a good deal of Goethe's prose, because these are new tones, an annunciation that the individual has inherited the earth and vastly extended his purview. Werther claims no less than all, because his estate knows no bounds. The passage quoted earlier closes with the purest expression of human yearning and human appetite, a sense of desire so fabulous that it becomes a foretaste of ineffable gratification:

> From the inaccessible mountain range to the wasteland which no foot has ever trod, and on to the end of the unexplored ocean, the spirit of the Eternal Creator stirs, rejoicing in every speck of dust which perceives Him and lives. —Oh, how often did I then yearn to take the wings of a crane which flew overhead, and make for the shore of the boundless sea, to drink from the foaming cup of infinity that effervescent rapture of life, and to feel for only one moment, in my limited mental powers, a drop of the bliss of that Being Who creates all things in and through Himself. (pp. 37-38)[12]

Here is the desire for intercourse with the Godhead, the hunger for union and fulfillment which Werther will transfer to Lotte under the name of human love.

This capacity for wonder and devotion, for something much larger and finer than the ordinary affairs of men, is, as Werther is to learn, a curse. In crashing through the pasteboard wall of human measure, Werther goes off the bourgeois map. The anthropocentric framework no longer holds. At first wedded to Nature, the picture of man progressively

shrinks while Nature grows. Nature is power, and power
knows no morality nor decorum. The world becomes a mag-
netic force field, creating and canceling at will, helter-skelter:

> Can you say "this is," when everything is transitory, when
> everything rolls by with the speed of a tempest and seldom
> lasts until its whole force is spent, but is swept along, alas,
> engulfed by the current and shattered on the rocks? There
> is not a moment that does not consume you and those close
> to you, not a moment in which you are not a destroyer, and
> necessarily so; the most innocent stroll costs the lives of a
> thousand poor little worms; one step destroys the laborious
> structures erected by the ants and tramples a small world
> into a miserable grave. Ha! it is not the rare, great misfor-
> tunes in the world that move me, not the floods that wash
> away your villages, nor the earthquakes that engulf your
> cities; my heart is undermined by the destructive power
> that lies hidden in . . . nature, which has created nothing
> that has not destroyed its neighbor, even itself. And so I
> stumble about in anguish, with heaven and earth and all the
> active forces around me; I see nothing but a monster
> that perpetually devours, eternally ruminates. (p. 38,
> amended)[13]

God has disappeared from the power equation now, and
Werther is gazing on the brute forces of life. There is no room
here for any type of containment or achievement. In this passage we see the key images and concepts of *Werther*, indeed of
Goethe's entire work. The central figure of destruction by the
floodwaters haunts Goethe's writing; it is ubiquitous in this
text, but it is equally prominent elsewhere, as metaphor for
self-destruction in *Tasso*, as actualized landscape that must be
contained in *Faust* II. Equally significant is the despair over
Bildung, the leveling awareness that formation is ever matched
by annihilation. Goethe's standard-setting *Bildungsroman, Wilhelm Meisters Lehrjahre*, is an effort to enforce form, to make
a pact with Nature, to funnel energy into social and decorous
channels. But, in *Werther*, no such compromise is conceivable.
These elemental forces are in human beings as well as in Nature, and *Werther* announces their indwelling power.

Already at the thunderstorm scene during the dance we get
a hint of the potential for panic and hysteria among civilized
people. Goethe describes, in some detail, the manic postures
and almost spasmodic behavior caused by fear. The link between the affections and the elements already prefigures the
stormy Ossianic landscapes which will take over the second
part of the book. As we might expect, the inner forces are almost always expressed in the metaphor of floodwaters:[3]

> Oh, my friends! Why does the torrent of genius burst forth
> so rarely, so seldom [burst in] high waves and [shake you]
> to the depths of your astonished souls?—Dear friends, there
> on both sides of the river, live unruffled gentlemen; their
> little summerhouses, tulip beds, and vegetable gardens
> would be ruined; they are, therefore, able to avert the
> threatening danger by building dams and ditches. (pp. 8-9,
> amended)[14]

That metaphor encompasses Werther's story: containment
unto death. He repeatedly describes his situation as a prison;
he refers to the horses that bite their own arteries for release;
he depicts death by sickness and passion with the same figure:
"Nature finds no way out of the labyrinth of confused and
contradictory forces, so man must die" (p. 36).[15] The imagery
of disease has often been remarked in *Werther*, but it must be
emphasized that Goethe is profoundly clinical even when he
is most lyrical. The *Ausweg* and *Labyrinth* are hardly metaphors, if we view them as the bloodstream of the human
being; passion is a biological, a pathological, reality in this
book. Often Werther is virtually asphyxiated, unable to find
air or release. In one grand sequence Goethe depicts Werther's
emotional distress in images that range from physiological
torture to sexual desire to death as outlet. Here the flood and
the labyrinth take on urgent erotic connotations and, as they
image the sought-after sexual congress, the desire to find a
way out (*Ausweg*) merges entirely with the frantic need to enter:

[3] The motif of water and flood is obviously an old topos in literature.
Among other writers, one may consult the work of Bernhard Blume and
Gaston Bachelard for discussion of the larger ramifications of this imagery.

When I have been sitting with her for two or three hours
and have feasted on her figure, her manner, the divine
expression of her thoughts, and then gradually my senses
become tense, a darkness appears before my eyes, I can
scarcely hear anything, my throat is constricted as though
by the hand of an assassin, and my heart beats wildly [to
get air to] my oppressed senses, but only increasing their
confusion—Wilhelm, often I don't know whether I really
exist. And at times—when melancholy [gets] the upper
hand and Lotte permits me the wretched comfort of shed-
ding my tears of anguish on her hand—I must [get away],
I must get outside and roam far through the fields; I then
find my pleasure in climbing a steep mountain, cutting a
path through an untrodden forest, through hedges which
tear me, through thorns which rend me. Then I feel a little
better. A little. And sometimes I lie down on the way,
overcome by weariness and thirst; sometimes in the depth
of night, when the full moon stands high above me in the
lonely forest, I sit down on a gnarled, crooked tree, to afford some relief to my aching soles, and then I doze off in
the twilight in an exhausted sleep. Oh Wilhelm! The solitary dwelling of a cell, the hair shirt, and belt of thorns are
the comforts for which my soul yearns. Good-by; I see no
end to this misery but the grave. (p. 40, amended)[16]

Late in the novel, shortly before his suicide, Werther actually encounters the realized flood, the swollen waters and
the true Ossianic landscape. Goethe is relentlessly making the
case for the exigencies of passion, the needs of need, and—just
as the lunar landscape of the soul becomes actualized in *Manon
Lescaut*, becomes the American landscape—the flood cannot
be held indefinitely in check in *Werther*. It must break into
reality, and it does so. It overflows the tranquil meadows and
lowlands, but for Werther it is too late.

Up to now I have tried to articulate the nature of Werther's
promise. I have suggested, as well, that he runs into a world
that chokes him, that dams him up. Yet, his tragedy is more
even than one of collision and containment. The analogy between natural and human forces is a flawed analogy, and

Goethe is a ruthlessly natural writer. He has Werther's discovery of Wallheim and Lotte coincide with Spring. But Werther soon sees that Nature is destructive as well as generative. As Spring yields to Summer and Fall, and Homer makes way for Ossian, Werther realizes the insidious disparity between Nature's cycle and man's cycle. What Nature does in a year, man does over a lifetime; what Nature repeats perenially, man can only project to an afterlife. Werther's life moves with the fatal rhythms of the seasons. Early in the text, the young man admires a country woman who can see falling leaves and "thinks of nothing, other than the coming of winter" (p. 393, my translation). Death haunts this book, death as the inevitable fifth season:

> Yes, it is so. As nature declines into autumn, so autumn begins within me and about me. My leaves are turning yellow and the leaves of the neighboring trees have already fallen. (p. 59)[17]

Even the magnificent hunger and capacity for response are time-bound, lent rather than possessed, virtues; they can be recalled. The winter landscape and the winter heart show no life:

> And this heart is now dead, no raptures flow from it any longer; my eyes are dry and my faculties, no longer invigorated by refreshing tears, cause my brow to be knitted in anxiety. I suffer much, for I have lost what was the sole joy of my life: the sacred, animating force with which I created worlds about me; it is gone! (pp. 65–66)[18]

The mournful, morbid, clinically depressed, prematurely aged young man, living in a torpor, whom we come to know as the book draws to a close, is a brutally *natural* phenomenon. When he proclaims, spiritually, "Isn't human fate just that: to do one's time, to drain the cup" (p. 468, my translation), we may interpret it as a kind of seasonal "readiness is all." People age and die in this brief, seemingly young, novel. Lotte spends much time with an old lady "nearing her end"; the old priest dies; his nut trees are cut down. Werther, in the letter

announcing his impending death to Lotte, states that his time
is up, that he has come full circle: "I want to die! —It is not
despair, it is the certainty that I have [completed my time] and
that I am sacrificing myself for you" (p. 81, amended).[19] He
will die, and their life will go on.

Much of the book's pathos hinges on whether such an exit
is permanent or not. " 'We shall be! . . .' " exclaims Lotte.
Nothing in nature disappears; " 'But, Werther, shall we ever
find each other again, and know each other again? What do
you believe? What do you say?' " (p. 42).[20] Is there a human
analog to the nature cycle? Can we even conceive of death,
when we know only life:

> Behold, we dream when we talk of death. I have seen many
> die; but so restricted is human nature that it has no feeling
> for the beginning or end of its existence. At this moment
> there is still mine and yours—yours, O my beloved. And in
> another moment—separated, parted—perhaps forever? —
> No, Lotte, no. —How can I pass away? How can you pass
> away? For we exist! —Pass away—what does that mean? It
> is just another word, an empty sound, which does not
> touch my heart. —Dead, Lotte! buried in the cold ground,
> so confined, so dark! (p. 89)[21]

This takes us, I believe, to the heart of Goethe's novel.
Werther is all openness and passion, but he himself is contingent and transient. He imaginatively and emotionally opens
himself to, and takes in, the universe; but physically he will
fill a hole. Rarely have human parameters been delimited so
starkly.

It is this awareness of transience and limits that gives such
beauty to Werther's passion. Most critics see in him the prototype of the egoist, the narcissist totally absorbed in his own
world.[4] And, indeed, *Werther* is point-of-view narrative with

---

[4] Wolfgang Kayser long ago wrote pertinently about the manner in which
Werther personalizes his world, imposes a point of view on all that he sees.
Even in innocuous details, such as "mein Homer," or "mein Wallheim," we
note the presence of a "colonizing" imagination. Kayser's remarks appear in
"Die Entstehung von Goethes *Werther*," *Deutsche Vierteljahrsschrift für Litera-
turwissenschaft und Geistesgeschichte* 19 (1941), 430–457.

a vengeance; if one excepts the fictive editor's intervention toward the end, the bulk of the narrative plunges us into
Werther's own perceptions, thereby opening the door for all
the charges of blindness and distortion which have been lev-
eled at him. But the great paradox, perhaps the great tragedy,
of this novel is that Werther alone points his view toward others. He alone seems capable of response. The story begins
with his elegiac mention of a former love, and it illustrates the
expansive possibilities of human intercourse:

> . . . I did feel the warmth of her heart, her noble soul, in
> whose presence I seemed to be more in my own eyes than
> I really was, because I was everything I could be. Good
> Heavens! Was there any faculty of my mind that was idle?
> Could I not unfold before her the whole marvelous feeling
> with which my heart embraces nature? Was our association
> not an endless stirring of the most delicate feeling, the keen-
> est wit, the nuances of which were all stamped with the
> mark of genius to the point of extravagance? (p. 5)[22]

Here is Werther's true calling, his genuine artistry: a mutual
development, a bringing into play of all his energies, an eternal weaving. Love is the arena for Werther's gifts. This affair
is merely alluded to, but the novel richly shows us Werther
loving. Lotte is merely the most obvious. She is the primary
fulfillment that he seeks, the overt divinity he worships. But
there is more. Werther befriends everyone, peasants and aris-
tocrats alike, murderers and madmen. The social affront he
suffers at the Count's reception is but an index of that defy-
ing, larger distance between human beings, that gap he repeatedly tries to bridge. He is haunted by the image of the
dying first love, the helplessness of the survivor to sustain the
sick one. In the face of another's death, all one's strength is
useless and taunting; Werther stands before the bed with the
feeling " 'that all your powers are powerless, and anxiety con-
vulses you, so that you would give anything if you could instill a drop of strength, a spark of courage into the dying creature' " (p. 23).[23] Werther's struggle is against human finitude.
He alone fights separation.

He does so alone, because the world depicted in this story

is content with maintaining distances between classes, between people. Werther is constantly admonished not to press so hard, to back off. There is something splendid about his refusal to compromise. The young man knows how isolated and brief existence is, and he wants relationship, empathy; he wants, ultimately, to build against time, to offset what the seasons take away.

However, his is a time for the *status quo*; there is no seeding here. The future will be harsh, for there is nothing to inherit. The story is filled with ominous signs: Werther must try to make good on a withheld legacy for his mother; Albert is away trying to straighten out money matters at the outset, and he receives unwelcome correspondence just when Lotte needs him most; most exemplary is doubtless the story of the young woman whom Werther befriends; at the beginning, she is awaiting the return of her husband, who is attempting, significantly enough, to put an inheritance in order; at the end, her condition is so radically altered, that we are not far from the fortunes of Lucky and Pozzo in *Godot*:

> "My dear sir, alas, my Hans has died." —He was the youngest of her boys. I was silent. —"And my husband," she said "returned from Switzerland and brought nothing back with him and if it weren't for some good people he would have had to beg his way home, he had contracted a fever on his journey." (p. 58)[24]

The world that Albert is managing and Lotte mothering is rotting away, outside their idyllic setting: it is the stage for madmen whose only happiness is in the asylum, for servants whom desire and convention force into rape; it is a place that is dying away, changing for the worst, leaving nothing to be replaced, not even nut trees. Werther's experience with the Count vigorously confirms his despair for human relations; he witnesses nothing but jealousy and in-fighting: "There is nothing they wouldn't take from each other: health, reputation, joy, recreation! . . . Sometimes I feel like begging them on my knees not to ravage their own insides so [furiously]" (p. 50, amended).[25] The reign of envy and suspicion and the absence of charity are probably to be expected among those

who have; but, the underlying coldness and indifference of
the others, for others, seems endemic to the race itself. In an
astonishing sequence, Werther overhears his precious Lotte
chatting with a friend:

> I heard them talking softly; they were telling each other in-
> significant trifles, town gossip: how this one was getting
> married, that one was sick, very sick. "She has a dry cough,
> her cheekbones protrude, and she has fainting spells; I
> wouldn't give a penny for her life," said the friend. "So and
> So is in a bad way too," said Lotte. "He's all swollen up,"
> said the other girl. —And my lively imagination trans-
> ported me to the bedsides of these poor people; I saw them
> turn their backs on life with the utmost repugnance, saw
> them—and Wilhelm, my little ladies were talking about it,
> well, as one would talk—about the death of a stranger. (p.
> 64)[26]

The ugly face of human callousness is laid bare in this tough
little scene. The matter-of-factness of the third person commentary ("He's all swollen up") displays the horrendous ac-
curacy of the lucid observer. Not so much the social structure,
rather the circumscribed, anaesthetized, nature of the living
self, its indifference for all that is not it, that is the obstacle,
the abyss between humans:

> I often feel like tearing out my heart and bashing in my
> brains at the thought that we mean so little to each other.
> Alas, the love, joy, warmth, and bliss which I do not con-
> tribute myself, no one else will give me, and even with a
> heart full of happiness I will not make anyone happy who
> stands before me cold and indifferent. (p. 65)[27]

Human responsibility consists in bridge-making, and, according to that standard, Albert and Lotte are deficient. The
natural state is inertia; there is so much more small talk than
big talk. Nowhere is such human inadequacy more brutally
shown than in Lotte's failure to alert Albert to Werther's
plight. Fear and embarrassment are doubtless partly account-
able, but there is indifference and forgetfulness as well: "The
table was set; a good friend, who had merely come in to ask

a question, and intended to go at once but stayed on, made the dinner conversation endurable. They forced themselves [, they talked, they gossiped, they forgot everything]" (p. 93, amended).[28] The difficulty of loving is seen to be almost muscular, an indigenous defect common to the species. The distance between human beings is very great, and one seems condemned to be a *fait divers* for the other. We have seen the blindness at the heart of *Manon Lescaut*, a blindness that is only exacerbated by need, by the desire for intimacy and oneness. In this novel, only Werther finds the way to bridge the gap. He does it the only way it can be done: the third person ("he's all swollen up") must be supplanted by the first person. Narration must come from the inside.

The I-narrative is often accused of carrying considerable narcissism with it; yet, in the final analysis, true generosity, empathy, and love can only come about when I becomes, or tries to become, the other. In his defense of suicide, Werther insists that understanding must follow empathy: "For only to the extent that we can put ourselves in another man's situation [*mitempfinden*] are we justified in talking about a matter" (p. 34).[5][29] Third-person understanding preserves its distance, but is therefore devoid of value:

> "It is in vain that a relaxed, rational person grasps the unhappy man's condition, in vain does he attempt to talk to him persuasively. Just as a healthy man standing at the bedside of a sick person cannot transfer to him even the slightest quantity of his own strength." (p. 35)[30]

The familiar image of helplessness returns, for Werther is obsessed with the need to go from the self to the other. And that is precisely what his narrative does. Werther imagines and speaks from beyond the self. When imagining the motives for suicide of a young girl, he stretches both his empathy and syntax to the hilt:

> "A decent young creature who had grown up in the narrow sphere of domestic duties, of a weekly schedule of tasks that

[5] Here, of course, the power of the German verb *mitempfinden* ("to experience with") is considerably diluted in the laborious English rendering.

included no prospect of amusement, except perhaps to stroll about town on Sunday with girls of similar station, dressed in the finery she had gradually accumulated; perhaps to go to a dance on the principal holidays, and for the rest to spend the odd hour gossiping with a neighbor, in complete emotional involvement, about the cause of a quarrel or an item of scandal. —Finally, her warm nature experiences deeper needs which are nourished by the flattery of men; her former sources of gratification lose their savor bit by bit, until she finally meets a man to whom she is irresistibly drawn by a hitherto unknown feeling, on whom she now pins all her hopes, forgetting the world about her, hearing nothing, seeing nothing, feeling nothing but him, the only one; longing only for him, for him alone. . . ." (p. 35)[31]

Here is the empathetic imagination, and its style, at work, the fiction-making mind of Goethe with his gift for discovering the "inner necessity" behind human action, but also the generous self-extension of Werther, who projects himself onto and into his world. Each encounter with the young farmhand enamored of his mistress testifies to Werther's openness, even to his prodigious effort at narration, at imagining from the inside. Werther is constantly humbled by the wonder of the world and the difficulty of translating it into language: "In fact, I would have to possess the gifts of the greatest poet to convey to you adequately [the expression of his face, the harmony of his voice], the hidden fire in his eyes" (p. 11, amended).[32] The desperate love story of the acquaintance moves Werther, tends to become his own—not by authorial analogy, but by the power of empathy and passion.

Because passion moves. When the farmhand finally commits murder, Werther understands and identifies, for it is his own inner drama that is being played out, also because he has absorbed the story of his friend: "an unconquerable feeling of sympathy took possession of him and he was seized by an indescribable desire to save the man. He felt him to be so unhappy, found him so innocent even as a criminal, and identified himself so completely with him that he was certain he could convince others too" (p. 75).[33] Of course he fails, for his friend and for himself.

Yet, it would be naive to read Goethe's novel primarily as a judgment of Werther. His reverence for power, his commitment to passion, and his openness to others are the ultimate tidings, the final news, that the book brings. Werther brings and disseminates knowledge of the heart, imagination from the inside, and he does not leave the world unchanged. At the end of the novel, Lotte has been profoundly affected; her relationship with Albert may no longer be intact, and the world of violent emotions has been entered.[6] The project of overcoming distance, of touching another, has succeeded, even if disastrously. The novel's preface reads *"You cannot withhold your admiration or your love from his spirit and character, nor your tears from his fate"* (p. ix).[34] Werther cannot "get" Lotte, but she finally "catches" Werther, just as the story of his life produced a mass wave of hysteria and, even, suicide. A more coercive, more enduring, force than he could know, Werther brings knowledge of the depths; he brings and he spreads; he is not unlike the pestilence, the all-embracing, all-destroying flood of which he speaks, the awful news that the soul can kill. The suicides caused by this tale must give us pause; they flagrantly transcend the decorous bounds of literary response, and they shrilly proclaim the proper and profound meaning of Goethe's novel: passion alone transcends distance, moves others, effects communication and understanding. Werther does not finally fail, because his story (even if not himself) outlasts the seasonal cycle. He does leave a legacy beyond death, perhaps the only successful inheritance of the novel: his letters, his supple and potent language for expressing and eliciting those feelings that exalted and destroyed him. In this small novel, the self takes its measure, both suffering and celebrating its limits and limitlessness.

[6] The penultimate sentence of the novel, "Lotte's life was feared to be in danger" (Man fürchtete für Lottens Leben), is more, I think, than a conventional expression of grief. If we view Werther as the introduction of passion and hunger and empathy in a world of distance and convention, then Lotte's "symptoms" at the close say something about Werther's enduring virulence.

Huis Clos: *Clarissa*

Like *Manon Lescaut*, Richardson's *Clarissa* dramatizes what we increasingly see as the double bind of individualist fiction: the conflict between self and society, and between self and other. The beleaguered Clarissa must fight on two fronts: against her father and all the Harlowes, and against Lovelace. And each of these combat zones is rich in nuance and suggestiveness. Critics such as Sale, Van Ghent, and Watt have demonstrated the spectacular fullness of the novel's conflicts: the Puritan myth of rake and virgin, the dalliance and intercourse between bourgeois and aristocrat, the familial tyranny.[1] In short, this long novel can no longer be seen merely as a study in consciousness and repression (although it is that), but as a subterranean key to the age, a document absolutely larded with psychic and social tensions for which literature is the ideal (and perhaps the only) expression.

Yet, the plot itself is, as in every Richardson novel, oppressively narrow, in Van Ghent's words, "a singularly thin and unrewarding piece of action—the deflowering of a young lady. . . ."[2] The variety of event and landscape, as seen in Defoe or Prévost or Fielding, is exchanged for an unswerving focus on the inner life of the two protagonists. *Moll Flanders* splendidly demonstrates the absorption of a picaresque plot into an integral life; Marivaux's Marianne ingests all events into her ever-growing ego. Both texts are deeply *affirmative*, a double "yes" to protagonist and setting, a belief that life (or plot) provides the ingredients for character. But, as Van Ghent points out, "the central action of Clarissa's story is a rape, an experience which might have assumed a position of

---

[1] See W. M. Sale, Jr., "From Pamela to Clarissa" in *The Age of Johnson*, ed. F. W. Hilles (New Haven: Yale University Press, 1949), the extremely influential essays on Richardson by Ian Watt in his *The Rise of the Novel* (Berkeley: University of California Press, 1957) and Dorothy Van Ghent's well-known piece on *Clarissa* in *The English Novel: Form and Function* (New York, 1953).

[2] *The English Novel: Form and Function* (New York: Harper and Row paperback, 1967), p. 62. It goes without saying that Van Ghent's comment sticks in the throat of the Feminist critics of the 1970s.

minor importance among Moll's adventures in adultery, big-
amy, and incest—conceivably an incident that Moll might
even have forgotten to make a 'memorandum' of."[3] In Richardson, the self is infinitely more swollen, virtually shutting
out the outside world, but it is also fragile, animated by principles more fine than mere survival. Accommodation begins
to be seen as cheap. Clarissa's self can say "no" to life, in order
to be true to itself. The making of a character, the accretive
movement of *Moll* and *Marianne*, becomes, here, a progressive unmaking. The social contract is no longer possible. William Sale has acutely described the existential leap which sep-
arates *Clarissa* from *Pamela* (and from all of Defoe or
Fielding):

> This pair cannot be tucked into the social structure as Defoe
> tucked his characters. There are moments when both Cla-
> rissa and Lovelace are tempted by the thought of their
> union; and marriage, as a symbolic act, is kept constantly in
> the forefront of the novel. But this story is no "love" story.
> It is not love for which Clarissa's old pious world is well
> lost; it is for a chance to live life more completely in con-
> formity with an ideal of conduct.[4]

Although modern criticism has shown that Clarissa uncon-
sciously yearns for what she denies, her story is nonetheless
one of incompatibility. Seen more graphically, *Clarissa* depicts
a harrowing dialectic between the inflated self and the shrink-
ing but lethal world.

The vertical world, in which events that would be banal in
Defoe's panorama now become deadly, is the perfect material
for epistolary fiction. The epistolary novel foregrounds consciousness and response, and it is rife with the potential for
blindness and solipsism. Richardson, as printer, was able to
exploit all phases of epistolary activity; as McKillop says, "the
writing of letters is only the beginning; they are copied, sent,
received, shown about, discussed, answered, even perhaps

---

[3] *Form and Function*, p. 60.
[4] W. M. Sale, Jr., "From *Pamela to Clarissa*," reprinted in *Samuel Richardson:
A Collection of Critical Essays*, ed. John Carroll (Englewood Cliffs: Prentice
Hall, 1969), p. 47.

hidden, intercepted, stolen, altered, or forged."[5] The actual
writing itself is illuminated and transformed into high drama.
Early on, Lovelace is described as "a great plotter, and a great
writer," one who "has always a pen in his fingers when he
retires" (I, pp. 17, 49).[6] If writing has sexual overtones here,
it is akin to death itself in the final part of the novel, where
Clarissa writes on, against doctor's orders, as if there were no
other activity worth her while. Beyond the very considerable
machinery of the letters, one is struck by the *ersatz* value of
the written word, its utility in replacing human presence. At
a critical juncture, Clarissa denies Lovelace entry to her, pro-
claiming "pen and ink must be, at present, the only means of
communication between us" (II, p. 510). In fact, pen and ink
seem to be the only means of communication whatsoever in
this novel. We see Clarissa writing her family even while she
is still living in the same house with them. Once gone, the letter takes on still more autonomy: it *is*, for the Harlowes, for
Miss Howe, Clarissa. They will never see her alive again, but
they will have access to her words. The letter is her bridge to
a world to which she can never, in person, return.

Above all, one has the grim sense that such an arrangement
suits Clarissa; hence it is imperative to understand and to assess her ineluctable transformation from woman to word.

We noticed, in the narratives of Moll and Marianne, that
the *histoire*, the history-story of a life, tends to achieve an excellence and integrity all its own. Moll assumes, at Newgate,
all the heterogeneity of her picaresque life, and Marianne is,
in the episode of the old soldier, finally desired exclusively as
the protagonist of her story, rather than as a flesh-and-blood
creature. In *Clarissa* this process is taken a step further.
Whereas Moll and Marianne achieve self through their
"story," Clarissa seems to be replaced by hers. She, more than
her counterparts in Defoe and Marivaux, needs the letters, becomes the letters, is available only in the letters. In part, it is
the "what they cannot have told you" syndrome so effec-

[5] A. D. McKillop, "Epistolary Technique in Richardson's Novels," reprinted in *Samuel Richardson: A Collection of Critical Essays*, p. 139.
[6] Samuel Richardson, *Clarissa Harlowe* (London: J. M. Dent and Sons Ltd.,
1932), 4 vols.

tively dramatized by Faulkner's Rosa Coldfield. Clarissa's
thoughts, her feelings, in fact her genuine experience, are hidden from the world, and letters alone can convey her version
of events. She is the ideal candidate for literature, since, without the inside view, she is a poor thing (as, indeed, her own
family and Mrs. Howe and still others take her to be). Appearances are against her. And appearances, as Clarissa
knows, count. Christopher Hill has shrewdly summarized her
damaged societal status:

> [Clarissa] had no sense of guilt: her conscience was clear.
> But she knew what society's verdict would be. Its standards
> are those of the Market: justification by faith was for Sun-
> days only. Society judges by events, not by motives. Cla-
> rissa knew it, and it was this that made her death inevitable.
> How could she have lived? There was no room in a com-
> mercial society for flawed goods.[7]

And, yet, the novel as a whole suggests a reprieve. Society
judges by appearances, but art goes a step further. Richardson's book, consisting largely of Clarissa's letters, is an ongoing alternative to outside judgment. In protesting to Mrs.
Norton, "that when my story is known I shall be entitled to
more compassion than blame" (III, p. 337), Clarissa is speaking to every reader the novel has had. Even the hard-hearted
Harlowes will "read" her properly, once she is dead. The
written word will triumph, will undo and redo appearances.
And this particular feat is paradigmatic of a recurrent desire in
all the fictions dealt with in this study: how to overcome appearances, to assert the inner picture, even to conquer life's
determinisms. The works to be dealt with in the following
chapter display the strange kind of breakthrough which Diderot, Sterne, and Rousseau were to achieve in this domain.
Clarissa, too, wins out, but her death is the necessary condition of her victory.

For the exchange is too arresting to be incidental. Clarissa's
story is told, but she is no longer there. It is a lethal dialectic:
the life feeds the story, and, once the story is full-blown, no

---

[7] Christopher Hill, "Clarissa Harlowe and Her Times," reprinted in *Samuel Richardson: A Collection of Critical Essays*, p. 117.

more life. All literature partakes of such parasitism, and there is doubtless something fine in such a dues-paying view of character: the life is depicted, *ab ovo*, and, at the end, the book is over, the character either dead or happy ever after, but the literary afterlife is permanently launched. Here is surely one of the temptations of autobiography. But, only in epistolary fiction do we see the living-writing dialectic fully enacted. And Clarissa is the extreme case of a character who becomes literature before our very eyes, who chooses to write herself to death, whose experience can be shared, not on earth but only in art. Raped though she is, Clarissa remains (as Lovelace knows only too well) ultimately virginal, promised to Christ and to her readers. And to them she delivers.

Why is her victory so Pyrrhic? Why does the story use up the life? The answer is not one of authorial whim. Richardson could not assuage his insistent readers with a happy ending, because he had created a protagonist with needs that no plot could gratify. Despite all her longings (which Watt and Van Ghent and others detect underneath the rhetorical flow), Clarissa remains intact, closed in upon herself, fighting for her integrity (i.e., her chastity, but much more too). She is the vibrant hungry self, the divine Clarissa, created for the very finest that life can provide, but, in the course of her experience, being "weaned from life," choosing letters and death. Her trajectory is worth studying, for it occupies a central position in the fictions studied in this book: the full-blown self, dispossessed.

When we first see Clarissa, she is manifestly queen of her world, and pride and darling of her family; no one is really surprised that Lovelace shifts his attentions for Bella to her, or that the despicable Solmes is so steadfast in his suit. What is strange is the young woman's strength of resistance, her powerful and shocking declaration of independence, in the article of marriage. Her property Clarissa is prepared to negotiate, but not her person. In refusing Solmes's offer, Clarissa asserts the inviolability of the self as an entity beyond exchange, an authority beyond that of capital:

> [Mr. Solmes] has even given hopes to your brother that he will make exchanges of estates, or at least that he will pur-

chase the northern one; for you know it must be entirely
consistent with the family views, that we increase our interest in this country. Your brother, in short, has given in
a plan that captivates us all: and a family so rich in all its
branches, and that has its views to honour, must be pleased
to see a very great probability of taking rank one day
among the principal in the kingdom.

And for the sake of these views, for the sake of this plan
of my brother's, am I, madam, to be given in marriage to
a man I never can endure! (i, p. 87)

Here is, indeed, the ugly bargain, and, in resisting it, Clarissa
displays her two most enduring beliefs: (1) the self is more
than property, and (2) the truest expression of self is will.
These beliefs are trumpeted throughout the novel, down to
the triumphant, grisly end. Let us consider the concept of
will, first, because it is the hallmark of the self, the first and
last trump of the individual, the animus that distinguishes self
from world. Whereas Lazarillo ultimately becomes an item in
the marketplace, and Moll and Marianne reveal their skill in
accommodation and absorption, Clarissa flaunts her will from
beginning to end. She defies Solmes, her family, and Lovelace, in the name of self. Her honesty toward Solmes is unheard of:

> Know then that I have invincible objections, sir, to your ad-
> dress. I have avowed them with an earnestness that I believe
> is without example . . . do not wish to have a young crea-
> ture compelled in the most material article of her life, in be-
> half of a person she cannot value. (i, p. 378)

Her repeated display of will must offend. Her uncle John Harlowe is not mistaken: "Must you have your will paramount
to everybody's?" (i, p. 314). Even her brother discovers,
much as Lovelace is later to find out, that physical force cannot subdue Clarissa; trying to keep her in the room through
violence, he finds himself bettered:

> And I struggled so vehemently to get from him that he was
> forced to quit my hand; which he did with these words:
> Begone then, Fury! How strong is will! There is no holding
> her. (i, p. 406)

Doubtless the surest and most succinct expression of will occurs just before Clarissa writes the fatal letter to Lovelace, accepting his aid in leaving the Harlowes. Clarissa, reminded that she must acquiesce and take Solmes, explodes in a dithyramb of denial:

> Indeed I never will! This, as I have said over and over, is not originally my father's will. Indeed I never will—and that is all I will say. (I, p. 428)

In this brief outcry, the word "will" is used no less than four times, and it powerfully illuminates Richardson's multiple strategies. "Not originally my father's will" foreshadows the ambivalent status of the father-Father which Clarissa exploits in her famous letter to Lovelace at the close of her life: "I am setting out with all diligence for my Father's House" (IV, p. 157). "My father's will" comes from higher reaches than James Harlowe occupies, and it is assuredly more in accordance with Clarissa's true needs. Each other mention of the word is absolutely ambivalent, signifying at once deed and time. "I never will" asserts both futurity and the self's control over it; it is the elemental pact between life and the self, wherein the individual bends time and event to his own needs. The naked self speaks in these lines, claiming its higher authority and affirming its autonomy in a *non serviam*.

This will be Clarissa's posture throughout her long Calvary. Richardson's novel is one of almost unmitigated antagonism, a combat from beginning to end. Clarissa asserts her integrity against the demands of her family, largely, it would seem, as preparation for the still more grueling trial that is to follow. Little in literature is comparable to the duel staged between Clarissa and Lovelace. Both are swollen warriors, sworn to protect their ego and have their way, determined never to yield. There is something pathological in the unswerving commitment of resources and energy that each displays, a maniacal narrowing of focus which transforms the entire novel into a homicidal battle. Lovelace stalks his prey throughout,[8] but his prey opposes him with arms that are

---

[8] Lovelace's letters are larded with images of the hunt; none is perhaps as well drawn as Letter LXXI (II, 245-249).

more than his equal. The rape itself leaves her *will* wholly intact, and, in that light, she dies victorious.

If, morally and psychologically, Clarissa resists valiantly during her entire ordeal, how does one properly take stock of the real changes that do occur in the novel? The answer may appear vulgar: the changes, the exchanges, are those of place and property. Richardson's greatness lies in his strange *economy*. Unending though this novel is, it deals with few issues indeed; but those few issues are far more ambivalent than first appears. More than any artist of his age, Richardson depicts the interconnectedness of economics and morals, of property and self. Even the language is contaminated: "Will," the battle cry of the naked self, the means of protecting the integrity of the individual, "will" also indicates those possessions and properties which the self leaves to others. Here is a radically different sense of futurity, an acknowledgement that the spirit may fly off to heaven, but here on earth we leave only *things*. Divine, Clarissa may be, but she moves among things. And she will discover that one cannot live without property.

At the outset, she is characterized as the darling of her grandfather, who expressed that love by leaving her a large part of his estate. Here is sufficient grounds for the sibling rivalry that is to do so much harm. Solmes, as we saw, offers a barter that the Harlowes cannot refuse. But the young woman with estate will be progressively despoiled. The process begins at home. At Harlowe Place, Clarissa is a virtual prisoner, held to her room, obliged to communicate with her own family by letters. The rebellious child is virtually excommunicated, and Richardson paints a remarkable picture of Clarissa's isolation in conjunction with the family's union. She unites them, as nothing else has; one distinctly feels that her separation is the catalyst for their harmony:

> My father is come home, and my brother with him. Late as it is they are all shut up together. Not a door opens; not a soul stirs. Hannah, as she moves up and down, is shunned as a person infected.
>
> The angry assembly is broken up. My two uncles and my Aunt Hervey are sent for, it seems, to be here in the morning to breakfast. I shall then, I suppose, know my

doom. 'Tis past eleven, and I am ordered not to go to bed. (I, p. 108)

Not until Kafka etches the suffering of his metamorphosed hero, Gregor Samsa, will literature show a comparable family drama, a comparably rigorous arrangement of isolated scapegoat and united collectivity.

The trip from closed doors at Harlowe Place to locked doors at Mrs. Sinclair's is not all that far. Faced with the threat of being imprisoned at her uncle Antony's house (equipped with moat, no less), faced with imminent marriage with Solmes, Clarissa breaks out. The crucial garden interview with Lovelace is filled with imagery of opening doors and penetrating realms:

[Lovelace speaking:] I must enter the garden with you— forgive me, but I *must* enter the garden with you. . . .

Dearest creature! interrupted he [Lovelace], holding my hand as I tremblingly offered to put the key to the lock. Let *me*, if you *will* go, open the door. . . . Who then shall assist you in your escape, if escape you would? From your chamber window only permitted to view the garden you must not now enter into, how will you wish for the opportunity you now have, if your hatred to Solmes continue? . . .

And then, freeing my hand, I again offered the key to the door. . . .

I was once more offering the key to the lock when, starting from his knees, with a voice of affrightment, loudly whispering, as if out of breath, *They are at the door, my beloved creature.* And taking the key from me, he fluttered with it, as if he would double-lock it. And instantly a voice from within cried out, bursting against the door, as if to break it open, the person repeating his violent pushes: *Are you there? Come up this* moment!—*this moment! Here they are—here they are both together! Your pistol this moment! your gun!* Then another push, and another. He at the same moment drew his sword, and clapping it naked under his arm, took both my trembling hands in his; and drawing me swiftly after him: Fly, fly, my charmer; this moment is all you have for it, said he. (I, pp. 483-484)

No more lyric nor passionate moment of the novel exists, than Clarissa and Lovelace fleeing Harlowe Place. The rape is notoriously unnarrated but the promise of passion is fully sensed here, and only here. Nowhere is Clarissa more pressed than here: the imagery of forced entries and bursting doors is omnipresent, creating a pulsating rhythm of coursing emotion and erotic desire. The configuration is beautifully double: penetration *by* the "gun" or the "naked" sword; penetration *into* a realm beyond walls or doors. Richardson is able to convey Clarissa's excitement and her suspicions simultaneously; his syntax becomes that of a poet, as he renders her fatal *geste*:

> Now behind me, now before me, now on this side, now on that, turned I my affrighted face in the same moment; expecting a furious brother here, armed servants there, an enraged sister screaming, and a father armed with terror in his countenance more dreadful than even the drawn sword which I saw, or those I apprehended. I ran as fast as he; yet knew not that I ran; my fears adding wings to my feet, at the same time that they took all power of thinking from me. My fears, which probably would not have suffered me to know what course to take, had I not had him to urge and draw me after him: especially as I beheld a man, who must have come out of the door, keeping us in his eye, running now toward us; then back to the garden; beckoning and calling to others, whom I supposed *he* saw, although the turning of the wall hindered *me* from seeing them; and whom I imagined to be my brother, my father; and their servants. (I, p. 484)

This admirable sequence, cinematic and breathless in its immediacy and point of view, well depicts the fatal flight. All is there: the family who must be left, the lover with naked sword, the joint physical exertion of the flight, the impossibility to see clear. But there is to be no open vista and no garden. The opening of the garden door is as fatal as the opening of the self. This "beyond" cannot be actualized in Richardson's imagination; in Clarissa he has created a self big with promise, but vulnerable and fragile, bent on preservation rather than on experience. The great irony of Richardson's novel lies in its symbolic typography, its many images of enclosure and imprisonment, ranging from the closed body to the locked room. The room at Harlowe Place yields to other closed quarters, equally sequestered, only more seamy.

Leaving her father's house is Clarissa's true violation. Clarissa repeatedly refers to this act as being "tricked out of herself." Herein lies the ambiguity of the novel. Can Clarissa, without her estate, remain intact, "at home" within herself? Can the self reign, sovereign, *in vacuo*? Or can Lovelace succeed in bringing her permanently "out of herself"? All of Lovelace's "art" is enlisted in this cause. The result is a siege of extraordinary intensity. Ironically enough, Lovelace's "art" consists precisely in simulating, or approximating, Clarissa's lost estate, Harlowe Place. Clarissa has lost a family: Lovelace invents one for her, calling it his own. We are close to burlesque, as Lovelace employs pimps and whores of his acquaintance to parade as Cousin Montague, Lady Betty, Captain Tomlinson.[9] Lovelace becomes very nearly demiurgic, creating an exact but perverse artificial replica of Harlowe House, the only difference being that Clarissa is now his prisoner, rather than her family's. It is the triumph of appearance:

> The house is to be taken in three weeks: all will be over in three weeks, or bad will be my luck! Who knows but in three days? Have I not carried that great point of making her pass for my wife to the people below? And that other

[9] The theatrical charade reaches, at times, such a level and degree of feint and delirious disguise that we seem close to farce and *guignol*. See, especially, the portion of Vol. IV which is entitled "Act II; Scene—Hampstead Heath, continued" (III, pp. 30-53). In this sequence, Lovelace, afflicted with gout, ensconced in great coat, missing teeth, hobbling up the stairs, and mumbling through his ague, corners Clarissa once more. Seeing her, he cannot maintain his pretense, and his burlesque art is exposed:

Up then came running a gentleman and his sister, fetched, and brought in by the maid who had run down; and who having let in a cursed crabbed old wretch, hobbling with his gout, and mumbling with his hoarse broken-toothed voice, was metamorphosed all at once into a lively gay young fellow, with a clear accent, and all his teeth; and she would have it, that I was neither more nor less than the devil, and could not keep her eye from my foot; expecting, no doubt, every minute to see it discover itself to be cloven. (III, pp. 41-42)

great one of fixing myself here night and day? What
woman ever escaped me, who lodged under one roof with
me? The house too, THE house, the people, people after
my own heart: her servants, Will and Dorcas, both *my* servants. *Three days*, did I say! Pho! pho! pho! *Three hours!* (II,
p. 222)

Lovelace is the demonic artist of the novel, the supreme
manipulator. Much of his craft consists in harnessing the
blind energies of others, and he gloats that the Harlowes have
abetted him every step of the way:

I knew that the whole stupid family were in a combination
to do my business for me. I told thee that they were all
working for me like so many underground moles; and still
more blind than the moles are said to be, unknowing that
they did so. I myself, the director of their principal motions; which falling in with the malice of their little hearts
they took to be all their own. (I, pp. 493–494)

Lovelace has skillfully become Clarissa's total environment.
Estranged from her family, she only has her correspondence
with Miss Howe as a bridge to a world beyond Lovelace (or
one of his agents).

Clarissa's entrapment grows on every page of the novel. It
is a tribute to Richardson's dramatic skill that the reader has
the sense of Clarissa going totally under, when Lovelace is finally able to intercept Miss Howe's letters as well. She has access to nothing that is not Lovelace. Richardson is giving us
a rigorously environmental picture of the self. All of Clarissa's fineness, including her will to deny, cannot alter her
presence and, consequently, her *locus*. Alive, she must be present somewhere; present, she can be invaded. No moral or
mental refinement can extract her from the *huis clos* into
which she is thrust. When Clarissa is absolutely entangled in
her antagonist's web, Lovelace strikes. Repeatedly. For there
is rape in this novel, and it is ultimately more than a hush-
hush, delayed-action affair of drugs and deflowering. Rape is,
rather, the violation of the self by another, the breaking and
entering of the other, the invasion and pillage to which Cla-

rissa is constantly subjected. Richardson does not describe Lovelace's sexual exploitation, but he can and does show Lovelace's suffocating nearness, his awful presence:

> She wrung her hands. She disordered her head-dress. She tore her ruffles. She was in a perfect frenzy. . . .
> She arose, Dorcas being about to withdraw; and wildly caught hold of her arm; O Dorcas! If thou art of mine own sex, leave me not, I charge thee! Then quitting Dorcas, down she threw herself upon her knees, in the furthermost corner of the room, clasping a chair with her face laid upon the bottom of it! O where can I be safe? Where, where can I be safe, from this man of violence? (III, pp. 238-239)

Even the most splendidly integral self takes up space, can be cornered. Lovelace's art, with its array of disguises, interception, and real imprisonment, creates a new estate for Clarissa that is akin to a nightmare, a kind of no-exit funhouse, with Lovelace at every door, every window, entering unseen, touching the body when it is uncovered, taking his pleasure, unstoppable. Tracking her, Lovelace corners Mrs. Lovick who gives us an image of the hounded Clarissa:

> We were forced to support her, she was so weak. She said:
> Whither *can* I go, Mrs. Lovick? Whither *can* I go, Mrs. Smith? Cruel, cruel man! Tell him I called him so, if he comes again! God give him that peace which he denies me. (IV, pp. 138-139)

Propertyless, Clarissa has no place to go; she can be arrested on the street. Lovelace threatens invasion right to the last pages of the novel, even beyond Clarissa's death. He is vampirish, insatiable.

Or perhaps, he is, in his own words, "imperial." Lovelace wants to possess her, materially, almost colonially. His entire being is bent on appropriating fully his property and her sole project, correspondingly, is to remain intact unto herself.

The elemental threat of Richardson's novel, opening up of the self, is envisioned as violation. The male desire for contact and penetration, so yearned for by Des Grieux and Werther, has metamorphosed into a nightmarish, exquisite, sense of vulnerability, capacity to be entered and violated. The full-blown self is infinitely delicate. It may be broken. One of its most pathetic guises is that of madness. After the rape, Clarissa bewails the loss of her self, and wants what is left to be placed in Bedlam, but alone, "locked up in some private mad-house" (III, p. 213). In a letter to Miss Howe, the terms are still blunter; the self is not lost, merely (!) damaged, and, above all, present and pressing, much the way Lovelace himself is:

> O my best, my dearest, my *only* friend! What a tale have I to unfold! But still upon *self*, this vile, this hated *self*! I will shake it off, if possible; and why should I not, since I think, except one wretch, I hate nothing so much? Self, then, be banished from *self* one moment (for I doubt it *will* for no longer), to inquire after a *dearer* object, my beloved Anna Howe! (IV, pp. 138-139)

Notice how persistent and perverse the pursuit has become. Her own inner being has resisted Lovelace, but it has suffered grievously in the process; Clarissa seems little more than a wound, an exposed, opened body. Richardson's book is clinical in its focus on how much invasion the self can withstand. Clarissa *could* have died on the spot, but Richardson keeps her alive, isolates her and observes. Clarissa is subjected to all the degradation her author can imagine, including a visit to prison. Her suffering is doubtless a kind of crucible, a burning off of excess pride, an initiation into humility; it is also a test to see what remains. [10]

[10] Nowhere is Richardson's pathos stronger than in the scenes of public degradation to which Clarissa is subjected. The notion of the intact self, the self that preserves, even at the cost of life, its integrity, is tested socially as well as psychically. Clarissa, who ever upholds decorum and even haughtiness, begins to *crack* under the weight of her experience. The outside world cannot be kept out, and the inside world cannot be kept in:

> But dost thou not observe what a strange, what an uncommon openness of heart reigns in this lady? *She had been in a prison*, she said, before a stranger in the shop, and before the maidservant: and so, probably, she would have said had there been twenty people in the shop. (III, p. 456)

What remains is chastened, if not chaste. Clarissa's ascent
begins when she reacquires property. At first, Bella proposes
a "Moll Flanders and Manon Lescaut solution" to her estranged sister: "you will think of going to Pennsylvania to reside there for some few years till all is blown over"; but Clarissa is going home, setting out with all diligence to her
Father's House. And that haven is not across the ocean. It is
closer at hand, closer even, we begin to realize, than Harlowe
Place:

> . . . a blush overspread her sweet face, on hearing . . . a sort
> of lumbering noise upon the stairs, as if a large trunk were
> bringing up between two people . . .
>
> In came Mrs. Smith: O madam, said she, What have you
> done? Mrs. Lovick, entering, made the same exclamation.
> Lord have mercy upon me, madam, cried I [Belford], what
> have you done! For, she stepping at the instant to the door,
> the women told me it was a coffin.
>
> With an intrepidity of a piece with the preparations, hav-
> ing directed them to carry it into her bedchamber, she re-
> turned to us: They were not to have brought it in til after
> dark, said she. Pray excuse me, Mr. Belford: and don't you,
> Mrs. Lovick, be concerned: nor you, Mrs. Smith. Why
> should you? There is nothing more in it than the usualness
> of the thing. I love to do everything for myself that I can
> do. I ever did. (IV, pp. 254-255)

In a stroke of genius, Richardson has capped his raped-maiden
story with an event at once perfectly poetic and perfectly pro-
saic. Clarissa's miserable room is broken and entered once
more, but the new intruder is welcome in her bedchamber.
The coffin is the ultimate estate, the quintessential portable
property; better than Harlowe House, it is called a "palace"
by Clarissa; it is to be furnished. It is her final, her only, abiding house. It is what a woman of property, accustomed to
paying her way ("I ever did"), requires. "I am setting out
with all diligence for my Father's House." One is tempted,
given the topography and room-drama of this novel, to say
that the emphasis should be placed on *House*, not on Father.
A place has at last been found: the coffin is inviolable.

The finest, and final, touch given to the coffin house comes toward the end:

> It [the coffin] is placed near the window, like a harpsi-chord, though covered over to the ground: and when she is so ill that she cannot well go to her closet, she writes and reads upon it, as others would upon a desk or table. (IV, p. 271)

Palace, house, and writing desk too. How could it be otherwise? Final refuge for the naked self, the coffin is safe, for, as Marvell says, "none, I think, do there embrace." Smallest, most imprisoning of rooms, the coffin is infinitely more spacious even than a palace; as writing desk, it houses Clarissa's ultimate expression of will: her will itself. Here Clarissa writes herself to death, because the letters and the will are her most potent extension into life. Closed to Lovelace, reduced to correspondence with her family and Anna Howe, Clarissa has ever used letters for contact. The will is her final letter, her own will expressed, *d'outre tombe*, disposing her property, crucially *opening* those hearts which remained closed. Herself absent, sequestered, even dead, the letters are alive, asserting her presence, receiving the tearful response which, alive and in person, she was denied. The coffin and the letter are the recipient of the virginal, intact, damaged but still closed, self. They are the palace and the wedding, the union and the communion, which experience itself could not provide. They are a place, a property, an estate, somewhere the self can live integrally. Richardson's loving focus on Clarissa's will, the battle as to who will execute it, the emotional impact of it—all this indicates Clarissa's triumph. Like the serpent devouring its tail (the emblem of the coffin), letters have a futurity which surpasses that of the death-limited individual, regardless of her strength or endurance. Clarissa, in fine bourgeois fashion, came into her estate.

The closed coffin and the letters are resonant figures of the self's privacy and inner kingdom; they are also forbidding images of closure, and the riches they convey can be negotiated only through absence and death. In *Clarissa Harlowe* Richardson has portrayed the disinherited self; the authority of the self is asserted in a final paroxysm of closure and will, but the letter alone is left to bear fruit. In Laclos, it will.

Languages of the Self: *Les Liaisons dangereuses*

In *Les Liaisons dangereuses* we see the most dazzling and vicious display of the power of the self in early fiction. Less character-based than the portraits of Werther, Clarissa, and Des Grieux, *Les Liaisons* is nonetheless a story of individualism gone wild; more than self-as-authority, we see in Laclos' epistolary novel the self deified. The high drama consists in the dangers of relationship, the *liaisons dangereuses*; for the self's power can be played out only in relationship, in controlling and manipulating others; and yet, Laclos demonstrates that relationship is concomitantly the desired or feared transcendence of self, seen as both loss and apotheosis. These two poles define the dialectic of love and pleasure which articulates the novel, two poles embodied by the two women, Merteuil and Tourvel, and fatally negotiated by Valmont.

Valmont and Merteuil are, in every sense, commanding figures. *"Conquérir est notre destin"* declares Valmont at the outset, and, in her masterful encounter with Prévan, Merteuil echoes him: *"Il faut vaincre on périr."* Yet, such bellicosity is reserved exclusively for the boudoir, for there is the true arena for conquest. In the tradition of Molière's Don Juan, the *"grand seigneur méchant homme,"* Valmont and Merteuil are staggering superman figures, closer to Sade than Stendhal, perhaps closest of all to Malraux in their thirst for power through eroticism.

The language of the novel consistently parodies both the religious and the chivalric traditions, as the duo consciously pervert all traditional codes. While remaining publicly within the pale of convention, they privately—in and through their letters—seek pure omnipotence through exploitation of their world. They perversely but genuinely aspire to the Godhead. We see this in Valmont's desire to replace the God that the pious Tourvel worships; we see it in Merteuil's systematic annihilation of Prévan. Jean-Luc Seylaz has written authoritatively about the mystique of reason and control in *Les Liai-*

sons.[1] Valmont and Merteuil effectively master life through analysis, achieving such power as to become fate for all the characters. Their range is impressive: it goes from the comedy of Valmont's theatrical rescue of a family in need (eliciting "Let us all kneel down before this image of God") to the sharp irony of Merteuil receiving letters from both Cécile and Mme. de Volanges with the identical plea: "It is from you alone that I expect some consolation." Moreover, as Seylaz has shrewdly argued, they assert their mastery through their astonishing *presence*: Valmont and Merteuil read virtually every letter; they compose (in both senses of the word) the letters in concert; what the others ignore, they know; what they do not know, they find out (e.g., Valmont's man conveniently intercepts mail by wooing Tourvel's servant). The whole plot seems little more than their sport, as they make and unmake people and reputations at will. They are insidiously where they should not be: Cécile acknowledges that Danceny is more swayed by Valmont's reasoning than by hers; Merteuil comes between mother and daughter, and destroys each. In short, the novel is theirs; they fill its every page, match and mismatch all the *liaisons*, create its every turn, procure and comment on all letters brilliantly, including their own.

Their triumph is one of intelligence, an intelligence so irresistible that Seylaz likens it to fascination in his chapter "*Le romanesque de l'intelligence.*"[2] Valmont and Merteuil demonstrate what you can do to people, and their exploits, in that realm, dwarf those of Sade. Every life that touches theirs is perfectly deformed and then annihilated by the end of the story. There is nothing left.

Why are they so successful? Largely because they understand their victims better than do the victims themselves. They understand the pressures of vanity and desire in all human gesture. They are specialists in pleasure, for they understand that it dictates all behavior.[3] Confirmed hedonists, they expose the sham of ethical categories and moral cosmetics.

---

[1] Jean-Luc Seylaz, *Les Liaisons dangereuses et la creation romanesque chez Laclos* (Geneva: E. Droz, 1958), pp. 83-155.

[2] Jean-Luc Seylaz, pp. 122-145.

[3] Merteuil effectively turns even the rake code upside down. Valmont need

They are manifestly 18th-century creations, and underlying
their strategy is the conviction that human beings are bodies,
and bodies are machines. Those machines may excite lust or
desire among the uninitiated, but, to Valmont and Merteuil,
the body is a delicate, familiar, instrument, transparent in its
workings, controllable. Rarely has such a clinical view of the
emotions been achieved. Valmont advances in his seduction
like a surgeon:

> While she was consoling me, a hand remained in mine;
> the pretty body leant upon my arm, and we were extremely
> close together. You have surely noticed in this situation
> how, as the defence weakens, demands and refusals take
> place at closer quarter; how the head turns away and the
> looks are lowered, while the sentences, all enunciated in a
> weak voice, become infrequent and broken. These valuable
> symptoms announce the consent of the mind [âme] in an
> unmistakable manner . . . (pp. 226-227)[4,1]

This is a universe so uniquely physical and generic that the
supposed ethical and personal underpinnings disappear from
the picture. The Présidente and Cécile are relentlessly *exposed*
in their affective and anatomical transparency; both women
speak a language of love concepts, but Valmont deciphers a
more immediate sensorial code, the only one he needs to
know. The rift between the love rhetoric and the body lan-

---

not pride himself on his so-called victories, since he merely abets and legiti-
mizes his "victims' " desire for pleasure in the first place:

Dites-moi donc, amant langoureux, ces femmes que vous avez eues,
croyez-vous les avoir violées? Mais, quelque envie qu'on ait de se donner,
quelque pressée que l'on en soit, encore faut-il un prétexte; et y en a-t-il de
plus commode pour nous, que celui qui nous donne l'air de céder à la force?
Pour moi, je l'avoue, une des choses qui me flattent le plus, est une attaque
vive et bien faite, où tout se succède avec ordre quoique avec rapidité; qui
ne nous met jamais dans ce pénible embarras de réparer nous-mêmes une
gaucherie dont au contraire nous aurions dû profiter; qui sait garder l'air de
la violence jusque dans les choses que nous accordons, et flatter avec adresse
nos deux passions favorites, la gloire de la défense et le plaisir de la défaite.
(p. 25)

[4] Choderlos de Laclos, *Les Liaisons Dangereuses*, tr. Richard Aldington
(New York: New American Library, 1962).

guage is so great that the reader has a feeling that two separate
worlds are in play, one a common currency that is utterly
bankrupt, and the other a lethal code known only to the se-
ducers. This knowledge of the senses is power. When Valmont discovers that Mme. de Volanges has been discrediting
him, he immediately plans a revenge that is erotic: "Ah! Her
daughter must certainly be seduced, but that is not enough,
I must ruin her; and since the age of this accursed woman pro-
tects her from my attacks, I must strike her through the object
of her affection" (p. 103).[2] There is something disquieting in
his choice of weapons; he becomes little more than an avenging phallus, waging a war against which there is no protection.

The view of the self as body reaches its culmination in the
portrayal of Cécile Volanges. She is the ultimate *thing*; her
body responds to all stimuli, while her mind dallies in adolescent fantasies. Merteuil gives the brutal diagnosis:

> . . . I know nothing so [banal] as the [easiness] of stupidity
> which yields without knowing how or why, solely because
> it is attacked and does not know how to resist. These sorts
> of women are absolutely nothing but pleasure machines.
>
> You will tell me that [we have only to make them that,]
> and that it suffices for our plans. Well enough! But do not
> forget that very soon everybody gets to know the [inner
> workings] of these machines; so, to make use of this one
> without danger, we must hurry, know when to stop, and
> then break it. (amended, p. 247)[3]

And that is precisely what happens, Cécile's machine is used,
broken, and discarded. Valmont fornicates with her, and she
thinks she is faithful to Danceny; he gives her a technical vocabulary for her sexual activity, so that the moral and emotional realms (which exist nowhere outside of her head) are
untouched; he impregnates her, and she even miscarries, all
the while unknowing. What is left of her finishes in a convent.

Here is an art of seduction that is actually a science of war,
a literally no-holds-barred war between the victims and the
conquerors. The technique used for the Présidente is comparable: verbal rhetoric and physical attack. The letters convey

the rhetoric, while all encounters are good for the body work. I have spoken of Valmont's wish to play God. Let us consider how consummately he controls all situations; at the very outset of his campaign, long before Tourvel registers what is happening (although her body knows), Valmont checks out the terrain:

> I arranged a walk so that we came upon a ditch which had to be crossed; and although she is very active, she is even more timid; you may imagine that a prude is afraid to take a leap. She was compelled to accept my help. I have clasped this modest woman in my arms! Our preparations and the crossing of my old aunt sent our gay devotee into peals of laughter; but as soon as I took hold of her, by an intentional awkwardness on my part our arms became mutually entwined. I held her breast against my own and, in that brief moment, I felt her heart beat faster. Her face was suffused by a charming blush and her modest embarrassment showed me *that her heart had beaten with love and not with fear.* And yet my aunt was as mistaken as you and said: "The child was afraid"; but the *child's* charming candour does not permit her a lie and she answered naïvely: "Oh no, but. . . ." That single word enlightened me. (p. 33)[4]

This charming, almost innocuous, passage is heinous in its implications. Valmont misses nothing, and he cannot be stopped. He arranges the walk, and he correctly assesses the movements of the body that he holds. A pulse beat, a tremble, a blush, these are the signs he reads, and that is a language over which there is no control. Tourvel has no idea how much she is saying. Perhaps the most arresting feature of this passage is its "naturalness"; Valmont does not need an isolated chateau or a secret abduction: a handshake, a kiss on the cheeks, a casual touching of bodies gives him all the information he needs. Intentionally or not, Laclos is depicting the vulnerability of the body in a social world: our conventions condone and even require handshaking, dancing, kissing. Clothes may cover our genitals, but the educated observer does not need that much to go on. Short of recluse, the body is exposed to touch and exploitation. The Présidente is diag-

nosed before she ever suspects she is ill. In the world of the
novel, only Valmont and Merteuil seem to have eyes, while
the others are blind. Each encounter between Valmont and
Tourvel is like an anatomy class. In the final seduction scene,
he describes her symptoms with cool professionalism:

> I then got up; and after a moment of silence I cast wild
> glances upon her which, however much they seemed to
> wander, were none the less clear-sighted and observant.
> Her ill-assured bearing, her quick breathing, the contrac-
> tion of all her muscles, her trembling half-raised arms, all
> proved to me that the result was such as I had desired to
> produce. . . . (p. 291)[5]

If Valmont is adroit at interpreting body language, Merteuil goes a miraculous step further: she *makes* body language.
What is involuntary and instinctive in most people, those irrepressible signs of interest and desire which the initiated can
decode, Merteuil has learned to control at will. She can repress what she feels; she can simulate what she does not feel.
Far more even than Moll or Marianne, Merteuil is a self-made
woman. Her education is a process of self-genesis: "I can say
that I am my own creation" (p. 175). There is a delirious kind
of auto-generation here; the body, ordinarily viewed as contingent and given, becomes, for Merteuil, the docile medium
of her high art, a potent tool, a precision instrument; nature
and instinct are still present, but they are utterly controlled
and disciplined. Hence, Merteuil is the consummate mask:

> That useful curiosity which served to instruct me also
> taught me to dissimulate; I was often forced to conceal the
> objects of my attention from the eyes of those about me
> and I tried to direct my own eyes at will; from this I gained
> that ability to simulate when I chose that preoccupied gaze
> you have praised so often. Encouraged by this first success,
> I tried to govern the different expressions of my face in the
> same way. Did I experience some grief, I studied to show
> an air of serenity, even one of joy; I carried my zeal so far
> as to cause myself voluntary pain and to seek for an expres-
> sion of pleasure at the same time. I worked over myself

with the same care and more trouble to repress the symptoms of an unexpected joy. In this way I acquired that
power over my features by which I have sometimes seen
you astonished. (p. 178)[6]

Thus, it follows that Merteuil's wedding night is essentially
"an opportunity for experience [expérience in French suggests
"experiment" as well]; I [noted] very carefully both pain and
pleasure and in these different sensations I saw nothing but
facts to collect and to meditate upon" (amended, p. 180).[7] It is
crystal clear that Prévan is no match for such prowess. Merteuil demolishes him with her art:

> . . . our eyes were very eloquent. I say our eyes; I ought to
> have said his eyes, for mine had only one expression, that
> of surprise. He must have thought I was astonished and ex-
> cessively [concerned] by the prodigious effect he was mak-
> ing on me. . . .
>   As he was [new to my circle], who were not numerous
> that evening, he owed me the customary attentions; and so
> when we went to supper he offered me his hand. When I
> took it I was malicious enough to make mine tremble
> slightly and to walk with lowered eyes and more rapid
> breathing. (amended, pp. 192-193)[8]

Prévan takes, of course, the false coins for the real, assumes he
is well on his way to victory, and is undone. The entire episode is a brilliant, speeded-up, parody of Valmont's pursuit of
Tourvel. Merteuil is utterly self-made, so disciplined as to be
a kind of super-machine, bent on manipulation and gratification. She represents the extreme limits of the pleasure syndrome, of maniacal self-sufficiency, a view of life that utterly
depersonalizes others, makes them the indifferent servants of
her will. Her life is a closed circle; she is, even in sex, the her-
metic self; pleasure, she realizes, is in us, not in the other; orgasm is impersonal and self-located:

> Ah! Keep your advice and your fears for those unbalanced
> women who rave of their "sentiment," whose [over-ex-
> cited] imagination would make one think nature had placed
> their senses in their heads; who, having never reflected, al-

ways confuse love with the lover; who, in their foolish illusion, think that the one man with whom they have
sought pleasure is the sole depository of it; who, being
truly superstitious, give the priest the respect and faith
which is due only to the divinity. (amended pp. 177-178)[9]

Merteuil is free and invulnerable behind her mask and
within her body; yet she knows that the individual heart is a
sanctuary that must be protected because it can be taken: "I
had descended into my own heart and I studied in it the heart
of others. There I saw that everybody keeps a secret in it
which he must not allow to be revealed . . ." (p. 182).[10] "Nouvelle Dalila," Merteuil seeks the heart of others while shield-
ing her own; no one in the book, and—I would argue—no
one outside the book, knows who she truly is.

At this point it is essential that we turn to the problem of
the book's form. Merteuil is incognito because of her philosophy of disguise; she is also unknowable, because she comes
to us through letters. Midway in the book, Merteuil repri-
mands the naive Cécile:

> You still write like a child. I see why that is; it is because
> you say everything you think and nothing you do not
> think. That is all very well between you and me who have
> nothing to hide from each other, but with everyone else!
> Above all with your lover! You will always seem like a lit-
> tle fool. You can see that when you write to someone it is
> for him and not for yourself; you ought then to try less to
> say what you are thinking than to say what [he wants most
> to hear]. (amended, p. 245)[11]

It is here that Les Liaisons dangereuses diverges radically
from the epistolary tradition around it; unlike La Vie de Marianne, Werther, La Nouvelle Héloïse or Clarissa, these letters
serve more as camouflage than as exposure. Marianne and
Moll and Werther achieve their authenticity and wholeness
ultimately through their confessions; the major characters of
Les Liaisons use the letters as disguise. And, since the novel is
composed wholly of letters, Laclos' book is a huge step forward into the epistemological jungle of modern fiction. If

each person writes in order to seduce rather than to confess, how can we know their true motives, their genuine feelings? Where is authority in this book?

At first, this assertion might appear extreme. Danceny and Cécile seem honest enough, but as their *liaisons* with Merteuil and Valmont develop, we witness an ambiguity in the letters of one, and understandable reticence in the other. Tourvel's initial letters to Mme. de Volanges and to Valmont himself do not accord with the nascent passion that Valmont (and the reader) easily observes. Perhaps the most illusory and treacherous semblance of truth lies in the correspondence of Valmont and Merteuil themselves. The reader sees soon enough that they lie to others, but they initially appear to be honest with themselves: the book seems to be an alternance of love letters to victims and of lucid strategical exchanges between conquerors. And, indeed, Valmont and Merteuil play the critic beautifully, reinterpreting letters of Tourvel and Cécile and Danceny with unerring judgment, frequently lessoning the reader who mistook the stated for the true; Merteuil does not hesitate to redo Valmont as well, and her letters to him are filled with words in italics, expressions he used and abused, deceptions that she exposes. As Seylaz has pointed out, the critical stature of Valmont and Merteuil adds immeasurably to their appeal and likens, dangerously likens, their work to that of the reader.[5]

The visible, acknowledged deceptions of *Les Liaisons dangereuses* in fact disguise, whereas they should highlight, the less visible, unacknowledged deceptions which run alongside. For letters carry an enormous dosage of deception within themselves. Human relations, even body-to-body and face-to-face, are murky, ambiguous, affairs; even with such presence, there is much room for misreading; and partners are alone in their conceptions even when they are together. Yet, a modicum of commonality is achieved; certain gross deceptions are not possible; the soul is solitary, but the other is still present. And the mutuality of bodies binds where consciousness would separate. Letters are, on the other hand, rigorously

[5] Jean-Luc Seylaz, pp. 131-134.

private, not to say solipsistic. The paper with its written characters must somehow replace or create the presence of people. A kind of scriptural emissary, the letter is dispossessed, bereft of the incredibly rich, tangible, more or less reliable, context which surrounds all human exchange; it is, instead, language alone, bodiless, unmoored. It is written in solitude and read in solitude, hence providing an awesome freedom of fabrication and interpretation; the umbilical cord between speaker and statement, statement and recipient, is not so much cut as separated into component times; each action is independent, ungraced by the checks and balances of human presence, freed from the allegiances which govern other exchange. Letters bestow on language an autonomy and potency which are emblematic of literature itself, the ideal realm of generated, rather than reflected, meanings. Merteuil's body and oral language are a triumph of generated meanings without referents. Deception is creative; lies are generative. Human relations need reliable concordance between signifiers and signified; letters are free-floating signifiers, and Valmont and Merteuil exploit their expressive freedom with brilliance.

In this light, the love letter is the ideal form of duplicity and creativity. What is a "love letter"? Where are its indices of truth and authority? Are the privacy of writing and the privacy of reading consonant with love? Nowhere is the prodigious freedom of the love letter better illustrated than in Valmont's impassioned statements written on Emilie's body; and it is worth quoting at length:

> After a [stormy] night, during which I have not closed my eyes; after having been ceaselessly either in the agitation of a devouring ardour or in the complete annihilation of all the faculties of my soul; I seek from you, Madame, the calm I need but do not hope to enjoy yet. Indeed the position I am in as I write to you makes me understand more than ever the irresistible power of love; I can scarcely preserve sufficient control over myself to put my ideas into some order; and already I perceive that I shall not finish this letter without being forced to interrupt it. Ah! May I not hope that some day you will share the [emotion] I feel at this mo-

ment? Yet I dare to think that if you really knew it you
would not be entirely insensible to it. Believe me, Madame,
cold tranquillity, the soul's sleep, the image of death, do not
lead to happiness; only the active passions can lead to it;
and, in spite of the torments you make me endure, I think
I may boldly assure you that at this moment I am happier
than you. In vain do you overwhelm me with your dis-
couraging severities; they do not prevent me from abandoning myself wholly to love and from forgetting in the
delirium it causes me the despair to which you surrender me.
It is thus I mean to avenge myself for the exile to which you
condemn me. Never did I have so much pleasure in writing
to you; never in that occupation did I feel so soft and yet so
keen an emotion. Everything seems to increase my raptures; the air I breathe is filled with voluptuousness; the
very table upon which I write to you, which for the first
time is devoted to that use, becomes for me the sacred altar
of love; how much it will be embellished in my eyes! I shall
have traced upon it the vow to love you forever! I beg you
to pardon the disorder of my senses. Perhaps I ought to
abandon myself less to raptures you do not share; I must
leave you a moment to dispel an ecstasy which increases
every instant, which becomes stronger than I am.
(amended, pp. 109-110)[12]

Here is a genuine "love-letter," conceivably the most authentic letter in the novel. Seylaz has spoken of Flaubert and
degradation of language in context of this letter,[6] and surely
the "genuineness" of the sexual ardor expressed by Valmont
is the perverse proof of his infidelity. But there is no simula-
tion here, no gap between signifier and signified, letter and
meaning: all the affective rhetoric is "justified"; the conventional outcries of "*Quoi!*" "*transport,*" "*ivresse,*" "*agitation,*"
etc., are entirely appropriate. Only the addressee is wrong. It
is the letter most in line with Merteuil's insistence that the
priest not be confused with the divinity, the lover with the
orgasm. The pleasure principle is relentlessly generic; for cop-

[6] *Ibid.*, pp. 94-95.

ulation purposes, most bodies are more or less alike, the climax achieved more or less identical, the partner more or less
indifferent; Valmont's letter is the quintessential impersonal
love letter.

I would like to emphasize the honesty of Valmont's letter,
because we need to be very careful about attaching labels of
"true" and "false" in *Les Liaisons dangereuses*. At a given point
in this novel—early for some, later for others—each reader
begins to realize that things are even less what they seem than
he thought. Not only are Cécile and Danceny and Tourvel
deluded—and their delusion constitutes the reader's superiority—but Valmont himself, and perhaps even Merteuil, are
playing a double game, one that involves prevarication and
disguise between each other, even to themselves. And, since
the novel is not a diary, but a sequence of letters, there remains no stable center, no single correspondent or moment
that one might deem reliable. All is show. Valmont's involvement with Tourvel far transcends what he can afford to acknowledge. Merteuil's play with Prévan and Danceny may be
more than play. Between the victors themselves is an abyss,
a realm of murky, unacknowledged feelings of vanity, jealousy, spite, desire, and—finally—hatred.[7]

The convenient schema of love letters and strategy letters
collapses, because all the letters now seem suspect, especially
those that *appear* most lucid and controlled. Valmont and
Merteuil, after appearing as comfortable, Olympian, reliable
narrators and manipulators, must be reassessed as implicated

[7] My entire interpretation is based on a crucial dynamic of reading,
whereby seemingly innocuous phrases are seen only in retrospect as foreshadowing. In particular, the growing rift between Valmont and Merteuil is
advertised long before it occupies center-stage. Referring, for example, to the
Prévan plan, Valmont acknowledges his bewilderment with Merteuil's letter:
"J'ai beau vous lire et vous relire, je n'en suis pas plus avancé; car, de prendre
votre lettre dans le sens naturel qu'elle présente, il n'y a pas moyen. Qu'avez-
vous donc voulu dire?" (p. 153). Still more ominous is a later confession of
Valmont's: "C'est une chose inconcevable, ma belle amie, comme aussitôt
qu'on s'éloigne, on cesse facilement de s'entendre. Tant que j'étais auprès de
vous, nous n'avions jamais qu'un même sentiment, une même façon de voir;
et parce que, depuis près de trois mois je ne vous vois plus, nous ne sommes
plus du même avis sur rien" (p. 271).

actors, manipulated themselves, part of a larger game than they had counted on. The innocuous background becomes the problematic foreground. The lethal truth of the novel begins to appear: relationship is deadly; all *liaisons* are *dangereuses*. Valmont and Merteuil is a relationship, and they will be destroyed; Valmont and Tourvel is a relationship, and they will be destroyed; Danceny and Cécile will be undone by Merteuil and Valmont, but also by their own wants. Mme. de Volanges will be grievously wounded by her daughter; Mme. Rosamonde will suffer the death of her nephew. At the outset, seducing and abandoning seems an elegant game, *très dix-huitième*, but, at the end, a grimmer, almost Greek view of passion and hubris has emerged.[8] People do not play with other people; *things* may be possessed, exchanged, and disposed of, but, let them be humanized, and the tone deepens. The vulnerability of self so feared by Clarissa emerges as Laclos' cardinal truth. There is a terrible reciprocity in *Les Liaisons dangereuses*, a reciprocity mirrored everywhere in the book's form with the swapping of letters and partners and sharing of information and bodies; but this mutuality is a kind of affective boomerang, revealing that nets trap both ways, that letters bind as well as divine, unite sender and receiver as well as deceive them.

The plot of the book is irrefutable. It *shows* us a Valmont in love, a Merteuil who is jealous. It shows, further, a Valmont who surely dies by choice at the hands of Danceny, for what other explanation is feasible? He is, and he has been, as Merteuil sovereignly informs him, in love with Tourvel. And this leads to the elemental but astonishing realization: his love letters, despite all disclaimers, are authentic, while his strategy

---

[8] Merteuil may be seen as the final apotheosis of the skin-artist whom we saw in the *Buscón*. Whereas skin can be resewn in Quevedo, Laclos reveals the hubris of making one's body one's medium. To be sure, very great and wondrous effects can be wrought by the freely signifying body; but the body's final allegiance is not to the shaping, designing mind of its occupant: death and affliction do not send visiting cards. Merteuil can simulate passion, but she cannot prevent smallpox. Like the rest of one's body, the face—docile and keenly expressive in good days—is a lent, rather than a given, commodity, an alien rather than controllable system. It has laws beyond the legislation of even a Merteuil.

letters are false. Or, rather, both sets of letters are true: Valmont is in love and he is desperately seeking to call it a game, to grant himself control. Here is Laclos' breakthrough: language cannot and does not lie, even though it ruptures our codes of fidelity and consistency. Each letter is an index of the self, a new guise, a new venture; even the most wildly improbable (e.g., Merteuil's to Mme. de Volanges) are rich portraits of the self's resources, its chameleon-like exercise of power and energy. Laclos—ever a military man—stages the fullest exercise of power ever depicted in fiction. Valmont and Merteuil are mad for assertion. In Merteuil we see the sovereignty of the self enacted in every key known: her will is fleshed out in language, gesture, and mask. She is the infinitely fertile progenitrex of meanings, spewing forth lies and casting herself to others in what seems a paroxysm of creativity. Sublimely unconstrained by truth or referent, Merteuil makes herself endlessly anew, far more potent than her male counterpart; she possesses the frightening purity of art itself, a performance coming from nowhere, demiurgically issuing onto the world.

The greatness of the novel lies in the fact that Laclos' vision ultimately contains and assesses Merteuil as well. The letters of *Les Liaisons dangereuses* tell a composite story that reverses and dwarfs the plans of its apparent manipulators. That story emerges ineluctably, writ large at the end, as visible and legible as the pox marks that now cover Merteuil's face, replacing all prior masks. A story of self-deception more than deception, it traces the evolving conflict of two codes, the love and the pleasure code. And its modus operandi is seduction, not control. Who is seducing whom in this novel? Valmont's love letters to Tourvel are responses rather than initiatives. She seduces him from the outset of the novel, and continues right up to his suicide at having lost her.

This love frightens Valmont immeasurably; what begins as frustration that a woman such as Tourvel could resist him so long ends as a consented, though unacknowledged, relationship. Above all, the spectacular seduction scene—despite its overtly theatrical character—betrays a Valmont caught up by feelings unlike any he has ever known:

I am still too full of my happiness to be able to appreciate it, but I am astonished by the [unknown] charm I felt. . . . Even if yesterday's scene carried me, as I now think, a little further than I intended; even if I shared for a moment the agitation and ecstasy I created; that passing illusion would now have disappeared, and yet the same charm remains. I confess I should even feel a considerable pleasure in yielding to it, if it did not cause me some anxiety. Shall I, at my age, be mastered like a schoolboy, by an involuntary and [unknown feeling]? No; before everything else, I must combat and thoroughly examine it. (amended, pp. 287-288)[13]

Note the parallel defense: resist the feeling and analyze the feeling. Not only is Valmont overcome by sensations he cannot control, but, worse still, those feelings originate from a single individual. That indeed would be a humiliation "of thinking I might depend in any way upon the very slave I have enslaved myself; that I do not contain the plenitude of my happiness in myself; and that the [ability to make me enjoy] it in all its energy should be reserved to such or such a woman, exclusive of all others" (amended, p. 288).[14]

Such feelings can be fought most characteristically by choking them with analysis, distancing and disciplining them into a letter: "I need to make an effort over myself to distract myself from the impression it made on me; it was [to help me do so] that I began to write to you" (amended, p. 225).[15] After the final "victory," Valmont again seeks refuge in letters: "Even when we separated, the idea of her did not leave me and I had to make an effort to distract myself" (p. 294).[16] The letter, which we have seen to be the ideal medium for creation *ex nihilo* and masquerade, is the last citadel for the beleaguered self. The letter-writer's privacy and isolation, his freedom from exposure, his respite from passion and opportunity for reflection: all combine to make the letter into a verbal equivalent of the secret, threatened, but guarded, heart of which Merteuil spoke.

But love ends solipsis and security; the protected but imprisoned self wants out; there can be no self-sufficiency. Thus

Valmont goes, for the first time in his life, beyond pleasure.
The pleasure cult and the body machines do not bind, for the
utility ceases with orgasm. Valmont encounters a person, and
his feeling outlives his sexual pleasure:

> It was with this naïve or sublime candour that she surren-
> dered to me her person and her charms, and that she in-
> creased my happiness by sharing it. The ecstasy was com-
> plete and mutual; and, for the first time, my own outlasted
> the pleasure. I only left her arms to fall at her knees, to
> swear an eternal love to her; and, I must admit it, I believed
> what I said. (p. 294)[17]

Within the hedonist, egocentric code of Merteuil, Valmont's
words have a revolutionary power. The book depicts the fallacy of the pleasure-machine code, and it does so magnificently in the mutual seduction scene itself. Replete with theatrical and military imagery, the scene begins in the purest
rake tradition. Valmont feigns and mimics with customary
professional skill, and victory seems assured. He praises his
own art: "[Up to now], my fair friend, I think you will find
I adopted a purity of method which will please you; and you
will see that I departed in no respect from the true principles
of this war, which we have often remarked is so like the
other" (amended, pp. 292-293).[18] Valmont's technique earns
him her body, but he cannot accede to her person. She resists,
and he describes her in impeccable clinical detail:

> Imagine a woman seated, immovably still and with an
> unchanging face, appearing neither to think, hear nor listen;
> a woman whose fixed eyes flowed with quite continual
> tears which came without effort. Such was Madame de
> Tourvel while I was speaking; but if I tried to recall her at-
> tention to me by a caress, even by the most innocent ges-
> ture, immediately there succeeded to this apparent apathy,
> terror, suffocation, convulsions, sobs and at intervals a cry,
> but all without one word articulated. (p. 293)[19]

Valmont is stumped. No amount of science will take him further. The body-machine concept must be abandoned. Only

by speaking of his happiness can Valmont bring Tourvel to make love with him. Tourvel gives herself, as a person, to Valmont, and in so doing, she transforms the pleasure ethos into a unique personal relationship; struck by her openness, her exposure, Valmont knows he is loved:

> For my observations I needed to find a delicate and sensitive woman who would make love her sole [concern] and who in love itself would see only her lover; a woman whose emotion, far from following the ordinary track, would start from the heart and reach the senses. . . . And then, it was necessary for her to add to all this the natural candour which has become insurmountable from the habit of yielding to it, which does not allow her to dissimulate any of the feelings of her heart. Now, you will admit that such women are rare; and I am ready to believe that but for her I should never have met with one perhaps. (amended, p. 308)[20]

One cannot stress enough Tourvel's absence of mask, her personal commitment toward her lover, because these are the bases of relationship and they are diametrically opposed to the hedonist principles he has lived by, up to now. And, these are the features of Tourvel that most seduce him. Tourvel alone in the novel assumes the burden of love, and she does so with simplicity and dignity:

> All I can tell you is that I was placed by M. de Valmont between his death or his happiness, and I chose the latter. I neither boast of it nor blame myself for it; I simply say what is. . . .
> I have then consecrated myself to your nephew; for his sake I [have forsaken all]. He has become the sole centre of my thoughts, of my feelings, of my actions. As long as my life is necessary to his happiness, it will be precious to me, and I shall think it a fortunate one. (amended, p. 299)[21]

Tourvel's brief happiness is characterized by generosity and certainty. Wholly vulnerable, she holds nothing back; she hints at a Valmont who, like her, has also grown into love:

I will confess I had noticed in him formerly an appearance of reflection and reserve which rarely left him and often brought me back, in spite of myself, to the false and cruel impressions I had been given of him. But since he has been able to yield unconstrainedly to the emotions of his heart he seems to guess all the desires of mine. Who knows whether we were not born for each other! If this happiness were not reserved for me—to be necessary to his! . . . And I feel it myself; this happiness one creates is the strongest bond, the only one which really binds. (pp. 306-307)[22]

These words are beyond irony. Tourvel's statement is a definition of relationship, of bonds (*liens*) which unite. And, as the title says, such relationships are dangerous. The fatal letter which Valmont sends her, with its refrain of *"ce n'est pas ma faute,"* is a step back into the generic pleasure code of orgasm and exchange. Tourvel is destroyed by the letter, and her final delirious visions evoke, with almost surreal power, the cost of love:

Pitiless in its vengeance, it has delivered me up to him who ruined me. It is at once [for] him and by him that I suffer. I try to fly from him, in vain; he follows me; he is there; he besets me continually. But how different he is from himself! His eyes only express hatred and scorn. His mouth only utters insult and blame. His arms embrace me only to rend me. Who will save me from his barbarous fury?

But what! It is he. . . . I am not deceived; I see him again. O my charming love! Receive me into your arms; hide me in your bosom; yes, it is you, it is indeed you! What disastrous illusion made me mistake you? How I have suffered in your absence! Let us not separate again, let us never be separated. Let me breathe. Feel my heart, feel how it beats! Ah! It is no longer fear, it is the sweet emotion of love. Why do you refuse my tender caresses? Turn that soft gaze upon me! What are those bonds you try to break? Why do you prepare that equipment of death? What can have so altered those features? What are you doing? Leave me; I shudder! God! It is that monster again! (amended, p. 358)

In a moment of great suffering and intensity, Tourvel has retold the story of *Les Liaisons dangereuses*. Valmont's pursuit, the world of masks, the metamorphosis of rhetoric and lust, the twin face of desire, above all, the cost of passion, of giving oneself, without mask and naked, to another—all this is expressed in Laclos' most lucid and tragic statement about relationship.

Tourvel represents an alternative to the closed manipulating self, and the beauty of her love seduces Valmont; but the gift of self, shown as problematic with Des Grieux and Werther and fearsome with Clarissa, is paid dearly in *Les Liaisons dangereuses*. The egomaniacal, self-deifying pleasure code has been transcended, but the love ethic is no less deadly. Collision marks Laclos' novel, as it finishes like a nuclear explosion, with letters scattered and hidden, bodies everywhere, lives destroyed. Rarely has the appeal of the other been evoked with such power: the other as victim, as machine, as God, as instrument of pleasure, as invitation to love. The letter runs the gamut from pretense of love to declaration of war, from means of discipline to means of death. It is ultimately a novel of massive failure: failure of reason and failure of love.

Laclos has depicted the double drama of self as god and the impossibility of love. The 19th century will not produce any rebel-hero (or creative artist) of a stature comparable to Merteuil, and not until Proust will the cost of relationship be measured so acutely.

Finally, there is perhaps no other novel in literature that deals so powerfully with the theme of self-creation. Language, although multiple and generative in *Les Liaisons dangereuses*, is still—tragically—wedded to mimetic fictions; creation and change, within this context, must betoken lie and betrayal. In Laclos' equation, the freedom of the self and the destruction of the other are inseparable. In Sterne, Diderot, and Rousseau we shall see the effort to transcend tragedy and mimesis; the self will find its arena for expression and assertion, but it must be safe, without danger, without relationship.

"We may have lost the war, but we had all the good songs."
—Tom Lehrer

THE LIFE AS BOOK

ALL LITERATURE is at the end of an umbilical cord that connects, equates, and trades off language against reality. Even the most mimetic text, claiming language exclusively as reflection of a prior reality, suggests by its own presence that language makes rather than reflects. Balzac may have had his sights on the *état civil*, but his world is every bit as much a word-world as Mallarmé's *Coup de dés*. Within the texts themselves, however, language is only one avenue, one means for actualization or assertion. There are others. Relationship and material success, survival and love, are fundamental goals and activities in Western literature.[1]

In the works studied thus far, language has not been recognized as the ultimate privileged activity, the final means of transcendence and achievement through art's Midas touch. Quevedo's Pablos found language to be a great resource, and Moll and Marianne achieve selfhood largely through confession and story; but other rewards and other appetites are at play in these texts. In the love stories, the full ecosystem is visible; the prowess of language is part of a larger system of forces: Des Grieux wants to move the man of quality, but his

[1] Lionel Trilling, in a very different context, has suggested that the larger cultural signification of James Joyce may be seen in terms of new programs replacing older, now defunct, reward systems. In particular, the figure of Stephen Dedalus appears as one untempted and unmoved by the "world," one who will therefore not make the archetypal journey through materialist lucre on to the finally recognized and valued goal of spirit and soul. See "James Joyce in His Letters," reprinted in *Joyce: A Collection of Critical Essays*, ed. William Chace (Englewood Cliffs: Prentice Hall, 1974), pp. 143–165.

tragic love for Manon is unredeemed by belletristic feats; Werther's sole aim is to project himself onto and into the world of Nature and Others, but his only accomplishment is a *pis-aller*, the epistolary record he leaves.

Human activities must be seen competitively: the need to eat, love, survive, and create is gratified variously. Pablos talks his dinner and Nemours talks his sex, but both feats are viewed ironically, as *ersatz*; Werther and Des Grieux want relationship, and words can take them only so far. For Des Grieux and Werther, language is not enough; for Clarissa, language does suffice as a medium of her will, but she must die in the process. In *Les Liaisons dangereuses* we begin to see the spectacular anarchic power of language, a potency for creation and deception which subverts both relationship and knowledge, for it insidiously mouths truths through its lies and mocks senders as well as receivers. *Les Liaisons dangereuses* is a tragic novel, not only because of the manifest destruction which follows in the wake of its sovereign sport, but also because it relentlessly places the freedom of language in context of the need for relationship.

What follows collision? Many have seen in the tragic 18th-century novels a forerunner of romantic and realist developments of the 19th century, a foreplay of the wars between self and society, self and other. Yet, there is also in the 18th century a post-antagonist, post-relational literature, a strange literature of resolution and transcendence, of celebrations of selfhood beyond all constraints seen up to now. In Diderot's *Neveu de Rameau*, Sterne's *Tristram Shandy*, and Rousseau's *Confessions* we find, perhaps, the most haunting and potent texts of the century, strange parables of by-pass and overpass, of the freedoms of language and imagination over and against the poverty of matter and experience. In these texts the self prophetically plays out its life as art, and the relational binds of the past are past.

The Imploding Self: *Le Neveu de Rameau*

Conceivably the most mercurial, multi-faceted, restless spirit of the 18th century is Diderot. He marks everything: art, music, science, theater, biology, physics, anthropology,

history, government, and, of course, literature. It is not easy
to assess his achievement, because we are still his inheritors;
the massive project of the *Encyclopédie* testifies to a gargantuan
appetite for the fruits of reason, the knowability of the world,
the effort to submit the real to logic and to language, to make
the whole consort available to all who could read. Complementing the idealism and commitment of the *Encyclopédie*
project (which consumed twenty-five years of Diderot's life)
are a host of writings evidencing equal faith in the goals of the
Enlightenment: the early texts on the theater, indicating his
belief in its potential as a moral influence in society, essays on
the deaf and dumb, a lively interest in all the artistic and scientific productions of his day.

Amid this variety there are nonetheless recurrent concerns:
there is, on the one hand, an almost superhuman effort at reform and progress, a belief in knowledge and its usefulness, a
faith in education and the power of reason; complementing
this lifelong belief, somewhat like a single bitter almond
among a host of good ones, are a handful of odd, impudent,
irresistible, texts, works which were never published during
Diderot's lifetime, works which flaunt the cynicism and skepticism which must have accompanied the philosopher's resolve and courage. *Le Neveu de Rameau* is such a bitter almond, a violent diatribe against the philosophers, a ruthless
and hilarious calling into question of all that went into the *Encyclopédie*; yet, like the bitter almond, the *Neveu* not only gives
the true flavor to the ensemble, but it illuminates the cost of
philosophy, the ways of financing the life of moral and intellectual idealism.

At first glance, the *Neveu* seems too frivolous to support
such claims. The nephew himself appears to be so bizarre, so
marginal, as to be unproblematic, an eccentric fool, an *original*
who amused Diderot. The dialogue form presents Myself as
a stable counterforce, a narrator more than a participant; for
him, the nephew is "a compound of elevation and abjectness,
of good sense and lunacy" (p. 8)[2,1] whose essential value is a
shock value:

_____

[1] Denis Diderot, *Rameau's Nephew and Other Works*, tr. Jacques Barzun (In-
dianapolis-New York: Bobbs-Merrill Company, 1964).

But for my part it is only once a year that I stop and fall in
with them, largely because their character stands out from
the rest and breaks that tedious uniformity which our education, our social conventions, and our customary good
manners have brought about. If such a character makes his
appearance in some circle, he is like a grain of yeast that fer-
ments and restores to each of us a part of his native individ-
uality. He shakes and stirs us up, makes us praise or blame,
smokes out the truth, discloses the worthy and unmasks the
rascals. It is then that the sensible man keeps his ears open
and sorts out his company. (pp. 9-10)[2]

The arrangement is clear: the nephew is to be a catalyst, interesting especially as a new lens, which will help the philosopher to sharpen his vision and to leaven his wisdom. The
nephew is a bit of a buffoon, a grotesque, and apparently un-
threatening harbinger of unwelcome truths. And unwelcome
they are. In a brilliant series of repartees, the nephew lays low
the entire scaffolding of the philosopher's program, and we
begin to realize that this oddball has some authority:

You think everybody aims at the same happiness. What an
idea! Your conception presupposes a sentimental turn of
mind which is not ours, an unusual spirit, a special taste.
You [then outfit this oddity with the name of] virtue, [you
call it] philosophy. But virtue and philosophy are not made
for everybody. The few who can, have it; the few who can,
keep it. Just imagine the universe philosophical and wise,
and tell me if it would not be [a bloody bore]. (amended,
pp. 34-35)[3]

The good life is the hedonist life: "to drink good wines, gorge
on choice food, tumble pretty women, sleep in downy beds—
outside of that, all is vanity" (p. 35).[4] Myself bravely goes
through his repertory. He begins with patriotism and receives
the most modern reply in the text: "Vanity! There are no
countries left. All I see from pole to pole is tyrants and slaves"
(p. 35).[5] Friendship is next: "Gratitude is a burden, and bur-
dens are to be shuffled off" (p. 35).[6] When the note of civic
duties is sounded, the nephew becomes still more vitriolic:

HE.   Vanity! What difference whether you hold a position or not, provided you have means, since you only seek
a position in order to get wealth. Discharge one's duties—
what does that bring you?—jealousy, worries, persecution.
Is that the way to get on? Nonsense! Pay court, pay court,
know the right people, flatter their tastes and fall in with
their whims, serve their vices and second their misdeeds—
there's the secret.
MYSELF.   Watch over the education of one's children?
HE.   Vanity! That's a tutor's business.
MYSELF.   But if a tutor, imbued with your principles,
neglects his duty, who will pay the penalty?
HE.   Not I anyhow. Possibly, some day, my daughter's
husband or my son's wife.
MYSELF.   But suppose that either or both plunge into
vice and debauchery?
HE.   Then that is part of their social position.
MYSELF.   If they disgrace themselves?
HE.   It's impossible to disgrace yourself, no matter
what you do, if you are rich. (p. 35)[7]

The voice of philosophy that speaks reason, virtue, education and reform, a voice that Diderot spent most of his life
articulating, is called an isolated, quixotic, unwanted voice.
The philosophers' world is a dream world; the real one is a
parasitic jungle, and the nephew is as shrewd a guide as Balzac's Vautrin is to be some seventy years later. Making it here
and now is the nephew's game, and the philosophers' cher-
ished (necessary) reward of the "long view" is, like the after-
life, perhaps just a wistful myth in comparison with the short
view:

MYSELF. . . . Which of the two, Socrates or the judge
who made him drink hemlock, is today the dishonored
man?
HE.   A great comfort to Socrates! Was he any the less
convicted? any the less put to death? (p. 13)[8]

The longest view that the nephew is prepared to take is the

one he can see with his eyes and smell with his nose, prefera-
bly no more than a meal away.

From his exchange with the nephew, Myself expects a surer
orientation, a clearer picture of his moral world. Instead, he is
brought into contact with a new universe, a sub-society of
parasites and cheats, a carnival that is animated by laws too
base and too basic for the *Encyclopédie* to deal with them. In a
striking passage of his *Lettres philosophiques*, Voltaire had suggested that the march of civilizations is better measured by
scientific than by military accomplishment, and that a new
optic was needed to assess cultures. The nephew, in like but
satirical manner, provides Myself with a new history of Europe, a panorama silhouetted by grand scoundrels and cheats,
conmen of stature. For example, Bouret has achieved such re-
nown with his dog trick that "All Europe marveled at it;
every courtier envied it" (p. 43).[9] If Bouret is "*le premier
homme du monde*," he has to protect his title against contenders
such as "the Renegade of Avignon," multiple traitor and arch
villain. New profiles, these, far from the greats of science and
war, but equally compelling in their own right. Here is the
nephew's proper milieu, the arena in which his talents have
their full play. His specialty consists in winning the day for
his patrons, and much art is needed to buttress his rhetoric:

When, for example, opinions are divided and the debate has
reached the highest pitch, no one listening and all talking at
once, you should be somewhat to one side, in the corner of
the room farthest from the battlefield, and your explosion
should be timed after a long pause so as to crash suddenly
like a bombshell among the combatants. No one has mastered this art like me. Yet my really surprising skill is in the
opposite vein. I have mild notes accompanied by smiles, an
infinite variety of faces expressing agreement. In these,
nose, mouth, brows, and eyes participate. I have a flexibil-
ity of spine, a way of twisting it, of shrugging or sagging,
of stretching out my fingers, of nodding and shutting my
eyes, of being thunderstruck as if I heard a divine angel's
voice come down from heaven—this it is to flatter. I don't
know whether you grasp the whole force of this last atti-

tude of mine. I did not invent it, but no one has surpassed me in performance. Just look! (p. 42)[10]

Rarely has language come so close to gesture. The nephew describes his art of persuasion, and he enacts it at the same time. Those last lines are addressed to the reader as well as to Myself: "I don't know whether you grasp the whole force of this last attitude of mine," for there is a prodigious energy at work here, a performance requiring great skill and finesse, a display that magnificently leaves language and explodes the page: "Just look!" (*Voyez, voyez*). Diderot's text and the nephew are actually producing their effects, and there seems to be a kind of pause, a blank space for the gesture to unfurl, and Myself must assent: "You are right. It is unique" (p. 42).[11] This is creation, not only in the sense that the nephew exhibits his art, but also that words, after gathering their momentum, explode into gesture and produce their effects, much as the sycophant-nephew must seduce through his own language. We shall see, later, that the true potency of *Le Neveu de Rameau* is to be found along precisely these lines.

Myself quickly categorizes and limits the spectacle: "No, I must admit that you have carried the art of making fools and abasing yourself as far as it can go" (p. 42).[12] I would like to stress the ambivalence of such commentary. The nephew's talent is no less refined and real, simply because it is in the service of flattery and seduction. Myself is repeatedly uneasy as he confronts the spectacle of technical virtuosity devoid of ethical value. The nephew, like Bouret, Palissot, and the Renegade of Avignon, is an artist, a man who uses his body and speech like a precision instrument for amoral ends, a man who appreciates skill and finesse whenever they appear: in crime and deception as well as music or art:

I [Myself] was beginning to find [it painful to be with] a man who could discuss a dreadful deed, an abominable crime, in the way a connoisseur in poetry or painting discusses the fine points of a work of art—or as a moralist or an historian points out the merit of an heroic action. I felt gloom overwhelming me. (amended, p. 62)[13]

Myself is disturbed, because he dimly perceives that skill and finesse are value-free notions, that the society circus may be appreciated in strictly aesthetic terms, and therefore music, morality, crime, and hypocrisy are interchangeable and indifferent fields where the artist performs. In this light, Myself is both seriously and genuinely distressed by the nephew's tone: "I confess I don't know whether you are speaking [sincerely] or [maliciously]. I am a plain man and I wish you would be good enough to talk plainly and leave your 'art' outside" (amended, p. 46).[14] But "*bonne foi*" and sincerity are inappropriate grids for the clowning, performing nephew; the nephew *is* his art, and therein lies his importance. However ridiculous Diderot and Myself paint him, the nephew nonetheless takes over the text, obsessively imposing himself, plying his art and sharing his perceptions. He is *there*, and no amount of moral erasure will get rid of him. He is nightmarish, appearing out of nowhere, giving and running the show, and, finally, disappearing into oblivion. There is an obscure urgency in this text, a muffled panic in presence of this buffoon who cannot be naysaid. Why?

I have already suggested that he embodies a solely aesthetic apprehension of things, and that is already unsettling. But, Diderot has endowed him with still more. The nephew is, ultimately, a practicing artist. But he is a very special kind. The evidence is abundant that, in traditional terms, he is a *failed* genius: he strikes his own forehead with desperation, but is forced to concede, " 'It seems to me nevertheless that I have something there, but I knock in vain, I worry it but nothing comes out' " (pp. 77-78).[15] Filled with premonition, he seeks to create: "When I take my pen by myself, intending to write, I bite my nails and belabor my brow but—no soap, the god is absent" (p. 78).[16] The nephew cannot create. Myself having experienced the nephew for the duration of the exchange, puts the question to him point blank:

. . . tell me how it is that with your remarkable power for understanding, remembering and rendering the most beautiful works of the great masters, with your contagious enthusiasm for them and for conveying them, you have never done anything that amounts to anything. (p. 76)[17]

It is a question that cuts to the heart of the work. The nephew is not a genius, not a Bohemian artist, not a *poète-mage*. The 19th century will furnish, *ad nauseam*, portraits of artists, but Diderot has done both less and more: not the known composer Rameau, but his nephew, not the man who creates art, but the one who experiences it. The nephew's achievements are both imaginative and imaginary: does that make them less significant? Early on, we see his generative mind at work:

> The whatever-it-is inside me speaks and says to me: "Rameau, you'd give a great deal to have composed those two pieces; if you had done two, you would surely have done two more; and after a certain number you would be played and sung everywhere. You would walk about with head erect, your mind would bear witness to your own merit. Other people would point you out and say—'That's the man who wrote those lovely gavottes.' " [And he sang the gavottes. Then with the appearance of a man deeply moved by a rush of happiness, he added with a moist eye, while rubbing his hands together:] "You would have a comfortable house" [measuring its breadth with his arms], "a good bed" [{and he stretched out carelessly on it}], "good wine" [tasting it with a smack of tongue against palate], "a good carriage and pair" [raising his foot to climb in], "pretty women" [whom he seized by the breast and gazed at voluptuously]. (translator's brackets, my braces for amendments, p. 17)[18]

Here again language magnificently spills over into other realms, spewing forth, becoming flesh, replacing the material world. Art, even more than desire, brings forth the most prodigious creations (can we call them otherwise?) from the nephew. In the figure of the nephew, Diderot has drawn a sublime but grotesque image of response to art; the nephew is not so much creator as viewer, reader, auditor, one liberated and magnified by the stimuli he receives. Again, not Rameau, but his nephew, the non-professional, the non-singled-out-by-fate, the man who bequeaths nothing, who has only the transient experience itself.[2] His fullest performance comes toward the close, and it must be quoted at length, for it displays the particular kind of creativity which redeems the nephew from sterility, and which the entire text is celebrating:

[. . . He jumbled together thirty different airs, French, Italian, comic, tragic—in every style. Now in a baritone voice he sank to the pit; then straining in falsetto he tore to shreds the upper notes of some air, imitating the while the stance, walk and gestures of the several characters; being in succession furious, mollified, lordly, sneering. First a damsel weeps and he reproduces her kittenish ways; next he is a priest, a king, a tyrant; he threatens, commands, rages. Now he is a slave, he obeys, calms down, is heartbroken, complains, laughs; never overstepping the proper tone, speech, or manner called for by the part.

[All the "woodpushers" in the café had left their chessboards and gathered around {him}. The windows of the place were occupied from outside by passers-by who had stopped on hearing the commotion. They guffawed fit to crack the ceiling. But he noticed nothing, he kept on, in the grip of mental possession, an enthusiasm so close to madness that it seemed doubtful whether he would recover. He might have to be put into a cab and be taken to a padded cell. . . .

[Yes, you too would have burst out laughing at the way in which he aped the different instruments. With swollen cheeks and a somber throaty sound, he would give us the horns and bassoons. For the oboes he assumed a shrill yet nasal voice, then speeded up the emission of sound to an incredible degree for the strings, for whose tones he found close analogues. He whistled piccolos and warbled traverse flutes, singing, shouting, waving about like a madman,

[2] To those who teach, who want to arouse in others a response to art (and I must be speaking to a large percentage of my readership), the nephew is a dazzling and disturbing figure. Dazzling, because his acuity in aesthetic matters is so authoritative, but disturbing, because he lays bare the excesses and inadequacy of "response" when it is undirected or unmoored.

being in himself dancer and ballerina, singer and prima
donna, all of them together and the whole orchestra, the
whole theater; then redividing himself into twenty separate
roles, running, stopping, glowing at the eyes like one possessed, frothing at the mouth.

[The heat was stifling and the sweat, which, mixed with
the powder in his hair, ran down the creases of his face was
dripping and marking the upper part of his coat. What did
he not attempt to show me? He wept, laughed, sighed,
looked placid or melting or enraged. He was a woman in a
spasm of grief, a wretched man sunk in despair, a temple
being erected, birds growing silent at sunset, waters murmuring through cool and solitary places or else cascading
from a mountaintop, a storm, a hurricane, the anguish of
those about to die, mingled with the whistling of the wind
and the noise of thunder. He was night and its gloom, shade
and silence—for silence itself is depictable in sound. He had
completely lost his senses. (translator's brackets, my braces
for amendments, pp. 67-68)[19]

Here we see the vistas, the extraordinary range and volume of
the nephew's performance. He becomes a world unto himself,
living out—momentarily—lives and passions unknown to
him. A century before Rimbaud's "*Je devins un opéra fabu-
leux*," the nephew becomes, in himself, "*tout un orchestre, tout
un théâtre lyrique*." The word "alienation" is rigorously appropriate, for the self is engaged in a prodigious feat of expansion
and metamorphosis. The scene closes in an extension of self
of such breadth that the human is eclipsed: birds at sunset,
murmuring waters, tempest, the shadows of night, silence.
We are strangely reminded of Werther's sense of being dispersed in Nature, but the tone here is radically different: frenetic, almost psychotic, reeking of perspiration and adrenalin.

Nothing, of course, remains. Depleted, almost deathlike,
his state has led Leo Spitzer to some remarkable pages on the
erotic rhythm of Diderot's prose, with the nephew's performance likened—stylewise—to sexual intercourse.[3] Yet, the eva-

---

[3] Leo Spitzer, *Linguistics and Literary History* (Princeton: Princeton University Press, 1948), pp. 135-191.

nescence of the nephew's experience is the inevitable cost and license for it; one can be, only momentarily and sequentially, the whole consort of passions and people in the nephew's repertory; one cannot remain them. The nephew, in his response to art, achieves multiplicity. He achieves it the only way the single, circumscribed human being can: through his mind. He is the creative imagination, the adventurous, cancerous self that spawns forth personae and avatars. Wedded and bound to no principles, he enjoys a freedom unknown to Myself. It is true that his flights are brief, his other selves virtual; but that is always the price paid by sanity for the pleasures of expansion; otherwise there is schizophrenia, permanent alienation, and the nephew wants none of that.

I have stressed the creative dimension of the nephew's mimicry, even though Diderot himself views it with some condescension and considers it a lower form of art; for the nephew outruns whatever Myself or the text can say about him. He is its *raison d'être*, whereas his own is never articulated. But, perhaps, it can be.

In the nephew's spectacular imaginative freedom we see the *force motrice*, the living center of the work. The mind is free and generative, regardless of one's program. And, as long as our flights and fancies are played out in the mind, in those cerebral precincts unpoliced by any laws, then our daytime agenda can remain intact. Therefore it is essential that the nephew spit out and display every single ounce of his antiphilosophy. The nephew is all of the selves—the lascivious, cynical, anarchic, corrupt selves—that Diderot chooses not to *remain*, although he cannot choose not to *be* them. Thus, the nephew calls education hogwash, speaks of molecular determinism far before Darwin, just as he saw a Europe of masters and slaves long before Marx proclaimed it. Just as the nephew, through art, becomes other people, Diderot, in and through this text, can become the nephew, right to the hilt. Like the bitter almond, perhaps more still like venom that must out, the nephew's potent voice must be heard. His poison is cathartic, not only because it contains large doses of anti-philosophical truth, but because it is the indispensable sewage system for philosophy itself. The nephew exposes the

carnival of the world, and his topsy-turvy vision is contagious. Embodied in the nephew's words and his very being is
the view of society as an endless charade of parasites and
cheats, *"les différentes pantomimes de l'espèce humaine"* (p. 108).
The nephew concludes that the king alone is exempt from
"taking positions," and, at this juncture, scant pages before
the end, Myself shows that he has absorbed, much like an innoculation, his share of the toxin; in a burst of insight, with a
panoramic sweep utterly uncharacteristic of his own tidy position-taking, Myself himself completes the lesson:

> The King? Even about him there might be something more
> to say. Don't you suppose that from time to time he finds
> near him a little foot, a little nose, a little curl that makes
> him perform a bit of pantomime? Whoever stands in need
> of another is needy and takes a position. The King takes a
> position before his mistress and before God: he dances his
> pantomime steps. The minister trips it too, as courtier, flat
> terer, footman and beggar before his king. The crowd of
> self-seekers dance all your positions in a hundred ways,
> each viler than the next, in front of the minister. The noble
> Abbé, in furred cape and cloak, dances attendance once a
> week at least before the official who appoints to benefices.
> Really, what you call the beggar's pantomime is what
> makes the world go round. Every man has his Bertin and
> his little Hus. (p. 83)[20]

This grandiose vision is one to which Myself could not
accede unaided. The dialogue form, with its binary oppositions, must be seen as a consort, a dialectic, a whole that is
greater than the sum of its parts. Not the nephew, but Myself
is to change and grow; but the nephew must point the way,
and he does so by his "position," i.e., his point of view and
his mode of being. The cynicism and doubt can be expressed
only through the procedural device of a free-speaking, but
non-binding, character. Let him be a trifle ridiculous, and he
is freer still. Finally, let the nephew's creative imagination
serve as a model for Diderot's own, a stimulus for pushing his
iconoclast further and further into nooks and crannies where
pieties still reign. Much like the chess games that Diderot is

observing, the entire dialogue is a shrewd contest of wit and intelligence. Only in this light does the celebrated opening page attain its fullest meaning:

> Rain or shine, it is my regular habit every day about five to go and take a walk around the Palais-Royal. I can be seen, all by myself, dreaming on D'Argenson's bench. I discuss with myself questions of politics, love, taste, or philosophy. I let my mind rove wantonly, give it free rein to follow any idea, wise or mad, that may come [along, much like] our young libertines along Foy's Walk, [who pursue smiling-faced, giddy courtesans with up-turned noses, abandon one for the next], pursuing all and clinging to none: my ideas are my trollops. (amended, p. 8)[21]

One is tempted to say that an entire facet of the Enlightenment is expressed in these lines: the life of the mind, the cultivation and pursuit of one's ideas, the meandering uncharted itinerary of thought, the taste for reflection, the fundamental association of thought and pleasure, an association borne out by the extended metaphor of *"mes pensées ce sont mes catins."* Here is the core of Diderot: the powerful connection between thinking and whoring, the pursuit of ideas as illicit pleasure, sport for the young, a trifle risqué, an enterprise so delicious that the form of the woman-thought takes on full shape and even flesh, with its marvelous promise of sophisticated pleasure and debauchery, the whole transformation so vivid and complete that we no longer know what precedes what, trollop or idea, idea or trollop. But control and security are never truly threatened: one trollop is exchanged for another, and, ultimately, there are no trollops, no sex at all, just a man sitting, alone, on a bench, daydreaming. This is safe. Titillating, perhaps even vertiginous, but quite safe. No pox and no arrests. All the naughtiness and risk-taking are in the metaphor, and that metaphor is the condition of Diderot's freedom: the revery is a privileged arena, a Pandora's box which may be opened at will, a space without censorship or constraint: from the daydreaming emerge the whore-thoughts whom Diderot pursues, the two phantoms who become Moi and Lui, who do battle over the good life. All of the nephew's virulence, the excursions into fantasy and the explosions of lunacy are, in fact, incursions and implosions, because the area to be explored, the figures to be wooed, pursued and made love to, come exclusively from the mind.

The mind is a free and safe place, safe in the sense that it is inviolate and beyond the reach of authority, but also wild, in the sense that one's Walpurgis nights and Saturday sprees may take place there, so that Diderot feels the need, once a day or once a year, to set adrift in those waters just as Ishmael needs, every so often, to go to sea. And literature can record the doings of the mind, doings unmeasured and unmeasurable any other way. For words and language, like the nephew's performance, can make something from nothing, can be infinitely generative without having to be possible.

But, implosions replace explosions when explosions are either undesirable or inconceivable. "My ideas are my trollops" is a narrative form of solipsis, of masturbation. The pursuit and the quest are indeed unchecked in *Le Neveu de Rameau* because we are dealing exclusively with figures of speech, a dream-scape rather than a hard world. The erotic quest has turned inward: how vastly different *"mes pensées ce sont mes catins"* is from the tragic, non-figurative, uninternalized desire of Des Grieux for Manon, of Werther for Lotte. *Le Neveu de Rameau* is post-relational, but it explicitly taps the same energies of desire; in the mind, in the unpoliced imagination, those energies may finally have their spectacular play. But the spectacle is solitary, a theater of one. Self-enactment is merely the acting self.

New Worlds and Old Worlds: *Tristram Shandy*

Whereas *Manon Lescaut* and *Clarissa* depict the impossibility of finding a place for passion, *Tristram Shandy*, a text largely without passion or landscape, nonetheless sets out to colonize realms of life and literature unheard-of before. The Old World may be more than the Harlowes' intransigency or Prévost's affair of corrupt institutions and lecherous old men or Goethe's stifling conventions and failed legacies; I would submit that *Tristram Shandy*, in a manner that resembles Joyce's

Ulysses, is built on and out of the fragments of crumbling traditions and institutions. In his fine essay on the tradition of
learned wit in *Tristram*, D. W. Jefferson's essential conclusion
is that "the theme of *Tristram Shandy* may be seen in terms of
a comic clash between the world of learning and that of human affairs."[1] Comic though that clash is, I think that Sterne
is depicting a cleavage, a gulf between the profuse materials
of scholastic authority and learning which appear on every
page of *Tristram*, and not only in the words of Walter Shandy,
but in Toby and Tristram as well, the constant web of erudite
allusion, on the one hand, and the already modern sense, on
the other, that humans are adrift, unmoored, cut loose from
these systems that used to give structure to life. The Past is
ubiquitous in *Tristram*; Greek, Latin, Dutch, and French
sources are cited, and often cited at considerable length, for
virtually every event in the novel, but Sterne is having his
pleasure with them, turning them into puns, exploding them
into fantasy. Let us consider the following learned discussion:

> Gastripheres, for example, continued Kysarcius, baptizes a
> child of John Stradling's *in Gomine gatris* &c. &c. instead of
> *in Nomine patris*, &c. —Is this a baptism? No,—say the
> ablest canonists; inasmuch as the radix of each word is here-
> by torn up, and the sense and meaning of them removed
> and changed quite to another object; for *Gomine* does not
> signify a name, nor *gatris* a father. —what do they signify?
> said my uncle Toby. —Nothing at all—quoth Yorick. —
> Ergo, such a baptism is null, said Kysarcius. (p. 247)[2]

Beyond the wordplay the thing itself, the ceremony and significance of baptism, does not remain intact, and that is because wordplay is inevitably corrosive. Corrosive but also
extensive, projective: Sterne's narrative strategy is to make a
revolutionary new purchase on language, discrediting old
realms but spawning and then occupying new ones. I do not

---

[1] D. W. Jefferson, "*Tristram Shandy* and the Tradition of Learned Wit," reprinted in *Laurence Sterne: A Collection of Critical Essays*, ed. John Traugott
(Englewood Cliffs: Prentice Hall, 1968), p. 162.

[2] Laurence Sterne, *The Life and Opinions of Tristram Shandy, Gentleman*, ed.
Ian Watt (Boston: Houghton Mifflin, 1965).

want to overstate my case: it is well known that the medieval
Christian tradition was resilient enough to house and tolerate
a considerable amount of parody and self-satire, but wordplay, in Sterne, is already on the way to becoming creative
rather than satirical, and, as such, it will be an indispensable
tool for Tristram in narrating his life and opinions; it will also
be a tool for Laurence Sterne to employ in completing a book
and in expressing a vision in a world where nothing can be
completed and everything has already been said.

Yorick's sermon on conscience, happily inserted among the
pages of Stevinus, nicely states the already modernist problems of authority, judgment, and orientation which beset
Sterne. Conscience is defined as "the knowledge which the
mind has within herself" (p. 95), and is therefore quite close
to the notion of consciousness; but Sterne is aware that conscience is unreliable, that, in all too many cases, "this domes-
tic God *was either talking, or pursuing, or was in a journey, or per-
adventure he slept and could not be awoke*" (p. 97). Conscience is
not to be trusted alone; it needs to be abetted by a law, a
firmer one than jurisprudence offers, one setting forth the
principles of morality and religion. But those principles themselves, augustly quoted from the Bible, the Sorbonne, and
other repositories of authority, are no longer sound, function
primarily as touchstones to punning and satire. We need laws,
but they are crumbling, we are reduced to conscience and
consciousness, but they are fallible. This was Sterne's situation, much as it is our own; it was his precise literary situation
as well, since he was clearly not to continue in the path of Defoe, Richardson, or Fielding, and his satire would be unlike
that of Pope or Swift. His solution, spiritually and literarily,
is to do his own thing: "to write a book is for all the world
like humming a song—be but in tune with yourself, madam,
'tis no matter how high or how low you take it" (p. 238). This
is no easy matter, for he must do battle with the critics constantly, those critics who judge all by rules and laws, and he
must also find his own thing. For the novelist, the Old World
is an aesthetic as well as a cultural issue. We have seen the role
that tradition and convention play in *Manon Lescaut, Werther*
and *Clarissa*; yet, Prévost, Goethe, and Richardson were con-

tent to use traditional forms of mimesis in their quarrel with tradition. Sterne goes a quantum leap further: he revolutionalizes the form of the novel, finding sustenance everywhere along the way: the innocuous givens of time, place, and sequence, comfortably relied on by mimetic fictioneers, are jostled and overturned by Sterne, yielding new vistas, adumbrating new realms. The hitherto transparent *conventions* of storytelling are brilliantly foregrounded by Sterne, energized and fictionalized in themselves: the words which used docilely to tell the novelist's story now tell their own. Sterne, beset by impotency at every turn, is to discover the potency of language: The crumbling Old World is to be, not overcome (as Des Grieux, Werther and Clarissa were to learn), but shaped anew.

How can a single writer reverse the Humpty Dumpty story and put the world back together again? Sterne's strategy is to stake out a new area where wholeness, authority and accomplishment will again be possible. It comes in the guise of a Gonopsychanthropologia, a depiction of the origin of the human soul. How does the self come to be what it is? Sterne gives us, comically but not altogether comically, four controlling factors: (1) the disposition of the animal spirits at conception, (2) the safety of the cerebellum at birth, (3) the wholeness and length of the nose, and if a male, of another organ as well, and (4) the name. And, on these fronts, as we all know, Tristram Shandy, hero of a genuine *Bildungsroman ab ovo*, is a cosmic loser: animal spirits dispersed, cerebellum smashed, nose crushed, other organ almost removed, and Tristram for a name. Nineteenth-century positivism produced fictions that would account for a person's character by his "background," his parents, his socio-economic conditions, heredity, and environment. Sterne is both funnier, and surely as close to the mark, in his insistence (rather, Walter Shandy's insistence) that the real formative stage of the self occurs between conception and birth. Whatever the scientific validity of Walter's position, Tristram emerges—unlike the richly endowed Des Grieux, Werther, and Clarissa—as a character cursed by Fortune and marked by the conditions of his birth. How can a success story be possible?

Most readers and critics assume that Sterne was not seriously concerned with Gonopsychanthropologia, but I would
suggest that he is vitally interested in offsetting the rigorous
determinism inherent in Walter Shandy's view, and that he is
showing you, all the time, just how he and you can conquer
such determinism. We are well into the fourth volume of
Tristram Shandy before we even get to all the details of Tristram's birth: Sterne has manifestly been up to other things, in
fact just about everything including the kitchen sink: anec-
dotes about Yorick, a Sorbonne document on baptizing foe-
tuses before birth, Uncle Toby's wound and his subsequent
hobbyhorse, Ernulphus' curse, the author's preface (midway
in the 3rd volume), considerable lore about sieges and fortifications, the immortal tale of Hafen Slawkenbergius, even the
story of Licetus "born a foetus, of no more than five inches
and a half in length, yet he grew to that astonishing height in
literature, as to write a book with a title as long as himself—
the learned know I mean his Gonopsychanthropologia, upon
the origin of the human soul" (p. 212). Tristram has taken a
long time in coming out, but, once there and permanently
disadvantaged, Walter is so struck down as to wish his child
had been Licetus instead, the five and one-half-inch foetus.
Five and one-half inches is not very big. Things are low as we
close Chapter 19 of Vol. 4. Chapter 20 goes as follows:

> What a rate have I gone on at, curvetting and frisking it
> away, two up and two down for four volumes together,
> without looking once behind, or even on one side of me, to
> see whom I trod upon! —I'll tread upon no one,—quoth I
> to myself when I mounted—I'll take a good rattling gallop;
> but I'll not hurt the poorest jack-ass upon the road—So off
> I set—up one lane—down another, through this turnpike—
> over that, as if the arch-jockeys had got behind me.
> Now ride at this rate with what good intention and res-
> olution you may,—'tis a million to one you'll do some one
> a mischief, if not yourself—He's flung—he's off—he's lost
> his seat—he's down—he'll break his neck—see!—if he has
> not galloped full amongst the scaffolding of the undertak-
> ing criticks!—he'll knock his brains out against some of

their posts—he's bounced out!—look—he's now riding like
a madcap full tilt through a whole crowd of painters, fid-
dlers, poets, biographers, physicians, lawyers, logicians,
players, schoolmen, churchmen, statesmen, soldiers, casu-
ists, connoisseurs, prelates, popes, and engineers —Don't
fear, said I—I'll not hurt the poorest jack-ass upon the
king's high-way—But your horse throws dirt; see you've
splash'd a bishop —I hope in God, 'twas only *Ernulphus*,
said I —But you have squirted full in the faces of Mess. *Le
Moyne, De Romigny*, and *De Marcilly*, doctors of the *Sorbonne* —That was last year, replied I —But you have trod
this moment upon a king. —Kings have bad times on't,
said I, to be trod upon by such people as me.

—You have done it, replied my accuser.

I deny it, quoth I, and so have got off, and here am I
standing with my bridle in one hand, and with my cap in
the other, to tell my story—And what is it? You shall hear
in the next chapter. (p. 223)

No five and one-half-inch foetus here, no problem with animal spirits, cerebellum, noses, and other organs, not even
names. Instead we have a prancing, galloping author, leaving
Tristram's birth because he is free to, taking apart critics because they deserve it and he can do it, bearing no malice but
nonetheless splashing Sorbonne bishops and trodding on the
king. Here we witness a celebration of strength, of potency,
of authority, of unbridled freedom; it is a peculiar sort of freedom, namely the kind that Sterne has been demonstrating and
even celebrating since the outset: the freedom of imagination
and language which is unshackled, unbound by the petty narrative business at hand of getting Tristram born, untrapped
by the determinist prison that Walter thinks his son has been
born into. Among the traditions which Tristram is free to
transgress is the linear fiction of fiction, the notion that things
must proceed 1, 2, 3 in a life or in a story: "Could a historiog-
rapher drive on his history, as a muleteer drives on his
mule,—straight forward;—for instance, from Rome all the
way to Loretto, without ever once turning his head aside
either to the right hand or to the left,—he might venture to

foretell you to an hour when he should get to his journey's
end;—but the thing is, morally speaking, impossible" (p. 28).
Our consciousness of life is multiple and simultaneous, and
the power of writing can overcome event and sequence
through digression and metaphor, for surely you have recognized that the man on the prancing horse, like Wallace
Stevens' capable young rider, is a metaphor of the imagination. We are corporally limited and determined, but we can
and do live in and through metaphoric extensions of reality.
The mind is its own place, and the hazards of birth may form
it, but they cannot control it.

The mind is its own place, and it—in keeping with the
dominant metaphor of the novel—is under siege. Sterne's
characters occupy their minds much like hermits, rarely going
forth to see what it is like outside. Humans, according to
Sterne, are without the advantages of some kind of Momus'
glass:

> ... had such a glass been there set up, nothing more would
> have been wanting, in order to have taken a man's charac-
> ter, but to have taken a chair and gone softly, as you would
> to a dioptrical bee-hive, and look'd in,—viewed the soul
> stark naked;—observed all her motions,—her machina-
> tions;—traced all her maggots from their first engendering
> to their crawling forth;—watched her loose in her frisks,
> her gambols, her capricios; and after some notice of her
> more solemn deportment, consequent on such frisks, &c.—
> then taken your pen and ink and set down nothing but
> what you had seen, and could have sworn to:—But this is
> an advantage not to be had by the biographer in this planet.
> ... (pp. 55-56)

And he later adds, "Our minds shine not through the body,
but are wrapt up here in a dark covering of uncrystalized flesh
and blood; so that if we would come to the specifick charac-
ters of them, we must go some other way to work"|(p. 56).
The muleteer may take the body straight from Rome to Loretto, but Sterne is recording a different trip. The route that he
chooses toward the inner life of characters is, of course, the
hobbyhorse, the ruling passions and fantasies of individuals

which establish their perceptual grid. Uncle Toby's is probably the most developed, and Sterne delights in exchanges such as the following, as Doctor Slop is holding forth on the advancement of medical technology: "Sir, it would astonish you to know what Improvements we have made on late years in all branches of obstetrical knowledge, but particularly in that one single point of the safe and expeditious extraction of the foetus,—which has received such lights, that, for my part, (holding up his hands) I declare I wonder how the world has —I wish, quoth my uncle Toby, you had seen what prodigious armies we had in Flanders" (pp. 108-109). This is more than a comic principle; it is also a recognition that the sounds and sights of the world are refracted, when human beings perceive them, into the preconceived frames inside of us.

"At best," as Benjamin Lehman says, Sterne's characters "understand one another only by fits and starts. A pervasive loneliness is at the core of each, as in life itself."[3] Blindness looms large in the novel of failed relationships, but there is nothing tragic in Sterne's book, not only because he renders the hobbyhorsical blinders as palpably laughable (especially in courtship between Toby and Widow Wadman), but also because the locked-up selves can still communicate through feeling. Sterne's cult of sensibility is the other side of this solipsism. Certain set pieces, such as the tearful death of Yorick at the outset, Uncle Toby's speech to the fly, the episode with the dying Le Fever—these scenes, dated as they may appear today, indicate that feeling and sentiment go where words cannot. This dimension of Sterne was prized by his contemporaries, but it is the very oddity of his text, an oddity which Doctor Johnson augured would not wear well, that constitutes its major appeal today. I would suggest that Sterne's narrative tricks are in collusion with his sentimentalism. Above all, as if to *enact* the bond of comradeship and tenderness depicted among characters, the book seeks a very special relationship with its reader. Early on, Sterne, much like Fielding in *Joseph Andrews*, addresses the reader as a fellow-traveller and ex-

---

[3] Benjamin H. Lehman, "Of Time, Personality, and the Author: A Study of *Tristram Shandy*," reprinted in *A Collection of Critical Essays*, p. 28.

presses hope that their acquaintanceship will grow into famil-
iarity and finally friendship. But, unlike in Fielding, to be
Tristram's friend is to meet him at least halfway, to make a
very different kind of voyage, to keep one's own imagination
as active as the author's is, even to project that imagination.

The reader is expected to fill in the asterisks, pursue the in-
nuendo, double the double-entendre. This, often enough,
works: the reader does the sexual imagining at hand, can feel
the hypnotic power of the Widow Wadman's eyes or the
sympathy between Walter and Toby; but, very often, this
kind of response to one of the characters cannot be forthcoming, because Sterne is busy doing tricks, prancing or digress-
ing, showing us his authorial sleight-of-hand tricks. Tristram's digressions are also, as he shrewdly says, progressive,
and a certain amount of interruption and ellipsis is good for a
man, whets his appetite and keeps him on his toes. Digressions are, we learn, "the sunshine—they are the life, the soul
of reading" (p. 55). But black pages, graphs, left-out chapters,
mind-boggling mix of chronology: the reader would have to
be a kind of emotional plastic man to sentimentally move into
all these items. Why all these pyrotechnics? Consider the following:

> I told the Christian reader—I say Christian—hoping he is
> one—and if he is not, I am sorry for it—and only beg he
> will consider the matter with himself, and not lay the blame
> entirely upon this book—
>   I told him, Sir—or in good truth, when a man is telling
> a story in the strange way I do mine, he is obliged contin-
> ually to be going backwards and forwards to keep all tight
> together in the reader's fancy—which, for my own part, if
> I did not take heed to do more than at first, there is so much
> unfixed and equivocal matter starting up, with so many
> breaks and gaps in it,—and so little service do the stars af-
> ford, which, nevertheless, I hang up in some of the darkest
> passages, knowing that the world is apt to lose its way,
> with all the lights the sun itself at noon day can give it—and
> now, you see, I am lost myself! (p. 351)

Going through *Tristram Shandy* is a strange voyage, a con-
tinuous search for that "northwest passage to the intellectual

world." The reader must consent to lose himself in Sterne's world if he is to grasp Sterne's meaning. Now there is a new kind of vicious taste, we are told, "of reading straight forwards, more in quest of the adventures, than of deep erudition and knowledge which a book of this cast, if read over as it should be, would infallibly impart with them" (p. 43). Let us take Sterne seriously here, not just when he speaks of erudition and of knowledge, but especially when he admonishes us not to read straight forwards, but to read over. To read for adventures is to seek out a certain thread of plot, whether it be Tristram's birth or Toby's amours; what is *not* connected with the birth or the amours is digressive, perhaps distracting; it has almost a different ontological status, for it is the non-story extra-language. If a text has only a few asides or rhetorical chapter headings, we can accept such a story non-story duality: but *Tristram Shandy* rubs our noses into it, flaunts the unimportance of its stories, wraps any and all linear plots into bowknots, or better still, slipknots. In short, Sterne reminds us over and over that the reality of his text is the reality, *not* of any tidy particularized story, but of language itself. Sterne revels in mixing levels of plot and time, in leaving characters frozen at keyholes and on beds, because they are all, in the final analysis, red herrings, and the only discourse that counts is that of the narrating Tristram. Tristram tells us: "All my heroes are off my hands;—'tis the first time I have had a moment to spare,—and I'll make use of it, and write my preface" (p. 142), because his heroes and his preface have equal rights in his project. There are no second-class words. As readers and critics, we underline what seems important and relegate the rest to some enormous murky room where "details" are stored. Sterne's belief in language is so democratic that it verges on anarchy. The words themselves are real and potent, capable of instant creation, even spontaneous combustion; a chapter closes with Toby and Walter shaking their heads together for different reasons: the next chapter sovereignly begins: "Holla!—you chairman—here's sixpence—do step into that bookseller's shop, and call me a day-tall critick. I am very willing to give any one of 'em a crown to help me with his tackling, to get my father and my uncle Toby off the stairs, and to put them to bed" (p. 214).

Language spawns meanings; regardless of the grammatical tenses, it creates presence; and it makes, in the mind of the reader, its own place. The prancing author who spattered bishops and trod upon the king happened only in language, and, of course, language is the New World of *Tristram Shandy*. This book generates new lands, magnificent places such as the Promontory of Noses. Where is the Promontory of Noses? When asked by Widow Wadman where he received his wound, Toby replied, "You shall see the very place, Madam" (p. 479). That place is neither Toby's groin, nor the particular trench near the citadel of Namur, but the realm of the mind. It is the culminating *double entendre* of the novel, indeed the culminating figure of my entire study: language creates a world, a place to live. The analogical, metaphorical, associational potency of language enables a vivid new lease on life, for it authorizes tangential realms and punning paths along which the hobbyhorsical mind can move. The syntagmatic course is not thereby halted; rather, it bifurcates, sets off in new directions, narrativizes vertically, along the axis of metaphor, rather than proceeding apace, like a muleteer. Sterne powerfully demonstrates the appeal of such new roads, showing them to be much more than the aberrant mistakes of lunatic characters, but more essentially a treasure-house of imaginative ventures. The Promontory of Noses points already to Rimbaud's "Promontoire," to dream-scapes and figural realms where exploration and activity may genuinely take place. Widow Wadman's *siege* on Uncle Toby, mirroring and imaging Toby's obsession with other kinds of sieges, brilliantly displays the potential of such an analogical, even a *comparative*, structure: Sterne marvelously inverts his amatory and his military discourses, creating high comedy and laying bare the essential sameness of love and war.

But that is not all. The comic framework and the stylistic foregrounding of Sterne's performance is untroubling: we laugh at the delightful mixture of languages and strategies, for the mimetic charge of Sterne's language, the strangely manipulable world of *signifiés*, is never dominant: war and love are *not* the same, but the links between them take priority in Sterne's text, and the endless digressions come to seem legitimate.

Let us, however, do some linking and associating and di-
gressing on our own, by returning (mentally) to a vastly different kind of *siege*, notably Lovelace's siege of Clarissa in
Richardson's novel. Richardson is dreadfully mimetic, and his
book is one precisely of imprisonment, of lack of room: for
Clarissa—and for Richardson—there can be no analogical reprieve, no metaphorical exit, no digression wherein the verbal
medium might aggrandize and open up the material. We are
talking about more than comedy and tragedy here; it is more
specifically a matter of language's projective and dodging
power and the kinds of stories that can be told. What Diderot
does to Prévost, Sterne does to Richardson: the mimetic donnée of the fable—erotic pursuit and siege—is internalized and
imploded, yielding a magnificent set of new departures, new
worlds, breaking the tragic limits of the mimetic love story
by transforming it all into verbal discourse. Cervantes and
Fielding had written novels of the road, but the only journeys
made in *Tristram Shandy* are made on hobbyhorses, not on
horses. And, he is also saying, hobbyhorses are our truest
and finest mode of transportation. When Thoreau said, "I
have traveled a great deal in Concord," he was talking about
the mobility of the mind, its ability to imagine and thereby
add to the pitiful data of our lives. Sterne shows repeatedly
that language can express that inner itinerary, that voyage
which transforms the reader into fellow-traveller just by virtue of reading. Reading itself is emblematic of the Sterne paradox and breakthrough: the body is immobile, the fingers
move slightly, the eyelids twitch, and nothing else shows
whatsoever: imagine a photograph of someone reading; all
the motion and life is internal. Sterne brings the inner mobility and freedom of the mind to language.

At the beginning of Vol. 5, Tristram asks the question
which must haunt all writers:

> Tell me, ye learned, shall we for ever be adding so much
> to the *bulk*—so little to the *stock*?
>
> Shall we for ever make new books, as apothecaries make
> new mixtures, by pouring only out of one vessel into an-
> other?
>
> Are we for ever to be twisting, and untwisting the same

rope? for ever in the same track—for ever at the same pace?

Shall we be destined to the days of eternity, on holy days, as well as working-days, to be shewing the *relicks of learning*, as monks do the relicks of their saints—without working one—one single miracle with them? (p. 259)

This quotation pointedly returns us to the old sources and traditions, the visible relics which clutter Sterne's book like a cathedral-junk shop, an Old World that can interest the writer only if he can transform it into a New World. *Tristram Shandy* does show things coming to life, but it is more than the child of Walter Shandy and his wife. Generation is everywhere. At one point Walter is trying to explain to Toby what an analogy is, and he is interrupted in the process: "Here a devil of a rap at the door snapp'd my father's definition (like his tobacco pipe) in two—and, at the same time, crushed the head of as notable and curious a dissertation as ever was engendered in the womb of speculation;—it was some months before my father could get an opportunity to be safely deliver'd of it" (p. 78). The metaphor, or more precisely the analogy, is one of childbirth, and what is being born is an idea. At another point, Tristram defines hypothesis: "It is the nature of an hypothesis, when once a man has conceived it, that it assimilates every thing to itself, as proper nourishment; and, from the first moment of your begetting it, it generally grows the stronger by every thing you see, hear, read, or understand" (p. 114). Hypothesis and metaphor are the very soul of creativity, for they extend the real. Sterne's book is not about the birth of Tristram, but more substantially and compositely about the birth of ideas, the life of the mind, that old Gonopsychanthropologia, the origin of the soul. Ideas have distinct advantages over people: they cannot be castrated or have their noses flattened; they are not subject to physical dangers because they are not corporeal; time and space do not worry them, since they generate their own; they do not even need to be possible:

Didst thou ever see a white bear? cried my father. . . .

A white bear! Very well. Have I ever seen one? Might I ever have seen one? Am I ever to see one? Ought I ever to have seen one? Or can I ever see one? (for how can I imagine it?)

If I should see a white bear, what should I say? If I should
never see a white bear, what then?

If I never have, can, must or shall see a white bear alive;
have I ever seen the skin of one? Did I ever see one
painted?—described? Have I ever dreamed of one?

Did my father, mother, uncle, aunt, brothers or sisters,
ever see a white bear? What would they give? How would
they behave? How would the white bear have behaved? Is
he wild? Tame? Terrible? Rough? Smooth?

—Is the white bear worth seeing?

—Is there no sin in it?

—Is it better than a black one? (p. 307)

Here is the prolific, generative, mind at work, spewing forth
hypotheses, making life beyond the niggardly categories of
logic and truth. Here is the writer at the crossroads of the
paradigmatic and syntagmatic resources of language, refusing
to choose, having his cake and eating it. This is the life-mak-
ing process that is celebrated throughout the book, that un-
derlies all the digressions, that replaces the story of Tristram's
birth with the graphic spectacle of its own. It is the life of
Tristram's mind, and, committed to language, it is Tristram's
book.

Sterne's novel works a miracle, because it gets onto paper
and into words the private mechanisms and private topogra-
phies which, given there is no Momus' glass for our kind, we
would never perceive otherwise. Not just our inner mind set,
but the tangential world of connotation is given expression in
Sterne. To understand *Tristram Shandy* is to read it *à demi mot*,
to enter into connivance with Sterne, who is ever decorous in
what he says but often bawdy in what he suggests. Sterne says
noses, and we know better;[4] he describes the fair Bedouine

---

[4] Surely, pornography must take honors in the category of fiction that enlists reader involvement. Pornography is a prototype of "generative" reading, for it counts on the reader to do the crucial extra imagining. This is especially true for the tongue-in-cheek variety that Sterne employs; the
notorious description of the fair Bedouine rubbing Trim's "knee" has led
Jean Jacques Mayoux to suggest that the reader is transformed into a voyeur
of a masturbation scene; the reader-spectator is obliged to "compromise himself to the point of becoming a responsible actor" ("Laurence Sterne," in *A
Collection of Critical Essays*, p. 110). There is, nowadays, much criticism de-

rubbing Trim's knee and above, and we keenly follow the action; he threatens to do a chapter on buttonholes, and our mind starts a wondering:

> Button-holes!—there is something lively in the very idea of
> 'em—and trust me, when I get amongst 'em—you gentry
> with great beards—look as grave as you will—I'll make
> merry work with my button-holes—I shall have 'em all to
> myself—'tis a maiden subject—I shall run foul of no man's
> wisdom or fine sayings in it. (p. 217)

Sterne alerts us to the multivalence of our language, multivalent because of all the additional realms of discourse which may be brought in, especially the censored realm of sexual discourse. Whiskers and knots will never be the same after Sterne. In the chapter on whiskers, we see how the Lady Baussiere becomes so obsessed with whiskers that she sees them everywhere and sees nothing else. We are warned that the unsaid meanings, the connotations, can so gain the upper hand, that some words will be discredited forever: night caps, chamber pots, spigots, and faucets. These are all reputable words, Old World words, but, at Sterne's hands, they show their backsides. That is, they do so only if we give our connivance.

Toward the end of this narrative, the dense metaphorical clusters tend to become luminous with meaning. Toby's fortifications and sieges not only mirror warfare itself, but take on their full value in the love battle with Widow Wadman, and the sexual skirmishes in the sentry box actualize the metaphor. Sterne seems to be saying that a powerful enough obsession will eventually leave the realm of thought and of language and become flesh. One of the finest lessons of *Tristram Shandy* is that our hobbyhorses may lead us into rather than away from life. When Tristram's brother Bobby dies unexpectedly, out come the relics and Walter becomes a speaking dictionary:

> "Returning out of Asia, when I sailed from Aegina towards Megara," (when can this have been? thought my un-

---

voted to "reader activity"; it would be interesting to investigate the role of
sexual imagining in such activity.

cle Toby) "I began to view the country round about. Aegina was behind me, Megara was before, Pyraeius on the
right hand, Corinth on the left. —What flourishing towns
now prostrate upon the earth! Alas! Alas! said I to myself,
that man should disturb his soul for the loss of a child,
when so much as this lies awfully buried in his presence—
Remember, said I to myself again—remember thou art a
man."—

Now my uncle Toby knew not that this last paragraph
was an extract of Servius Sulpicius's consolatory letter to
Tully. —He had as little skill, honest man, in the fragments,
as he had in the whole pieces of antiquity. —And as my
father, whilst he was concerned in the Turky trade, had
been three or four different times in the Levant, in one of
which he had staid a whole year and a half at Zant, my uncle Toby naturally concluded, that in some one of these pe-
riods he had taken a trip across the Archipelago into Asia;
and that all this sailing affair with Aegina behind, and Megara before, and Pyraeius on the right hand, &c. &c. was
nothing more than the true course of my father's voyage
and reflections. —"Twas certainly in his manner, and many
an undertaking critick would have built two stories higher
upon worse foundations. —And pray, brother, quoth my
uncle Toby, laying the end of his pipe upon my father's
hand in a kindly way of interruption—but waiting until he
finished the account—what year of our Lord was this? —
"Twas no year of our Lord, replied my father. —That's impossible, cried my uncle Toby. —Simpleton! said my
father,—Twas forty years before Christ was born.

My uncle Toby had but two things for it; either to suppose his brother to be the wandering Jew, or that his misfortunes had disordered his brain. (pp. 267-268)

Relics though they are, Walter's remembered fragments are
being put to a humane use that is as serious as it is comic. It is
legitimate and wise for the activities of the mind to offset the
disasters of the flesh. Those old writers are proving their met-
tle and, much like Fielding's Parson Adams, Walter has travelled and seen a great deal more than Toby or anyone can
know. His ship voyage is a nautical version of the ubiquitous

hobbyhorse. The games of *Tristram Shandy* are not unlike the quilts woven by shell-shocked soldiers; the play of the fingers and the play of the mind can offset the disasters visited upon the body and the soul. Sterne's view of language as natural resource, as saving grace, is the view of a therapist: "A blessing which tied up my father's tongue, and a misfortune which set it loose with good grace, were pretty equal" (p. 266). The parity implied by this vision is civilized and humane, for it measures human event in a wonderfully rich and elastic manner, allowing us to recoup, mentally, what we lose, materially.

But Tristram himself commands fully and finally our interest as the figure in whom life and mind merge. If the narratives of Toby, Walter, Trim, and others are discontinuous, the narrative of Tristram, i.e., his project of describing his life, subsumes them all and never falters. He has found potency and economy. Nothing can be extraneous to him, since he has only one project: to display, *through* a narrative, the quality of his mind. The play of that mind, its inner voyages and games—this is Sterne's new setting. At one point he claims that the fame of his book will counterbalance the evils that have befallen him as a man. Not so much the fame of the book as the very nature of the book will redress the misfortunes of his life. The determinist prison that the body is subject to can be exploded through thought and language alone. The impossible is only a ten-letter word; Tristram suavely proves that he is in three places at once as he writes from Lyon about two visits to Auxerre and simultaneously about his arrival in Lyon; the times of memory and writing time itself are interwoven in a rich tapestry, because the mind can enjoy just such liberty. The mind knows no limits, and Tristram goes on to add that "the measure of heaven itself is but the measure of our present appetites and concoctions" (p. 376). Heaven, the last bastion of the Old World, has been miraculously novelized, metamorphized, and internalized. Desire, perhaps even more than thought, is the animating force, the demiurge of Sterne's world, financing both the benevolence and the pornography, endlessly potent in its visions and fabrications. There is no life so poor or maimed, so truncated, that it can-

not be converted into a rich and whole book. Tristram's misfortunes are transformed as they become merely the materials
of his life, and literature—rather than England or France—becomes the field where he lives.

But no one has ever died in literature, since words do not
know time. Consciousness, thought, desire, and language
permit us to make a figure of our life and to splatter bishops
and kings while doing it; they enable us to be in three places
at once, to mix luxuriantly our levels of discourse. But the
person behind the entire operation, the house for the generative mind, is rooted in time and space. Book 7 depicts Tristram's journey through France, his flight from Death, and it
is an integral part of the novel. Our bodies are in time.
Churches and books may remain fixed, but Janatone evolves:
"But he who measures thee, Janatone, must do it now—thou
carriest the principles of change within thy frame" (p. 373).
Sterne's characters are frequently frozen in dramatic postures
and left for whole chapters, but living people follow other
laws:

> Time wastes too fast: every letter I trace tells me with what
> rapidity Life follows my pen; the days and hours of it, more
> precious, my dear Jenny! than the rubies about thy neck, are
> flying over our heads like light clouds of a windy day,
> never to return more—everything presses on—whilst thou
> art twisting that lock,—see! it grows grey; and every time
> I kiss thy hand to bid adieu, and every absence which fol-
> lows it, are preludes to that eternal separation which we are
> shortly to make.—
> —Heaven have mercy upon us both! (p. 469)

Here is a wisdom beyond comedy, a tragic sense of evanes-
cence which accounts for the intermittent stasis *within* the
novel. Time is too often dealt with as a literary problem, but
it only appears in literature because it is a *human* problem, one
that literature can miraculously resolve. Language and desire
can spawn new worlds, and Toby's hobbyhorse moves him
back and forth between England and Flanders quicker than
the flash of an eye. But Tristram's vile cough punctuates
every book of this prancing novel, and the spectre of impo-

tency—not a man with an unloaded gun, but a man containing, as we all do, a time bomb—that spectre must eventually kill desire. *Tristram Shandy* indelibly traces the connections, the blood-line between Old Worlds and New Worlds, determinism and freedom, life and art.

The Written Life: *Les Confessions*

No study of the enabling and redemptive powers of language can close without a discussion of Rousseau. Whereas his sole novel, *Julie ou la nouvelle Héloïse*, picks up a number of the threads of this study (the self-in-time, the notion of the love-letter, the strategies for sublimating desire), it is nonetheless to the *Confessions* that we must turn for the most dazzling display of the life as book. It may be argued that the *Confessions* are not a novel, but my fundamental purpose in studying them is to show how Rousseau exploits the powers of language to rewrite and to "reright" the life as a fiction.

Rousseau's *Confessions* recast every phase of my book. In them we see, writ large, each central moment of the trajectory of self: the marginal self that is severed from and sacrificed to the world; the drama of recognition, disguise and exhibitionism; the collision of full-blown self with society and the other; the ultimate project of self-enactment through language and book. In Rousseau's tortured autobiography we see a virtual curtain-call of my characters, a re-sounding and resounding of my early themes, the whole entourage called forth—somewhat like that haunting Last Judgment that Rousseau repeatedly invokes, book in hand—to be seen for what it is: words, mere words, magic words. Rousseau's life, in the *Confessions*, moves dizzily through the parabola I have charted, from the hungry promenading music-making self that is to inherit the world to the manic ghost who has been utterly dispossessed, seeking only a refuge, from which the value and fullness of his life might be re-experienced and recreated—and thereby salvaged—in words.

Not that Rousseau ever accepted the redemptive power of language. He knew its power too well ever to trust it, and he could not forgive its mediating status, the unbridgeable chasm separating it from the things it bespeaks. But the absence on which language is predicated could, he tragically and sovereignly came to understand, be turned to advantage. The *Confessions* both record and are that act of understanding.

The Fall from Grace and the encounter with the contingent world have already been registered in this study: Lazarillo's bruising contact with the stone statue, Pablos' fall from Boy King into excrement and Simplicius' stint as disguised calf are all proto-realist excursions into adaptation and secular lifemanship; likewise, the Princess of Clèves experiences the twin tarnishing of passion and court, and she, like Simplicius at the close of his story, understandably chooses to exit from the "world." Rousseau's version of being expulsed from the Garden of Eden is crucially related to his discovery of language as mediating instrument and of men as opaque rather than transparent. Falsely accused of breaking a comb, Rousseau realizes, to his horror, that language simply will not *prove* his innocence. He *says* he is innocent; he is not believed. Here we have, from the older writer's perspective, the exodus from the garden:

> There ended the serenity of my childish life. From that moment I never again enjoyed pure happiness, and even today I am conscious that memory of childhood's delights stops short at that point. We stayed some months longer at Bossey. We lived as we are told the first man lived in the earthly paradise, but we no longer enjoyed it; in appearance our situation was unchanged, but in reality it was an entirely different kind of existence. No longer were we young people bound by ties of respect, intimacy, and confidence to our guardians; we no longer looked on them as gods who read our hearts; we were less ashamed of wrongdoing, and more afraid of being caught; we began to be secretive, to rebel, and to lie. (pp. 30-31)[1]

The gods, too, have exited, for men can no longer read into one another's hearts. Here is the perpetual crisis of Rousseau's life: to make his heart and soul visible. The childhood trauma

[1] Jean-Jacques Rousseau, *The Confessions of Jean-Jacques Rousseau*, tr. J. M. Cohen (Penguin Books, 1953).

of falling from transparent grace into verbal opacity is likened
to another, equally archetypal, memory, this time of a literal
expulsion from the walled city: Rousseau's prose moves into
the present tense, as he relives his initiation as Outsider:[2]

> I was returning with two comrades. A mile and a half from
> the city I [hear] the sound of the tattoo[;] and [increase] my
> pace. Then I [hear] the drum-roll[; I run at full speed; I ar-
> rive] out of breath[;] and bathed in sweat, my heart pound-
> ing. I [see] from the distance the soldiers at their posts. I
> [run toward them] and [shout] breathlessly. It was too late.
> [At] twenty paces away I [see] them raise the first bridge.
> I [tremble at the sight of these] dreadful horns rising in the
> air, a sinister and fatal augury of the inevitable fate which
> from that moment awaited me. (amended, p. 49)

Rousseau is marked by this seminal experience of exclusion.[2]
Instead of efficacious transparent language, he finds the tower
of Babel; locked out of the community, he is, like Lazarillo
and Pablos, on his own. His entire career may be seen as an
effort to open up the walled city, but to do so in the only way
he is to be vouchsafed: through "forging" a language of his
own. In the latter part of his life, with plenty of good reasons,
Rousseau voluntarily chooses the withdrawal that was forced
on him from the outset. The Princess de Clèves, we may recall, left the Court, straightway to die. Rousseau, in his
strange way, leaves the City to live. He does what he has to,
knowing, obscurely, that he has to: "The choice I made to
write and conceal myself is precisely what I needed"
(amended, p. 116).[3] *Ecrire* always means, in some sense, *se
cacher*, language itself being a disembodied emissary, consigned to the pages of a book, bringing tidings of a physical

[2] For an illuminating view of literature as "return" to the community, see
Jean Starobinski, *Jean Jacques Rousseau: La transparence et l'obstacle* (Paris: Gal-
limard, 1971), pp. 153–165. I would like to acknowledge a broad general debt
to Starobinski; much of my reading of Rousseau is indebted to his work.

[3] Peter Brooks has given us an admirable study of the concept of worldliness in French 18th-century thought and fiction: *The Novel of Worldliness*
(Princeton: Princeton University Press, 1969). Brooks understandably does
not deal with Rousseau, who functions very much as a "counter culture" figure.

self that is never coextensive with it. While absence may be the conditions of writing, it nonetheless creates a scandal if the writer fully adheres to it. What Diderot and the other *philosophes* seem to have been unable to brook was the absence of Rousseau's *person*, replaced, as it was, by his word. *"Il n'y a que le méchant qui soit seul,"* wrote Diderot, stinging his hermit friend to the heart. In the atmosphere of worldliness which characterized 18th-century France, Rousseau's behavior is simply unheard of. (Whereas the life of the recluse is a credible option for Simplicius in the turmoil of the Thirty Years' War, to leave Paris is quite unthinkable in mid-18th century.) The man of letters has a crucial relationship to society at large. But the *cercles* and the *philosophes* were not only of the world; they wanted to change the world as well.

So did Rousseau. Throughout his life, Rousseau could devise only one way of changing the world: to *expose* himself. He is the swollen, gargantuan[4] self whose every discovery is inner, whose odyssey consists of an inner voyage, one that he felt had never yet been recorded in literature. As Starobinski has pointed out, the authority of all his work is internal: in the "Discours sur l'inégalité parmi les hommes," the famous noble savage theory posits both a quasi-mythic past and a hazy future where virtue and wholeness might be possible; yet, both these historical moments are red herrings, because Rousseau demonstrates throughout that he can recreate "unspoiled man" merely by going into himself.[5] Innocence is within. He is its measure; his only task is to liberate the inner man. Self-exposure would thus be a social and universal act: Rousseau's mission is to reveal the Truths he harbors. Innocence, law, morality, even God, are no longer to be found in Nature or in the heavens or in institutions: they reside in the self. With the ardor of a genuine Encyclopaedist, Rousseau sets out to inventory and catalog himself.

[4] Auerbach significantly entitled his discussion of Rabelais, "The World in Pantagruel's Mouth"; if Rabelais depicts the early Renaissance hunger for absorbing knowledge and "ingesting" the world itself, then Rousseau prophetically announces the inner retreat, the discovery or making of a universe inside the self.

[5] See Starobinski, pp. 25-33.

Self-exposure may also be, as we know, an obscenely private act. Rousseau's exhibitionism, chronicled at the beginning of the third book, is indeed directed toward a public, but
there is little that is edifying in it:

> I haunted dark alleys and lonely spots where I could expose
> myself to women from afar off in the condition in which I
> should have liked to be in their company. [The thing] they
> saw was [not] obscene, I was far from thinking of that; it
> was ridiculous. The absurd pleasure I got from displaying
> myself before their eyes is quite indescribable. There was
> only one step for me still to make to achieve the experience
> I desired, and I have no doubt that some bold girl would
> have afforded me the amusement, as she passed, if I had
> possessed the courage to wait. (amended, pp. 90-91)[4]

Rousseau's exposed body does not bring him the desired sexual partnership (*le traitement désiré*), but rather a labyrinthine
chase replete with castrating nemesis:[6] "In a moment I was
caught and seized by a big man with a big moustache, a big
hat, and a big sword" (p. 91).[5] Other kinds of exposure must
be found, which will influence the public and effect the necessary release as well. Joseph Andrews' body is commensurate with his self; Marianne's program of self-exposure moves
from the flesh to the soul; Rousseau seeks a kind of recognition and legitimacy that is similar to theirs, but his "confessions" will replace as well as depict his person.

His person did not do too well. Recorded historical event,
Rousseau realizes, is a very crude affair. The meaning of his
own life is scandalously misinterpreted and misunderstood by
others. The true account is known only by him: the inner motives behind the public gestures, the feelings behind the
words, the soul behind the person. In writing about his life,
Rousseau discovers the awesome shaping power of the artist.
He becomes his own Pygmalion, adding to the paltry known
events a rich overlay of motive, an aura of feeling and a large,
indispensable personal context, in which the "data" themselves fit in humbly, showing a new, inevitable, inevitably in-

[6] See *ibid.*, pp. 203-211.

nocuous, face, demonstrating the powerful teleology of
Rousseau's *vita nuova*. To write about one's life is always to
*re*write one's life. It matters not whether Rousseau lied or
whether he invented details. What counts is that "facts" of his
life are now shorn of their awful intrinsic meanings, their in-
dicting, unitary significance; above all, the deadliest quality of
one's past acts, the pastness of them, their immovable, unchangeable status, this too is marvelously, effortlessly, overcome by the magic of writing. Rousseau deliciously trots out
his sins: the stolen ribbon, the abandoned epileptic, the for-
saken children; these items not only "trot," they also pirou-
ette, show multiple colorations, allow their teller innumerable
alibis. The process is always the same: a fulsome *mea culpa*, a
reminder to the reader that such honesty is unique, and then
the inevitable "inner motives" which will complete the picture and exonerate Rousseau: he accused the girl, Marion, of
stealing the ribbon because he *actually* wanted to give it to her
himself; he was just a child, etc.; he consigned his children
away because Thérèse's family would have corrupted them;
he did it out of love, etc. And where no legitimizing alibi can
be found, he is left in the ultimately gratifying position of enjoying his misery. For the dreadful "otherness" of these
events is gone now: there is only Rousseau, evoking them,
turning them over in his mind, presenting them leisurely on
the page, adjusting them this way and that, in short, controlling his past in writing, whereas his past controlled him in life.
What started as a moral imperative: to expose one man's innocence and to render it universal, has now become a creative
exercise, *sui generis*, a process of writing that always invents
even when it confesses.

Rousseau needed whatever measure of control over events
that he could muster. If the Baroque alienation from the
world echoes my first chapter, and his multiple quest for recognition is reminiscent of Fielding and Marivaux, the theme
of collision—embodied in *Manon Lescaut, Werther*, and *Clarissa*—seems a veritable hallmark of his career. He collides
equally with society at large and with the individuals in it. No
one is too small to bump into Rousseau. The *Confessions* stage
an unending series of confrontations, meetings where the an-

tagonism is frequently veiled during the actual exchange but
carefully discerned and highlighted by Rousseau in his crucial
afterthought activity. Rousseau's public image is clearly delineated: he dares to be the only virtuous man in a corrupted
world, thereby providing an invaluable role-model service. In
so doing he offends public mores far more drastically even
than Des Grieux; his anguish at being misunderstood and re-
jected cuts even deeper than that of Werther; the hounding
and physical displacement he undergoes are as extreme as
those suffered by Clarissa. The dichotomy between his al-
truistic program (he will display virtue to the World) and the
role foisted on him as enemy of the people very nearly drives
him mad:

> As I sought in vain for the cause of this unanimous hostil-
> ity, I almost believed that the whole world had gone mad.
> Could the writer of *Perpetual Peace* be a spreader of discord,
> the creator of the Savoyard Vicar be an infidel, the author
> of the *New Héloïse* a wolf, and that of *Émile* a madman!
> (pp. 545-555)

Each of these texts, he feels, is a guarantor not only of his zeal
for public welfare but—perhaps even more importantly—of
his personal integrity as well.

Self-exposure is no simple matter. Rousseau experiences,
ever more acutely, the discrepancy, even the polarity, between his inner sense of self and the public image that is
flaunted at him.[7] How do we bring the inner world to light
and to life? Let us recall Sterne's mention of Momus' glass, a
kind of window in a man's chest which lets us look in, a literal
transparency for which Rousseau yearns but which Sterne
recognizes as denied to man. Literature, as Sterne beautifully
illustrates throughout *Tristram Shandy*, thrives precisely on
opacity:

> . . . had the said glass been there set up, nothing more
> would have been wanting, in order to have taken a man's
> character, but to have taken a chair and gone softly, as you

---

[7] It is more than obvious that Rousseau's *Dialogues* take such schizophrenic
division and cast it into its appropriate dramatic, exteriorized form.

would to a dioptrical bee-hive, and look'd in,—view'd the
soul stark naked;—observ'd all her motions,—her machin-
ations;—traced all her maggots from their first engendering
to their crawling forth;—watched her loose in her frisks,
her gambols, her capricios; and after some notice of her
more solemn deportment, consequent upon such frisks,
&c.—then taken your pen and ink and set down nothing
but what you had seen, and could have sworn to: —But this
is an advantage not to be had by the biographer in this
planet . . . our minds shine not through the body, but are
wrapt up here in a dark covering of uncrystalized flesh and
blood; so that if we would come to the specifick characters
of them, we must go some other way to work. (*Tristram
Shandy*, pp. 55-56)

Of all mortals, Rousseau was probably the least suited for
transparency. Everything he tells us in the *Confessions* confirms the image of a man endlessly checked and choked, containing worlds within while stammering or fuming without,[8]
spending a considerable amount of his time in a daze, plagued
by bladder dysfunction, exquisitely aware of what he has to
offer and just as keenly attuned to the flawed transmission
process that *presents* him as less than he is, as other than he is.
The relationship with Mme. de Warens is poignant and
unique, because she alone accepts him as he is, loves the entire
person, the flesh and the soul.

He himself cannot quite manage so much. One detects an
underlying sense of worthlessness: he remembers being afraid
to buy pastries, because he invented an entire, threatening
scenario:

As I come to the pastrycook's I catch sight of the women
behind the counter and can already imagine them laughing
amongst themselves and making fun of the greedy young-
ster. Then I pass a fruiterer's, and look at the ripe pears out
of the corner of my eye; the scent of them tempts me. But
two or three young people over there are looking at me; a

[8] See, among other episodes, Rousseau's "profession de foi" before the
Consistoire at Geneva, p. 465 (Fr.). Starobinski devotes several pages to the
rubric, "Sans pouvoir proférer un seul mot," *op.cit.* pp. 165-168.

man I know is standing in front of the shop; I can see a girl
coming in the distance. Is not she our maidservant? My
short sight is constantly deceiving me. I take everyone who
passes for someone I know. I am frightened by everything
and discover obstacles everywhere. (p. 45)[7]

In the episode with Zulietta, the Italian courtesan, we see a
still more paralyzing fear. On the point of having intercourse
with this beautiful woman, Rousseau simply cannot carry it
off: he cannot believe that his person is worthy of desire: "She
comes and throws herself at my head, at mine although she
knows I am a nobody, although my merits, which she cannot
know, would be nothing in her eyes. There is something in-
comprehensible about this" (p. 301).[8] He then imagines that
there must be a hidden flaw, and one of Zulietta's strangely
formed nipples is enough to incapacitate him. It is as if he
were maimed by disjunction between inner promise and
outer achievement. Rousseau desperately wants to unite the
public with the inner self, but he himself is singularly unable
to effect such a blend. He experiences total sexual fulfillment
only once in his life, but he does not do so as Rousseau; instead, he is Dudding, a young Englishman on the make. Dud-
ding-Rousseau assembles his constituent pieces and achieves
unimpeded sexual communication with Mme. Larnage; their
sexual intercourse is significantly described as a language:[9]
"She had given me that confidence, the lack of which almost
always prevents me from being . . . myself. For once I was
myself. Never have my eyes and my senses, my heart and my
mouth, spoken so eloquently" (p. 239).[9] This passage, I
would submit, contains the quintessential Rousseau; as Dudding, the sexual exchange achieves the status of language, but
as Rousseau, the speech act will achieve the status of sex.
Rousseau's person contains a plenitude of desires, urges, im-
pulses, and feelings: the tragedy of his life and the modernity
of his work consist in the bittersweet solution he found: language will be called on to express and even to enact the in-

[9] I am indebted here to the unpublished Ph.D. dissertation of Michael
O'Dea, "Language and the Problem of the Self in Rousseau, Wordsworth
and Holderlin," Brown University, 1978.

nocence and the love and the fullness that he can externalize in no other way.

Nothing exemplifies more sweetly the balm and resources of literature than a comparison of Rousseau's epoch-making novel *Julie* with his tempestuous relationship with Sophie d'Houdetot. Whether or not the "real" passion is the reliable model for the love story is unimportant. This passion was, for Rousseau, the real thing: "As I have already said, this time it was love, love with all its strength and all its violence" (p. 414):[10] the kiss which Sophie customarily reserves for him is described in terms worthy of *Julie* and prophetic for Proust:

> [That sole,] fatal kiss, even before I received it . . . so fired my blood that my head was dizzy, my eyes were dazzled and blind, and my trembling knees could no longer support me. I had to stop and sit down; my whole bodily mechanism was in utter disorder; I was on the point of fainting. (amended, p. 414)[11]

Here is Rousseau in all his vulnerability, all his volatility. His person is very much in play here, pressing him to the point of swooning. Virtually brimming over, Rousseau's ecstatic longing threatens all stability;[10] we are reminded of his earlier lament: "Physical pleasure! Is it the lot of man to enjoy it? Ah, if ever in all my life I had once tasted the delights of love to the full, I do not think that my frail existence could have endured them; I should have died on the spot" (p. 210).[12] Rousseau-Sophie will not repeat Dudding-Mme Larnage. Instead, Rousseau will retain his balance while sublimating his passions. He does it twice: once in the novelistic form of Saint-Preux and Julie, but also in the subsequent transformation

---

[10] Rousseau is very frank in discussing his difficulty in achieving sexual control:

Naturellement, ce que j'avais à craindre dans l'attente de la possession d'une personne si chérie était de l'anticiper, et de ne pouvoir assez gouverner mes désirs et mon imagination pour rester maître de moi-même. On verra que, dans un âge avancé, la seule idée de quelques légères faveurs qui m'attendaient près de la personne aimée, allumait mon sang à tel point, qu'il m'était impossible de faire impunément le court trajet qui me séparait d'elle. (pp. 223-224)

into language and fiction which we see in the *Confessions* themselves. Sophie, he admits to us, was never tempted by him, although he negotiated a number of almost obscene bargains with her;[11] as time passes, however, he builds a fiction of mutual passion and renunciation, a fiction which now begins to honor them both:

> For however faithful, however estimable Mme d'Houdetot might be, she was after all a woman; he was away, opportunities were frequent, temptations were severe, and it would have been very difficult for her always to defend herself with equal success against a more persistent lover. It undoubtedly said much for her and for me that in such a situation we should have imposed limits on ourselves which we never allowed ourselves to infringe. (pp. 429-430)

Rousseau has ascribed a *beau rôle* to himself that the earlier commentary flatly denies; in addition, Sophie has now been co-opted by the fiction and has been outfitted with a reciprocal passion as well. Here are some of the rewards of literature, of *"écrire et se cacher"*; renunciation, as Marivaux's Marianne discovered, is the infinite Royal Way of the self.

Writing may well assuage his erotic hunger more fully and more safely and more reliably than sexual congress ever

---

[11] Consider, for example, the initial description of Sophie's diplomacy in responding to his passion:
Elle ne comprit rien d'abord à la sotte humeur avec laquelle je recevais ses caresses: mais mon coeur, incapable de savoir jamais rien cacher de ce qui s'y passe, ne lui laissa pas longtemps ignorer mes soupçons; elle en voulut rire; cet expédient ne réussit pas; des transports de rage en auraient été l'effet: elle changea de ton. Sa compatissante douceur fut invincible; elle me fit des reproches qui me pénétrèrent; elle me témoigna, sur mes injustes craintes, des inquiétudes dont j'abusai. J'exigeai des preuves qu'elle ne se moquait pas de moi. Elle vit qu'il n'y avait nul autre moyen de me rassurer. Je devins pressant, le pas était délicat. Il est étonnant, il est unique peut-être qu'une femme ayant pu venir jusqu'à marchander, s'en soit tirée à si bon compte. Elle ne me refusa rien de ce que la plus tendre amitié pouvait accorder. Elle ne m'accorda rien qui pût la rendre infidèle, et j'eus l'humiliation de voir que l'embrasement dont ses légères faveurs allumaient mes sens n'en porta jamais aux siens la moindre étincelle. (p. 524)

could. Speaking to Sophie in the garden, Rousseau found *words* commensurate with his heart:

> It was in that wood, sitting with her on a grass bank be-
> neath an acacia in full flower, that I found a language really
> able to express the emotions of my heart. It was the first
> and only time in my life, but I was sublime, if such a word
> can describe all the sympathy and seductive charm that the
> most tender and ardent love can breathe into the heart of a
> man. (p. 414)[14]

Words spoken in a *tête-à-tête* are annunciatory, not of physical love-making, but of more words, emissaries of Rousseau that inflame hearts and stir senses. *"Ecrire et se cacher"* may be the greatest aphrodisiac of all: Rousseau's work will seduce, will effect the sexual contact so threatening or unavailable in its immediacy. The reaction to his play, "Le Devin," hand-somely illustrates such an arrangement. Already during the first scene, Rousseau the spectator perceives a *"murmure de sur-prise"*; this response is soon amplified: "Around me I heard a whispering of women who seemed to me as lovely as angels, and who said to one another under their breath: 'That is charming. That is delightful. There is not a note that does not speak straight to the heart' " (p. 353).[15] Rousseau is achieving at last what his exhibitionism in Turin failed to: sexual re-sponse. Arousing the women in the theater arouses, in turn, Rousseau, very nicely approximating the *"traitement désiré"* sought after in Turin:

> The pleasure of affecting so many pleasant people moved
> even me to tears, which I could not restrain during the first
> duet, when I noticed that I was not the only one who wept.
> . . . I soon surrendered myself, completely and unre-
> servedly, to the pleasure of savouring my glory. And yet I
> am sure that sexual passion counted for more at that mo-
> ment than the vanity of an author; if there had only been
> men present I am positive that I should not have been de-
> voured, as I continuously was, by the desire to catch with
> my lips the delicious tears I had evoked. (p. 353)[16]

Rousseau's language, especially in his love novel, endows him with a potency and seductiveness available to him in no other way: "the women especially were wild about the book and its author. Such was their infatuation indeed that there were few of them, even of the highest rank, whose conquest I could not have made if I had attempted it" (p. 504).[17] In short, writing may offer leverage, a potential for affective assault: "Whoever can read those two letters without his heart softening and melting with the same emotion which inspired me to write them, had better close the book" (p. 408).[18] Granting even the presence of convention and affective fallacy, we are nonetheless far from the man who saw in the unreliability of language a sign of man's fall from grace. Rousseau has discovered that the ideal society he can act upon is the society of readers; to this projected community he can display and exhibit his self with unlimited freedom, while still being protected.

The reader, then, is Rousseau's final partner, to be wooed, convinced, and coerced. Rousseau exposes himself ever more hugely, because, the fuller a say he has, the more assuredly he can command assent. The *in-extremis* image of the Last Judgment is repeatedly invoked, a final court of appeal which readers have always constituted for authors; Rousseau's *Confessions* will guarantee his innocence, and his self-exposure will induce a comparable self-revelation among his readers: the affective community and communion—the one he could never achieve in his person—will be complete:

> ". . . Eternal Being[,] . . . let the numberless legion of my fellow men gather round me, and hear my confessions. Let them groan at my depravities, and blush for my misdeeds. But let each one of them reveal his heart at the foot of Thy throne with equal sincerity, and may any man who dares, say 'I was a better man than he.' " (amended, pp. 4-5)[19]

Listening, blushing, moaning, confessing, Rousseau's readers respond to his language with precisely those powerful emotions that he himself so loved and feared throughout his life. No other hermit can have known the appeal of others as acutely as did Rousseau. His senses overpower him, his blood rushes, his body tingles, he is ready to lose himself at every turn. Rousseau seems to have been terrifyingly available. He argues against the theater in Geneva, because he knows only too well the power of empathy, the spectator's helpless response to the play. [12] He has an ongoing sense of being manipulated by others, because he knows that a caress or a blush will turn him into putty. In moments of sexual passion, he invariably loses, we are told, his faculty of hearing, vision, and movement. He fears losing still more, he hints; he is worried about premature ejaculation with Mme. de Warens, with Zulietta. [13] Control is decidedly not his forte.

Writing offers control. *"Ecrire et se cacher"* is to move others while holding onto oneself. Writing prolongs pleasure.

Writing quite simply prolongs. It repeats his life, eradicates closure, makes ongoing what was finite and over:

> Precious and ever-regretted moments, begin to run your charming course again for me! Flow one after another

---

[12] For just these reasons Rousseau is able to make a passionate plea against the establishment of a theater in Geneva. To be sure, he does not want Geneva to resemble Paris; but the more determining psychic reasons for his distrust of theater have to do with his terrible vulnerability. It is no surprise that he understood Molière's *Misanthrope* so well, or that he "married" Racine's *Bérénice*: empathy is his forte as well as his weakness. See "Lettre à M. d'Alembert sur son Article 'Genève' dans le septième volume de l'Encyclopédie, et particulèrement sur le projet d'établir un théâtre de comédie en cette ville," in Jean Jacques Rousseau, *Du Contrat social ou Principes du droit politique* (Paris: Classiques Garnier, 1960), esp. pp. 150-158, 164-165.

[13] In Rousseau's early sexual apprentice experiences in Turin, there is considerable distaste for sexuality itself, especially in its physical details. I am thinking, in particular, of the masturbation scene to which Rousseau is a (more or less hypnotized) party, which culminates in the following manner:

> Je me dégageai impétueusement en poussant un cri et faisant un saut en arrière, et, sans marquer ni indignation ni colère, car je n'avais pas la moindre idée de ce dont il s'agissait, j'exprimai ma surprise et mon dégoût avec tant d'énergie, qu'il me laissa là: mais tandis qu'il achevait de se démener, je vis partir vers la cheminée et tomber à terre je ne sais quoi de gluant et de blanchâtre qui me fit soulever le coeur. Je m'élançai sur le balcon, plus ému, plus troublé, plus effrayé même que je ne l'avais été de ma vie, et prêt à me trouver mal. (p. 72)

through my memory, more slowly, if you can, than you
did in your fugitive reality! What shall I do to prolong this
touching and simple tale, as I should like to; endlessly to
repeat the same words, and no more to weary my readers
by their repetition than I wearied myself by beginning
them for ever afresh? (p. 215)[14, 20]

Note the temporal privileges of language: *"prolonger," "redire
toujours," "répéter"*: language is the agent of memory, and, together, they resurrect. The passage itself seems delicious and
savored, a slow-motion recall which language alone can manage. They bring back to life an experiential record that is not
only buried by time but was never transmitted or transmit-
table even in the past: "Indeed if it all consisted of fact, deed,
and words, I could describe it and in a sense convey its meaning. But how can I tell what was neither said, nor done, nor
even thought, but only relished and felt, when I cannot ad-
duce any other cause for my happiness but just this feeling?"
(p. 215.)[21] Memory and language are intrinsically pleasurable,
for they alone make circular and fluid our biological lives that
are linear and finite. Moreover, the act of memory and the act
of writing are wonderfully cooperative and coextensive, each
nourishing and stimulating the other. Finally, writing realizes
the grand social and unavowable private need for exposure:
no more scenes of paralysis and mute anguish, no more *après
coup* frustration wherein the brilliant retort comes only too
late; at last, the economy and synchronization have been
found: all his brilliance, his feelings, his imagination, will be
displayed, with the lightning-like immediacy of writing: the
timeless, redemptive present of *écriture*.

Thus, writing allows Rousseau to assemble his component
parts and to present the full portrait. The total exposure will
include all that "they cannot have told you," the dates, facts,
and the events, but also feelings, imaginings, and yearnings.

---

[14] Repeatedly, one has the sense that Rousseau is the most privileged of his
readers. Aware that his narrative may appear banal to an umsympathetic
reader, he avows: "Je sais bien que le lecteur n'a pas grand besoin de savoir
tout cela mais j'ai besoin, moi, de le lui dire" (p. 22).

The *Confessions* will give vent and scope to the felt but un-realized life, and Rousseau is a singularly viable candidate for such narration. His imagination and desires were so power-fully creative, grasped and so altered the external data of his life, that he justifiably felt that others could not possibly "know" him or his true story. In amorous matters, the timid suitor lusted his full, but did so in the safe precincts of the mind: "Consequently I have possessed few women, but I have not failed to get a great deal of satisfaction in my own way, that is to say imaginatively" (p. 28).[22] One is tempted to speak of compensation, perhaps of sublimation, and doubtless Rousseau does harness his imagination for *ersatz* purposes. When going through puberty, he tells us he created a type of elaborate mental security system, a veritable inner structure for channeling riotous desires into viable (harmless) outlets. This system is nothing less than a theory of literary genesis:

> My senses, which had been roused long ago, demanded de-lights of which I could not even guess the nature. I was as far from the reality as if I had been entirely lacking in sex-uality. My senses were already mature, and I sometimes thought of my past eccentricities, but I could not see be-yond them. In this strange situation my restless imagina-tion took a hand which saved me from myself and calmed my growing sensuality. What it did was to nourish itself on situations that had interested me in my reading, recalling them, varying them, combining them, and giving me so great a part in them, that I became one of the characters I imagined, and saw myself always in the pleasantest situa-tions of my own choosing. So, in the end, the fictions I suc-ceeded in building up made me forget my real condition, which so dissatisfied me. My love for imaginary objects and my facility in lending myself to them ended by disil-lusioning me with everything around me, and determined that love of solitude which I have retained ever since that time. There will be more than one example in what follows of the strange effects of that trait in my character which seems so gloomy and misanthropic. In fact, however, it

arises from my too loving heart, from my too tender and
affectionate nature, which find no living creatures akin to
them, and so are forced to feed upon fictions. (p. 48)[23]

Rousseau's entire life is adumbrated in this passage: the retreat
from contingency into the imagination, the radical discrepancy between misanthropic appearance and inner tenderness,
the ability of Jean-Jacques to metamorphose himself into another, the safety offered by the inner realm against sexual danger. To be sure, there is a persistent thread of causality linking
Rousseau's two arenas; he would appear to recoup, inside,
what he fears or fails to do, outside.

But, we would do well not to overprivilege the contingent
world. It may be possible to speak of choice as well as causality, electing the inner world rather than retreating to it.
Every text studied in this book acknowledges and serves the
authority of consciousness, soul, and imagination over the
tangible substance of the phenomenal world (including one's
own body). Rousseau presents the equation in its most elemental and sublime form; we appear to be made, he is saying,
for so much more than actually comes to pass.[15] The brutal
discrepancy between desire and realization, yearning and enactment, his well-nigh infinite resources and the paltry stage
he occupies, all this leaves him with a profound sense of being
cheated by life's niggardliness. Events do not and cannot
measure up:

How could it be that, with a naturally expansive nature
for which to live was to love, I had not hitherto found a
friend entirely my own, a true friend—I who felt so truly
formed to be a friend? How could it be that with such in-
flammable feelings, with a heart entirely moulded for love,
I had not at least once burned with love for a definite object? Devoured by a need to love that I had never been able

[15] One of the recurring phrases throughout the *Confessions* is "être né pour
quelque chose," to be born or destined for something. Here is the imperious
teleology at the heart of his work, the powerful sense of promise and disap-
pointment.

to satisfy, I saw myself coming to the gates of old age, and dying without having lived.

These melancholy but moving reflections drive me back upon myself with a regret that was not without its own pleasure. It seemed to me that fate owed me something she had never given me. To what purpose had she sent me into the world with [the keenest of] faculties, if they were to remain to the end unused? (amended, pp. 396-397)

"Promises not kept" seems to be the theme of his life; not merely the betrayal of friends, but the breaking of a larger pact, the scandal of unused passions, unspoken emotions, unmade loves, unheard warnings, and unshared life. The most intolerable inequality among men is the shameless disproportion between our sensed resources and our recorded accomplishments.

Rousseau bridges the chasm in a prophetic manner. He makes his own world: "The impossibility of attaining the real persons precipitated me into the land of chimeras; and seeing nothing that existed worthy of my exalted feelings, I fostered them in an ideal world which my creative imagination soon peopled with beings after my own heart" (p. 398).[25] Rousseau, like Proust, is determined to realize the immense repertory he carries within him. One may view all his artistic productions as versions of self-enactment which could be actualized in no other way: the outsider articulates the rights of the people; the frustrated, would-be, aging lover writes the romance of the century; the orphaning father writes the treatise on education; the hermit writes his confessions. The writing, he hopes, will right the record. The written text is to compete with history, because the fully exposed written self dwarfs the contingent, phenomenal one.

The *Confessions* both record Rousseau's failure and embody his victory. At the end of his life, tired even of his inner society (*"peuplé d'êtres selon mon coeur"*), he comes to grips with his ultimate quarry: *"être moi-même."* In himself is the world: his past, the places he has been, the people he has known and loved and hated; he is the locus of all this reality. The last pages of the *Confessions* describe his sojourn on the Ile de Saint-Pierre, a stay that he was to immortalize in his final work, *Les Rêveries d'un promeneur solitaire*. Already in this text we see the haunting island imagery, the final turn inward:

> It seemed to me that on that island I should be further re-moved from men, safer from their insults, and more for-gotten by them; freer, in a word, to surrender to the pleas-ures of idleness and the contemplative life. I should have liked to be so cut off on that island as to have no more traffic with mortal men . . . (p. 589)[26]

He compares himself to that other island dweller, Robinson Crusoe, both creators of "an imaginary dwelling" (pp. 765-766). Yet, Rousseau's exclusive self-cultivation and self-ex-ploration contrast so vividly with Defoe's protagonist that we may indeed measure the scope of this study by comparing Jean-Jacques' island reveries with the husbandry and industry of Crusoe. Crusoe, as Ian Watt has shown, is *homo economi-cus*,[16] and he splendidly transforms his island into a bustling agrarian community of one; Rousseau, as he is to demonstrate unforgettably in the 5eme Promenade of the *Rêveries*, seeks to sound his own depths, to quiet out the world so that he may descend into the deepest reaches of himself. The harmonious world that he finds within—so calm and restful in comparison to the travails of the senses and the nerves—is reminiscent of the eye of the storm, the insular Tahiti which haunted Mel-ville; the path to it, Rousseau has shown, is out of the world and into the self.

This inner sanctuary is not visible. Rousseau's last written text is devoted to mapping out this special island estate; it, somewhat like Clarissa's will, constitutes his final legacy. He not only renders public what is utterly private; he also creates as well as describes. In the last analysis, language must invent, even the most scrupulously accurate use of words; for the words betoken and create things which would not exist with-out the words. The words alone remain, and they establish a

---

[16] See Ian Watt, *The Rise of the Novel* (Berkeley: University of California Press, 1957), pp. 60-92.

homeland from which he cannot be expulsed; they are the
medium through which he recaptures and relives and relays
his past experience. Lazarillo becomes a town crier, and
Rousseau meditates on an island. Lazarillo details the goods
he receives in return for favors his wife lends out; Rousseau
articulates the inner motives and longing that attended and
dwarfed his life. Both are town criers. But Rousseau is displaying samples never before seen or attended to, in literature.
Indeed, the island wisdom is the condition of his solitude and
his link with men; writing enables him quite simply to die to
the world while creating his existence for a permanent society
of readers. The equation is complete: the life has become the
book.

CONCLUSION

ROUSSEAU'S *Confessions* have, I hope to have shown, effectively concluded my study by displaying virtually every phase in the drama of self-enactment. Like the serpent which eats its own tail (inscribed on Clarissa's coffin), Rousseau takes us full circle, showing us that the coercive public and social world (the one so authoritative in the picaresque and baroque fictions) can ultimately be dealt with by the linguistic formula: *écrire et se cacher.* The self may choose to master its environment and to enact its relationships through internalization, by means of language.

Language and thought may well constitute that "full circle" which the linear biology of the body denies. Indeed, the circle and the line may be emblematic for the two kinds of fictions dealt with in this book: the generative and the mimetic. The body, like discursive prose, moves only one direction: forward, or endward or deathward. *"Immer zu, immer zu,"* Büchner's Woyzeck cries, and he echoes the relentless chronometry of life itself; Aristotle's prescriptive beginning, middle, and end, and Shakespeare's famous stages of life, bespeak a fundamental paradigm that is crucially *imposed* in art while *suffered* in experience. We may begin our novels wherever we want, but such latitude is not available in our personal duration. Mimesis is the cornerstone of Aristotle's aesthetic, because art must, he feels, respect and reflect the body's sojourn in time and space. The *point d'honneur* of mimetic art, then, is not to flinch in the face of the twin nemises: closure and contingency. The life, like the story, must end; the trip is one-way. The greatest virtue of mimesis is fidelity, and it dictates a staunch, utterly unswerving, adherence to the deadly facts of life: every event is over when it is over, the show stops for no one, your life brings your death. Taken to its extreme, the mimetic novel offers neither play nor replay, but is wedded to a tyrannical unitary system, an arrangement of finite events and objects that is disposed and disclosed, as it were, on a treadmill. The character goes through experiences, and then it is over.

It goes without saying that no one has ever seen a mimetic novel of the type I am describing. The body cannot go backwards or sidewards or imagine a future that has not come, but the mind can. And, of course, so does fiction. The body ages, but we remember its (and our) youth. By performing the miracle of recall, the mind incessantly transcends the barriers of chronos, transforms the biological line into the mental circle, repossesses what seemed over. Such mobility magically extends the parameters of the self's whereabouts in time and space, for the mind is free to travel back to all the places that the body has left; it is even free to travel to places that the body has never been. It follows, then, that the self moves along two separate axes: (1) the linear, unchangeable, relentless route of the body, and (2) the circular, even spiral, trajectory of the mind that invents its own itinerary. Of paramount interest to this study has been the interplay between those two axes; not only does every life frame that interplay, enmesh and interweave the performances of mind and body; but the novel is the sole literary genre to capture this mind-body dialectic. Neither poetry nor drama allow that fuller panorama we find in fiction: the co-existence of self, setting and time, the combination of inner and outer vantage points, the symbiosis between thinking, speaking, and doing. Because the novel is privy to the mind's operations, it may, through its strategies of presentation, break the non-stop advancement of the body and approximate the circles, ellipses, and pirouettes of consciousness itself.

How, then, can one assess the development charted in this study? What does it mean when the sparse inner life of Lazarillo, essentially snuffed out by the authority of the contingent world, is followed by the increasingly swollen egos of Marianne, Werther, Clarissa, and is finally completed by a sublime reversal whereby the self retreats entirely into the inner life, but, in so doing, energizes that realm so potently that it can proceed to swallow the world? Is there a historical, or at least a psycho-social, grid that we can impose on this sequence of fictions? Doubtless such a grid would tell us something about individualism, the sense of and desire for self-hood, as it relates to the (cultural, economic, social, aesthetic, and psychic) history of Western Europe from the Renaissance to the French Revolution.

No such large synthesis is going to be articulated in these final pages. Perhaps others can attempt such an undertaking.

We customarily interpret such changes of style and form in the light of literary schools and of cultural history; when we narrow in, it is usually to take into account the known "facts" of the biography. I would propose a far more elemental "source" for literary performance: the plight of character, the authority granted to gesture versus thought, the choice of the mimetic over the symbolic or generative—these strategies issue from authorial reaches beyond the scrutiny of literary history. The literature itself is *prima facie* evidence here: other than the art itself, what indices do we have of the writer's position along these axes, or his choice of energies? Can it surprise us that the potency of language tends to replace, to become, the potency of the author? As the author moves through time, he may well privilege the resources of his verbal medium: i.e., the capacity of words to make new worlds rather than to describe old ones, to create rather than to reflect experience, ultimately to enjoy liberties to which the flesh is not and cannot be heir. If my chapters chart a "history," it is an evolution known to all writers. And to non-writers as well.

I would prefer to interpret my findings and my evolution in the light of freedom and bondage, the interplay between the line and the circle which fiction mirrors. It is quite possible that my sequence of texts connotes nothing of historical interest, that the progression from marginal self to the written life is not even obliquely related to any or all historical

changes that took place in Europe between 1550 and 1789.
The history I am charting is indeed the history of the self, but
in a literal sense: the history of a single self, a single body,
every-body. The phases delineated in my study belong to
every life-story. The hunger for the good life can be assuaged
in multiple ways: food for Lazarillo, punning for Pablos,
thieving for Moll, recognition for Marianne, Manon for Des
Grieux, Lotte for Werther, the ultimate pleasure and freedom
of writing itself for Tristram and Rousseau. Gratification and
fulfillment are thus negotiated in quite different ways, and the
composite view of these novels should enhance our sense of humane coping. Seen together, these novels disclose the things
they could not say separately.

Here is, of course, the *raison d'être* of comparative criticism.
Let us juxtapose, for example, *Manon Lescaut* and *Tristram
Shandy*, as alternate strategies for survival and fulfillment.
Within each text we can see the relics of an old world, and
each protagonist—Des Grieux and Tristram—has to create a
new world. Des Grieux collides head-on with his society;
from beginning to end he asserts his passion, his new ethic,
and, at the end, he simply runs out of space to live, right off
the map. Tristram, on the other hand, transforms his serious
problems into the comic materials of his life, and he transcends the determinist limitations of his birth and even of his
mortality through the celebration of language and literature.
What was violent conflict or passionate gesture in *Manon Lescaut* is viewed humorously or hobbyhorsically in *Tristram
Shandy*. Finally, Prévost and Sterne are, themselves, creating
new worlds, new kinds of novels, each seminal in its own
way. Prévost stresses the affective, pathological dimension of
his protagonist, and he develops a sensuous style to embody
Des Grieux's feelings. Above all, Prévost's book is mimetic,
and it thereby places the two lovers squarely in conflict with
their world, with no escape routes, no hidden arenas of fantasy or dream. Prévost can neither break nor interfere with
the logic of his story. Both narrative and ethical authority are
granted to the needs of his character, the desires of the self.
Manon already looks to the 19th-century novel of antagonism
and revolt, of the romantic hero versus the degraded society,

and he also points to the dilemma of French realism, so
acutely described by Marxist critics such as Lukacs or Gold-
mann. He carries another message too: the drama of the self,
if presented through mimesis, can end only in defeat. Sterne's
new novel points directly to *Ulysses*; unlike the conflict novels
of Prévost, Richardson, and Goethe, *Tristram Shandy* is a
novel of comic transcendence; through metaphor and analogy, through the discovery of consciousness and language as
autonomous but "travelable" realms, Sterne explodes the mimetic tradition and the linear narrative, thereby vastly enlarg-
ing our world. The reader is in, in a different way, for pornography makes the reader fictionalize; Tristram's
pyrotechnics both display the quality of his soul and flaunt the
primacy of his medium. Tristram will be saved by his book.

The mimetic tradition honors certain precious allegiances,
however, certain priorities which already begin to be blurred
in Sterne and will disappear altogether in much modern fiction: these priorities are: (1) the body has got to make it if the
soul is going to, (2) if you do not win, you lose, (3) no amount
of authorial pzazz can erase or offset the tragedy of the narrated lives. Sterne magnificently connects his narrative with
his anatomy, his monkey-business with his serious business,
and Tristram's narrative tricks are directly related to his determinist dilemma. In later writers it will be possible to salvage a rather questionable life through formidable art, to
transform the human material into aesthetic material and
thereby win in the work whatever the character loses in the
life. Artistic treatment will tend to replace the solid but no
longer credible or attainable rewards of life: Moll, Pip, Rasti-
gnac, Emma Bovary want to make it in this world; Strether,
Stephen Dedalus, Marcel, Roquentin, and a host of others are
content to internalize, sublimate, or else write a book about
their experiences. What is compelling about the early fictions—even those that issue in *écriture*—is that the "inward
turn," or the foregrounding of consciousness, or the play of
virtuality, can never be seen merely as authorial *fiat*: the redemptive powers of language and consciousness and writing
are always enlisted to save the life, to salvage a self that can be
actualized in no other way.

If the movement from Lazarillo to Rousseau depicts the coming of age of fiction, it also mirrors, somewhat more simply still, the coming of age. The sum of energies and the amount of hunger in a person's life may be constant over the years, but the roads taken and the choices made will differ in different times of life. For children and young people the circle and the line must look marvelously alike: the body's future seems so unlimited, its past so brief, that there can be little awareness of determinisms, trade-offs, and the like; as the writer ages, the appeal of the circle, the peculiar freedoms of thought and language, must come to seem increasingly precious. Can it be accidental that many writers begin mimetic and end symbolic? The career of Goethe and Joyce is illuminating here: *Werther* and *Urfaust* depict the hunger for immediate gratification, for knowledge in the flesh, for unconstrained self-assertion; as Goethe matures, the motif of renunciation looms larger and larger; finally, the second part of Faust seems literary light years older than part one; the bourgeois drama of Faust and Gretchen has become a world stage, a realm of unlimited verbal magic and symbolic event in which Goethe achieves a staggering synthetic vision of Western culture; but the individual story of Faust has become merely a part of the mosaic. Joyce's development is equally enlightening: he achieves, in *The Dubliners*, a sparseness and toughness that earned the admiration of Pound and can still resist the symbolizing efforts of his current critics; the *Portrait* is his "collision" novel, the story of a swollen consciousness that seeks to fly past all nets that would constrain it; *Ulysses* is arguably literature's fullest embodiment of how the self negotiates between the line and the circle: Bloom, more than any character in fiction, is wise about freedom and determinism, about the axes of the body and the mind, the trade-offs between gesture and imagination; above all, *Ulysses* announces the growing prowess of language itself, language as a survival strategy and compensation for Bloom, but also language as inebriating play for Joyce; *Finnegans Wake*, somewhat like the second part of *Faust*, is the consummate verbal universe, the reservoir of myth and archetype in which individual gesture and need have little or no role to play.

The generative axis of the mind is the route of consciousness itself. Human beings are "free" to double back, mentally,
to times and places forever gone, physically. The circle authorizes us to construct a shape for our open-ended, chrono-
metric lives. In the course of this study we have seen that the
inner life may be an impossible luxury item (*Lazarillo*) or an
unpoliced, vertiginously free, place of its own (*Le Neveu de
Rameau*, *Tristram*, Rousseau); it is that full spectrum that ultimately commands our interest. The positions arrived at in
single texts are profoundly complementary; only by seeing
them together can we properly gauge their secret rationales,
their hidden costs. Because our own life is long and we each
are living out our life-story, it is good that we achieve a comparative overview of fiction's survival strategies. Fulfillment,
as the term indicates, may legitimately range from filling our
belly to filling the blank page. Writers do not discover the
barriers of contingency (men have died forever), but they
demonstrate, all the time, our peculiar freedom.

It should be clear that readers, just as much as writers, have
partie liée with the enabling powers of language. In the context
of this study, self-enactment has been assessed as a grim, life-
or-death affair, and I have repeatedly invoked the notions of
survival and coping. But, self-realization through language
and thought is also a leisurely, aristocratic venture, a sovereign way of overcoming the dreary limits of time, space, and
matter. It confers prowess, *droits de seigneur*, even divine rights
to all of us who are—and we all are—*roturier* in the flesh.
Through language our entire repertory can be played out;
thought enables us to see and taste what can be experienced in
no other way. We read books because life is always poor. The
mind alone can outdo Midas by making something out of
nothing.

No one has better illustrated the scope and exhilaration of
imaginative travel than Wallace Stevens; in his poem, "Someone puts together a pineapple," he beautifully demonstrates
how the generative mind creates a new world. The poet's
imagination "opens up" the pineapple into twelve possible
metaphoric extensions; he then adds:

These casual exfoliations are
Of the tropic of resemblances, sprigs
Of Capricorn or as the sign demands,
Apposites, to the slighest edge, of the whole
Undescribed composition of the sugar-cone,
Shiftings of an inchoate crystal tableau,
The momentary footings of a climb
Up the pineapple, a table Alp and yet
An Alp
                    (*The Palm at the End of the Mind*, pp. 298-299)[1]

Here is the lush, spawning yet delicate, activity of the imagination that makes hemispheres and tableaux simultaneously,
that endows pattern and grandeur to the mean phenomenal
world. The loveliest lines of the poem are perhaps "The momentary footings of a climb/Up the pineapple, a table Alp and
yet/An Alp." The imagination travels and climbs, achieves
vistas and makes conquests, is deliciously imperial as it colo-
nizes the world it invents. This is the stuff of fiction. Here is
the peculiar freedom of language and imagination: to project
and then to explore a domain open to the mind alone. The
body never does get very far, but Thoreau had, as he said,
"traveled a great deal in Concord." There is much that the
body cannot afford to experience: sickness, madness, death,
perhaps ecstasy, perhaps even mountain-climbing. Imagination enables us to approach and, *somehow*, to appropriate what
we dare not encounter in the flesh. Language both records and
provides the vehicle for these forays. In dealing with the
forms of self-enactment, I have assessed both language and
gesture in terms of cost and reward; Stevens, in insisting that
his imaginative quest is both "a table Alp and yet/An Alp,"
reminds us of our two axes, our essential doubleness. A kind
of humane equilibrium is adumbrated, a balance between the
two realms, a warning that neither can be lived in exclusively,
that the beauty and value of each comes from the other.
    Stevens also adds, in this poem, "This is everybody's

---

[1] Wallace Stevens, "Someone Puts Together a Pineapple," in *The Palm at
the End of the Mind* (New York, Vintage Books, 1972), pp. 298-299.

world." The splendid adventures of the soul may be doomed to take place in the imagination. But we know that the mind is not always on holiday or mountain climbing. The inner world—as the novel of consciousness is later to demonstrate—is no more easily colonized or personalized than New Orleans or London or Paris. The imperial self which ever seeks to impose or to retain its form is obliged to fight for its life wherever it goes. "Inside" defies us, as much as "outside" does. The free spaces of thought do not seem to be our own. Mundanely, amorphously, impersonally, language and imagination go through *their* games and routines in *our* heads, displaying, it would seem indiscriminately and incoherently, the bric-a-brac and fragments of our lives on the screen of our consciousness. The buzzing does not stop. We all sense that the inner world dwarfs the outer world, not in significance but in volume. Despite the claims of psychoanalysis, the assurance that we store only what is significant, that the proper analysis of our mental picture will reveal a coherent pattern—despite all this, we suspect that there is much in our heads that means nothing to us, that is the result of pollution rather than storage, that flaunts our permeability rather than our cogency.

Does the stuff of consciousness secretly beckon us toward self-enactment? Leo Bersani has brilliantly used the figures of center and circumference to denote, on the one hand, a recognizable, consistent core of self, a so-called (restrictive) identity, and, on the other, the dizzying freedom of circumference, of all the virtual selves created by consciousness and desire but rarely actualized in experience.[2] As I have suggested, however, this inner world may be just as impersonal and threatening of "self" as the alien outer world. Interior monologues, even such as that of Leopold Bloom, are often as random as a shopping list. Selfhood, to some extent, must mean assuming the list, yoking into the ineluctable integrity of our person all that happens in and to us. It is a recognition

---

[2] See, especially, Leo Bersani's *Balzac to Beckett: Center and Circumference in French Fiction* (New York: Oxford University Press, 1970) and *A Future for Astyanax: Character and Desire in Literature* (Boston: Little, Brown, 1976).

that all our verbal and mental freedoms are lodged and housed in one body that will probably live only once. We make our meanings centripetally, confronting the world both in us and beyond us, but insisting on its possible relation *to* us. It is that homing desire, that perhaps conservative and preservative effort to achieve and retain our own form, to be today recognizably like we were yesterday (not identically, only recognizably), to realize that the differences between now and our life ten years ago are *our* differences, that constitutes the challenge and the value of "self" as a concept in literature and in life. What is at stake is ultimately no more nor less than the shape and meaning of a life. So much precedes, forms and outlasts us: language, the accidents of time, space and genes, the countless forces which beset and condition us during our stay. Whether we speak of Heideggerian *Geworfenheit* or give our preference to Stevens' more genial view:

> From this the poem springs: that we live in a place
> That is not our own, and much more, nor ourselves
> And hard it is, in spite of blazoned days.[3]

the homelessness of our condition is unarguable. No less beggared than Lazarillo, no less orphaned than Marianne, no less disinherited than Clarissa, no less expelled than Rousseau, we nonetheless make our estate out of the shape of our life. We connect and fuse, by our sovereign desire to do so, what is separate and alien. There is no grander colonizing effort than the formation of a life.

Proust often remarked how miraculous it is that we wake up as the same individual who fell asleep scant hours earlier, given the extraordinary experiences we encounter during our dreams. But dreams are merely the most flagrant hiatus in our precarious sense of identity. Each moment has its anarchic appeal; each day is filled with adventures where we are other and with eddies where we are no one. How, then, can we speak of years and decades? How can we conceivably enter into professions and relationships? Many, no doubt, feel that inertia and routine take all the honors, but that may well be a

---

[3] Wallace Stevens, "Notes Toward a Supreme Fiction," *ibid.*, p. 210.

short-sighted and niggardly view. Life itself is so mobile that those old, scoffed-at, virtues—consistency, fidelity, identity—appear almost miraculous and chivalric in their effort to halt flux and impose form. The making of character is no less than an aesthetic and moral adventure, a deployment of energies both inwardly and outwardly, a confident letting go and a generous perseverance. To yoke the myriad world outside us to the equally multiple one within, and thereby to make and retain a self over time, these are prodigious attempts to stand up straight in a world that goes dizzily around, and, as such, they bear tribute to a uniquely human work of art. In the face of contemporary claims for more freedom, more consciousness, more mobility, let us not forget the value of self as repository, as (fictive) home for the variety of experiences we undergo. Self-realization, enacted in so many guises throughout the books we have discussed, is more than survival and affirmation: it is the creation of integrity where there would be discreteness and the celebration of pattern and sameness where there would be anarchy. These fictions, from *Lazarillo* to the *Confessions*, display something fine.

Self is not an anachronism. It may be, as Stevens would say, the "supreme fiction" of our lives, as it goes about colonizing, corralling, and taking stock of its multiple estates; as joint caretaker and voyager, it both assesses and experiences the double trajectory in the body and in the mind. Writing may serve the entire enterprise. It may speak of the body and the belly as well as the new worlds open to lying and imagining; it has futurity as well, and can speak of us when we can no longer speak. Its unavowed sympathies must lie with the inner world, because it is so uniquely suited to convey, even to make that inner world. In that world, language is the coin of the realm; it is the only human resource guaranteed to enrich the species. Art, and, to a much lesser degree, criticism, has always constituted a kind of "Open Sesame" whereby such treasures might be glimpsed and even exchanged. The writer, including this literary critic, performs, by his words, a speech act and a gesture of self-exposure and a measure of self-enactment that can happen in no other way. To end a book is to express a fundamental faith in the power of the word.

Notes of Original Language

The Marginal Self

Lazarillo de Tormes

Source: *La vida de Lazarillo de Tormes*, ed. Julio Cejador y Frauca (Madrid: Espasa-Calpe, S.A., Clásicos Castellanos, 1969), pp. 59-60. All quotations are taken from this edition.

[1] Yo por bien tengo que cosas tan señaladas y por ventura nunca oydas ni vistas vengan a noticia de muchos y no se entierren en la sepultura del oluido . . . (pp. 59-60)

[2] . . . mas, de que vi que con su venida mejoraua el comer, fuyle queriendo bien . . . (p. 70)

[3] . . . senteme como solia, estando recibiendo aquellos dulces tragos, mi cara puesta hazia el cielo, vn poco cerrados los ojos por mejor gustar el sabroso liquor, sintió el desesperado ciego que agora tenia tiempo de tomar de mí vengança y con toda su fuerça, alçando con dos manos aquel dulce y amargo jarro, le dexó caer sobre mi boca, ayudandose, como digo, con todo su poder, de manera que el pobre Lázaro, que de nada desto se guardaua, antes, como otras vezes, estaua descuydado y gozoso, verdaderamente me pareció que el cielo, con todo lo que en él ay, me auía caydo encima. (pp. 87-88)

[4] Començó a prouar el angelico calderero vna y otra de vn gran sartal, que dellas traya, e yo ayudalle con mis flacas oraciones. Quando no me cato, veo en figura de panes, como dizen, la cara de Dios dentro del arcaz. (p. 124)

[5] . . . moria mala muerte, tanto que otra cosa no hazia en viendome solo sino abrir y cerrar el arca y contemplar en aquella cara de Dios, que ansi dizen los niños. (p. 128)

[6] ". . . agora cerrando los agujeros del arca, cerrasse la puerta a mi consuelo y l'abriesse a mis trabajos." (p. 131)

[7] Y como la antiquissima arca, por ser de tantos años, la hallasse

sin fuerça y coraçon, antes muy blanda y carcomida, luego se me rindió y consintió en su costado por mi remedio vn buen agujero. Esto hecho, abro muy passo la llagada arca y, al tiento, del pan, que hallé partido, hize segun deyuso esta escripto. (p. 133)

[8] Torna a buscar clauos por la casa y por las paredes y tablillas y a taparselos. Venida la noche y su reposo, luego era yo puesto en pie con mi aparejo y, quantos él tapaua de dia, destapaua yo de noche.

En tal manera fué y tal priessa nos dimos, que sin dubda por esto se deuió dezir: Donde vna puerta se cierra, otra se abre. (p. 134)

[9] Leuantose y asiome por la cabeça y llegose a olerme. E como deuió sentir el huelgo, a vso de buen podenco, por mejor satisfazerse de la verdad y con la gran agonia que lleuaua, asiendome con las manos, abriame la boca mas de su derecho y desatentadamente metia la nariz. La qual él tenia luenga y afilada y a aquella sazon con el enojo se auia augmentado vn palmo. Con el pico de la qual me llego a la gulilla.

Y con esto y con el gran miedo que tenia y con la breuedad del tiempo, la negra longaniza aun no auia hecho assiento en el estomago, y lo mas principal, con el destiento de la cumplidissima nariz, medio quasi ahogandome, todas estas cosas se juntaron y fueron causa que el hecho y golosina se manifestasse y lo suyo fuesse buelto a su dueño. De manera que, antes que el mal ciego sacasse de mi boca su trompa, tal alteracion sintió mi estomago, que le dio con el hurto en ella, de suerte que su nariz e la negra malmaxcada longaniza a vn tiempo salieron de mi boca. (pp. 98-99)

[10] "Este, dezia yo, es pobre y nadie da lo que no tiene; mas el auariento ciego y el malauenturado mezquino clérigo, que, con darselo Dios a ambos, al vno de mano besada y al otro de lengua suelta, me matauan de hambre, aquellos es justo desamar y aqueste de auer manzilla." (pp. 176-177)

[11] . . . preguntandome muy por extenso de dónde era y cómo auia venido a aquella ciudad. (p. 151)

[12] Y comienço a cenar y morder en mis tripas y pan y dissimuladamente miraua al desuenturado señor mio, que no partia sus ojos de mis faldas, que aquella sazon seruian de plato. Tanta lastima aya Dios de mi, como yo auia dél, porque senti lo que sentia y muchas vezes auia por ello passado y passaua cada dia. Pensaua si seria bien comedirme a combidalle; mas, por me auer dicho que auia comido, temiame no aceptaria el combite. Finalmente, yo desseua aquel peccador ayudasse a su trabajo del mio y se desayunasse como el dia antes hizo, pues auia major aparejo, por ser mejor la vianda y menos mi hambre. (pp. 170-171)

[13] Yo simplemente llegué, creyendo ser ansi. Y, como sintió que

tenía la cabeça par de la piedra, afirmó rezio la mano y diome vna gran calabaçada en el diablo del toro, que mas de tres dias me duró el dolor de la cornada y dixome:

"Necio, apprende: que el moço del ciego vn punto ha de saber mas que el diablo."

Y rió mucho la burla.

Paresciome que en aquel instante desperté de la simpleza en que como niño dormido estaua.

Dixe entre mi:

"Verdad dize éste, que me cumple abiuar el ojo y auisar, pues solo soy, y pensar cómo me sepa valer." (pp. 77-78)

[14] En el qual el dia de oy viuo y resido a seruicio de Dios y de vuesta merced. Y es que tengo cargo de pregonar los vinos, que en esta ciudad se venden, y en almonedas y cosas perdidas, acompañar los que padecen persecuciones por justicia y declarar a bozes sus delictos: pregonero, hablando en buen romance. (p. 232)

[15] Y acuerdome que, estando el negro de mi padrastro trebejando con el moçuelo, como el niño via a mi madre e a mi blancos y a él no, huya dél con miedo para mi madre y, señalando con el dedo, dezia: "¡Madre, coco!"

Respondió él riendo: "¡Hideputa!"

Yo, aunque bien mochacho, noté aquella palabra de mi hermanico e dixe entre mi: "¡Quantos deue de auer en el mundo, que huyen de otros, porque no se veen a si mesmos!" (pp. 71-72)

[16] De manera que, continuando la posada y conuersación, mi madre vino a darme vn negrito muy bonito . . . (pp. 70-71)

[17] Porque, allende de ser buena hija, y diligente, seruicial, tengo en mi señor acipreste todo fauor y ayuda. Y siempre en el año le da en vezes al pie de vna carga de trigo, por las pascuas su carne y quando el par de los bodigos, las calças viejas, que dexa. E hizonos alquilar vna casilla par de la suya. Los domingos y fiestas casi todas las comiamos en su casa. (pp. 234-235)

[18] Hasta el dia de oy nunca nadie nos oyó sobre el caso; antes, quando alguno siento que quiere dezir algo della, le atajo y le digo:

"Mirá, si soys amigo, no me digays cosa con que me pese, que no tengo por mi amigo al que me haze pesar. . . ." (p. 240)

La Vida del Buscón

Source: Quevedo, Francisco de, *El Buscón*, ed. Américo Castro (Madrid: Espasa-Calpe, S.A., Clásicos Castellanos, 1973).

[1] Yo, viendo que era batalla nabal, y que no se había de hacer a caballo, comencé a apearme; mas tal golpe me le dieron en la cara,

que yendo a empinarse, cayó conmigo en una—hablando con perdón—privada . . . (p. 29)

² "Pablo, abre el ojo que asan carne; mira por ti, que aquí no tienes otro padre ni madre." (p. 63)

³ . . . me parecía estaba con mi proprio padre y con mis hermanos. (p. 64)

⁴ . . . aquel maldito que estaba junto a mí se pasó a mi cama, y se proveyó en ella, y puso la ropa . . . (p. 64)

⁵ . . . torné a dormir, y como entre sueños me revolcase, cuando desperté halléme sucio hasta las trencas. (p. 65)

⁶ . . . porque tal detrozo como yo hice en el ante, no le hiciera una bala en el de un coleto. Vino la olla, y comímela en dos bocados casi toda, sin malicia; pero con priesa tan fiera, que parecía que aun en los dientes no la tenía bien segura. Dios es mi padre, que no come un cuerpo más puesto el montón de la Antigua de Valladolid—que lo deshace en veinticuatro horas—, que yo despaché el ordinario, pues fué con más priesa que un extraordinario el correo. (p. 171-172)

⁷ . . . subieron la comida . . . en unos mendrugos de platos y retacillos de cántaros y tinajas . . . Sentáronse a comer, en cabecera el demandador, los demás sin orden. . . . Sorbióse el corchete tres de puro tinto, brindándome a mí; pero yo agüelo. El porquero hacía más razones que decíamos todos. . . .

Parecieron en la mesa cinco pasteles de a cuatro; y tomando un hisopo, después de haber quitado las hojaldres, dijeron un responso todos, con un *requiem aeternam*, por el ánima del difunto cuyas eran aquellas carnes. Dijo mi tío: "Ya os acordáis, sobrino, lo que os escribí de vuestro padre": vínoseme a la memoria. Ellos comieron, pero yo pasé con los suelos solos; quedéme con la costumbre, y ansí, siempre que como pasteles, rezo una avemaría por el que Dios haya.

Dieron fin a dos jarros, que hacían casi cinco azumbres; y así, el corchete y el de las ánimas se pusieron las suyas tales, que trayendo un plato de salchichas, que parecían de dedos de negros, dijo uno que para qué traían pebetes guisados. Ya mi tío estaba tal, que alargando la mano y asiendo una, dijo—con la voz media áspera y ronca, y los ojos nadando en mosto—: "Sobrino, por este pan de Dios, que crió a su imagen y semejanza, que no he comido mejor cosa en mi vida." Yo—que vi al corchete que, alargando la mano, tomó el salero, y dijo: "Caliente está este caldo," y que el porquero se llenó el puño de sal, diciendo: "es bueno el apetitillo para beber," y se lo chocló en la boca—, comencé a reír por una parte, y a rabiar por otra. Trajeron caldo, y el de las ánimas tomó con entrambas manos una escudilla, diciendo: "Dios bendijo la limpieza"; y alzándola para sorberla, por llevarla a la boca, la llevó al carrillo; y volcándola, se puso todo de arriba abajo que era vergüenza; y él, como se vió así, fuése a levantar; y como pesaba algo la cabeza, quiso ahirmar sobre la mesa (que era destas movedizas), trastornóla toda y manchó a los demás; tras esto decía que el porquero le había empujado. El porquero que vió que el otro se le caía encima, levantóse, y alzando el instrumento de hueso, le dió con él una trompetada, y asiéronse a puños; y estando juntos los dos, y teniéndole el demandador mordido de un carrillo, con dos vuelcos y alteración, el porquerizo vomitó cuando había comido en las barbas del demandador. Mi tío, que estaba más en juicio, decía que quién había traído a su casa tantos clérigos. Yo que los ví, que ya en suma multiplicaban, metí en paz la brega, desasí a los dos, y levanté del suelo al corchete, el cual estaba llorando con gran tristeza. Eché a mi tío en la cama, el cual hizo cortesía a un velador de palo que tenía, pensando que era uno de los convidados. (pp. 135-138)

[8] Hacíase toda entre gallos, ratones, jumentos, raposas, lobos y jabalíes, como fábulas de Isopo. Yo le alabé la traza y la invención, a lo cual me respondió: "Ello cosa mía es, pero no se ha hecho otra tal en el mundo, y la novedad es más que todo; y si no, salgan a representarla; será cosa muy famosa."

—"¿Cómo se podrá representar—le dije yo—, si han de entrar los mismos animales, y ellos no hablan?"

—"Ésa es la dificultad, que, a no haber ésa ¿había cosa más alta? Pero yo tengo pensado de hacerla toda de papagayos y tordos, que hablan, y meter para el entremés monas." (pp. 108-109)

[9] . . . comieron una comida eterna, sin principio ni fin . . . (p. 35)

[10] Cenaron, y cenamos todos, y no cenó ninguno. (p. 40)

[11] Mandáronme leer el primer nominativo, y era de manera mi hambre, que me desayuné con la mitad de las razones, comiéndomelas. (p. 40)

[12] . . . sonaba en ellos el eco de cualquier palabra. (p. 48)

[13] . . . salió de la cárcel con tanta honra, que le acompañaron doscientos cardenales, sino que a ninguno llamaban eminencia. (p. 17)

[14] Ítem, habiendo considerado que esta seta infernal de hombres condenados a perpetuo concepto, despedazadores de vocablos y volteadores de razones, han pegado el dicho achaque de poesía a las mujeres, declaramos que nos tenemos por desquitados con este mal que les han hecho, del que nos hicieron en Adam. Y por cuanto el siglo está pobre y necesitado de oro y plata, mandamos quemar las coplas a los poetas, como franjas viejas, para sacar oro y plata, pues en los más versos hacen sus damas de todos metales como estatuas de Nabuco." (pp. 114-115)

¹⁵ . . . había salido capitán en una comedia, y combatido con moros en una danza. A los de Flandes decía, que había estado en la China; y a los de la China, en Flandes. Trataba de formar un campo, y nunca supo sino espulgarse en él; nombraba castillos, y apenas los había visto en los ochavos. Celebraba mucho la memoria del señor don Juan, y oíle decir muchas veces de Luis Quijada que había sido honrado amigo. Nombraba turcos, galeones y capitanes, todos los que había leído en unas coplas que andan desto; y como él no sabía nada de mar—porque no tenía de naval más que el comer nabos— . . . (p. 175)

¹⁶ . . . hervían devotos. Al fin me puse como pude; podíase ir a ver las diferentes posturas de los amantes: cuál, sin pestañear, mirando, con su mano puesta en la espada y la otra en el rosario, estaba como figura de piedra sobre sepulcro; otro, alzadas las manos y extendidos los brazos a lo seráfico, recibiendo las llagas; cuál, con la boca más abierta que la de mujer pedigüeña, sin hablar palabra, le enseñaba a su querida las entrañas por el gaznate; otro, pegado a la pared, dando pesadumbre a los ladrillos, que parecía medirse con la esquina; otro, se paseaba como si le hubieran de querer por el portante, como a macho; otro, con una carta en la mano, a uso de cazador con carne, que parecía llamaba al halcón . . . pero de la de arriba, adonde estaban las monjas, era cosa de ver también; porque las vistas era una torrecilla llena toda de rendijas, y una pared con deshilados, que ya parecía salvadera, ya pomo de olor. Estaban todos los agujeros poblados de brújulas: allí se veía una pepitoria, una mano o un pie; en otra parte había cosas de sábado: cabezas y lenguas, aunque faltaban sesos; a otro lado se mostraba buhonería: una mostraba el rosario, otra, el pañizuelo; en otra parte asomaba un guante; por otra, un listón verde; unas hablaban algo recio otras tosían; cuál hacía la seña de los sombrereros (como si sacara arañas), ceceando. (pp. 250-253)

¹⁷ "Todos empuñaron aguja y hilo para hacer un punteado en un rasgado y otro. Cuál, para culcusirse debajo del brazo, estirándole se hacía L; uno, hincado de rodillas, remedaba [quizá remedando] un 5 de guarismo, socorría a los cañones ['pliegues abullonados de as calzas'] otro, por plegar las entrepiernas, metiendo la cabeza entre ellas, se hacía un ovillo. No pintó tan extrañas posturas Bosco como yo vi." (note, pp. 162-163)

¹⁸ . . . tan juntos, que parecíamos herramienta de estuche. (p. 161)

¹⁹ "Poca fe tienes con la religión y orden de los caninos; no falta el Señor a los cuervos ni a los grajos, ni aun a los escribanos, ¿y había de faltar a los traspillados? Poco estómago tienes. (p. 167)

²⁰ . . . y aún no bastaba, porque ya no reparaban sino en que pedía para otros, y no se preciaba de la sopa. (p. 176)

[21] ... que como tenemos por enemigo declarado al sol, por cuanto nos descubre los remiendos, puntadas y trapos, nos ponemos abiertas las piernas a su rayo, y en la sombra del suelo vemos la que hacen los andrajos y las hilachas de las entrepiernas; y con unas tijeras hacemos la barba a las calzas; y como siempre gastan tanto las entrepiernas, quitamos cuchilladas de atrás para poblar lo de adelante; y solemos traer la trasera tan pacífica por falta de cuchilladas, que se queda en las puras bayetas: sábelo sola la capa, y guardámonos de días de aire, y de subir por escaleras claras o a caballo. (pp. 149-150)

[22] Estamos obligados a andar a caballo una vez al mes, aunque sea en pollino, por las calles públicas; y obligados a ir en coche una vez en el año, aunque sea en la arquilla o trasera . . . (p. 151)

[23] ... y porque no le conociese, soltó de detrás de las orejas el cabello, que traía recogido, y quedó nazareno, entre Verónica y caballero lanudo; plantóse un parche en un ojo, y púsose a hablar italiano conmigo. Esto pudo hacer mientras el otro venía . . . (p. 166)

[24] ... era caballero de alquiler . . . (pp. 165-166)

[25] ... que haría que pareciese que se ardía la casa . . . (p. 196)

[26] Hubo fama de que reedificabe doncellas, resucitaba cabellos y encubría canas. Unos la llamaban zurcidora de gustos; otros, algebrista de voluntades desconcertadas . . . (pp. 17-18)

[27] ... era adquiridora de voluntades y corcheta de gustos . . . (p. 75)

[28] ... y en lo que ella era más extremada era en hacer doncellas no lo siendo. (p. 227)

[29] ... y era tan maldito, que nos obligaba a traer las traseras con carlancas, como mastines, y no había quien osase ventosear, de miedo de acordarle dónde tenía las asentaderas. (p. 186)

[30] ... la cara toda acuchillada. Tenía nones las orejas y pegadas las narices, aunque no tan bien como la cuchillada que se las partía. (p. 187)

[31] Tenía una potra muy grande, y atábase con un cordel el brazo por arriba, y parecía que tenía hinchada la mano y manca, y calentura, todo junto. (p. 234)

[32] Trataba en vidas, y era tendero de cuchilladas, y no le iba mal; traía la muestra de ellas en su cara, y por las que le habían dado, concertabo tamaño y hondura de las que había de dar. Decía: "No hay tal maestro como el bien acuchillado"; y tenía razón, porque la cara era una cuera, y él un cuero. (pp. 261-262)

[33] ... dos cuerpos de corchetes de sus malditas ánimas . . . (p. 267)

[34] Pasábamoslo en la iglesia notablemente, porque al olor de los retraídos vinieron putas, desnudándose para vestirnos. Aficionóseme la Grajal, y vistióme de nuevo de sus colores . . . (pp. 267-268)

Simplicissimus

Source: Grimmelshausen, Hans Jacob Christoffel von, *Der abenteuerliche Simplicissimus* (Darmstadt: Wissenschaftliche Buchgesellschaft, 1966).

[1] . . . denn fressen und saufen, Hunger und Durst leiden, huren und buben, raßlen und spielen, schlemmen und demmen, morden und ermordet werden, totschlagen und wieder zu Tod geschlagen werden, tribulieren und wieder gedrillt werden, jagen und wieder gejaget werden, ängstigen und wieder geängstiget werden, rauben und wieder geraubt werden, plündern und wieder geplündert werden, sich fürchten und wieder gefürchtet werden, Jammer anstellen und wieder jämmerlich leiden, schlagen und wieder geschlagen werden; und in Summa nur verderben und beschädigen und hingegen wieder verderbt und beschädigt werden, war ihr ganzes Tun und Wesen; . . . (p. 46)

[2] Wiewohl ich nicht bin gesinnet gewesen, den friedliebenden Leser mit diesen Reutern in meines Knans Haus und Hof zu führen, weil es schlimm genug darin hergehen wird: So erfordert jedoch die Folge meiner Histori, daß ich der lieben Posterität hinterlasse, was für Grausamkeiten in diesem unserm Teutschen Krieg hin und wieder verübet worden . . . (p. 15)

[3] Er sagte: "Bub bis fleißig, loß di Schoff nit ze wit vunananger laffen, un spill wacker uff der Sackpfeiffa, daß der Wolf nit komm, und Schada dau, denn he is a solcher veirboinigter Schelm und Dieb, der Menscha und Vieha frißt, un wenn dau awer farlässi bist, so will eich dir da Buckel arauma." Ich antwortet mit gleicher Holdseligkeit; "Knano, sag mir aa, wei der Wolf seihet? Eich huun noch kan Wolf gesien." "Ah dau grober Eselkopp," repliziert' er hinwieder, "dau bleiwest dein Lewelang a Narr, geit meich wunner, was aus dir wera wird, bist schun su a grußer Dölpel, un waist noch neit, was der Wolf für a veirfeußiger Schelm is." (p. 12)

[4] Hoho, gedachte ich, dies sind die rechten Käuz! dies sind die vierbeinigten Schelmen und Dieb, davon dir dein Knan sagte, denn ich sah anfänglich Roß und Mann (wie hiebevor die Amerikaner die spanische Kavallerie) für ein einzige Kreatur an, und vermeinte nicht anders, als es müßten Wölfe sein, wollte derowegen diesen schrecklichen Centauris den Hundssprung weisen, und sie wieder abschaffen. (p. 14)

[5] . . . da wurde ich eines großen Manns gewahr, in langen schwarzgrauen Haaren, die ihm ganz verworren auf den Achseln herum lagen, er hatte einen wilden Bart, fast formiert wie ein Schweizerkäs, sein Angesicht war zwar bleichgelb und mager, aber

doch ziemlich lieblich, und sein langer Rock mit mehr als tausen
Stückern von allerhand Tuck überflickt und aufeinandergesetzt, um
Hals und Leib hatte er ein schwere eiserne Ketten gewunden wie
S. Wilhemus, un sah sonst in meinen Augen so scheußlich und für-
chterlich aus, daß ich anfing zu zittern, wie ein nasser Hund, was
aber meine Angst mehret', war, daß er ein Kruzifix ungefähr sechs
Schuh lang an seine Brust drückte . . . (pp. 20-21)

[6] . . . dieser alte Greis müßte ohn Zweifel der Wolf sein, davon mir
mein Knan kurz zuvor gesagt hatte: In solcher Angst wischte ich mit
meiner Sackpfeif hervor, welche ich als meinen einzigen Schatz noch
vor den Reutern salviert hatte; ich blies zu, stimmte an, und ließ
mich gewaltig hören, diesen greulichen Wolf zu vertreiben . . . (p.
21)

[7] . . . ich trat ihm nach gegen ein großes Haus zu, allwo ich im Saal
Männer, Weiber und ledige Personen so schnell untereinander her-
umhaspeln sah, daß es frei wimmelte; die hatten ein solch Getrippel
und Gejohl, daß ich vermeinte, sie wären alle rasend worden . . . am
Schweiß, der ihnen über die Gesichter floß, und an ihrem Geschnauf
konnte ich abnehmen, daß sie sich stark zerarbeitet hatten; aber ihre
fröhlichen Angesichter gaben zu verstehen, daß sie solche Bemühun-
gen nicht sauer ankommen. (p. 93-94)

[8] . . . gleich darauf erhub sich zwischen diesen beiden ein Gelispel,
daraus ich zwar nichts anders verstund, als daß sich das eine Teil über
den bösen Geruch desselben Orts beklagte, und hingegen der ander
Teil das erste hinwiederun tröstete; "Gewißlich schönste Dame,"
sagt' er, "mir ist versichert von Herzen leid, daß uns die Früchte der
Lieb zu genießen vom mißgünstigen Glück kein ehrlicher Ort ge-
gönnet wird; aber ich kann daneben beteuren, daß mir Ihre holdse-
lige Gegenwart diesen verächtlichen Winkel anmutiger macht als das
lieblichste Paradeis selbsten." Hierauf hörte ich küssen, und ver-
merkte seltsame Posturen, ich wußte aber nicht was es war oder be-
deuten sollte, schwieg derowegen noch fürders so still als ein Maus.
Wie sich aber auch sonst ein possierlich Geräusch erhub, und der
Gänsstall, so nur von Brettern unter die Stiege getäfelt war, zu
krachen anfing, zumaln das Weibsbild sich anstellte, als ob ihr gar
wehe bei der Sach geschehe, da gedachte ich, das sind zwei von den
wütenden Leuten, die den Boden helfen eintreten und sich jetzt hier-
her begeben haben, da gleicherweis zu hausen und dich ums Leben
zu bringen. (pp. 99-100)

[9] "Lieber guter Freund, weil ich dein Bestes zu suchen unterstehe,
erfreue ich mich, daß ich hier allein mit dir reden kann; ich weiß, daß
du kein Narr bist, wie du dich stellest zumalen auch in diesem elen-

den und verächtlichen Stand nicht zu leben bebehrest. Wenn dir nun
deine Wohlfahrt lieb ist, auch zu mir als einem ehrlichen Mann dein
Vertrauen setzen willst, so kannst du mir deiner Sachen Bewandtnis
erzählen, so will ich hingegen, wo möglich, mit Rat und Tat bedacht
sein, wie dir etwa zu helfen sein möchte, damit du aus deinem
Narrnkleid kommest." (p. 157)

[10] Mit diesem Musterschreiber, welcher auch wie sein Vater Ulrich Herzbruder hieß, machte ich ein solche Freundschaft, daß wir
ewige Brüderschaft zusammen schwuren, kraft dessen wir einander
in Glück und Unglück, in Lieb und Leid nimmermehr verlassen
wollten. (p. 165)

[11] "Ach Freund," sagte er, "um Herzbruders willen gebt mir auch
zu essen!" Da er solches sagte, ging mirs durchs Herz, und befand,
daß es Herzbruder selbsten war, ich wäre beinahe in Ohnmacht ge-
sunken, da ich ihn in einem so elenden Stand sah, doch erhielt ich
mich, fiel ihm um den Hals und setzte ihn zu mir, da uns denn beiden, mir aus Mitleiden und ihm aus Freud, die Augen übergingen.
(p. 381-382)

La Princesse de Clèves

Source: Lafayette, Mme. de, *La Princesse de Clèves*, in *Romans et Nouvelles*, ed.
Émile Magne (Paris: Garnier Frères, 1958).

[1] . . . elle faisait souvent à sa fille des peintures de l'amour; elle
lui montrait ce qu'il a d'agréable pour la persuader plus aisément sur
ce qu'elle lui en apprenait de dangereux; elle lui contait le peu de sincérité des hommes, leurs tromperies et leur infidélité, les malheurs
domestiques où plongent les engagements; et elle lui faisait voir,
d'un autre côté, quelle tranquillité suivait la vie d'une honnête
femme, et combien la vertu donnait d'éclat et d'élévation à une personne qui avait de la beauté et de la naissance; mais elle lui faisait voir
aussi combien il était difficile de conserver cette vertu, que par une
extrême défiance de soi-même et par un grand soin de s'attacher à ce
qui seul peut faire le bonheur d'une femme, qui est d'aimer son mari
et d'en être aimée. (p. 248)

[2] . . . elle l'épouserait même avec moins de répugnance qu'un
autre, mais qu'elle n'avait aucune inclination particulière pour sa personne. (pp. 257-258)

[3] Elle ne se trouva plus la même disposition à dire à sa mère ce
qu'elle pensait des sentiments de ce prince qu'elle avait eue à lui parler de ses autres amants; sans avoir un dessein formé de lui cacher,
elle ne lui en parla point. (p. 270)

[4] Mme. de Tournon m'était infidèle et j'apprends son infidélité et sa trahison le lendemain que j'ai appris sa mort, dans un temps où mon âme est remplie et pénétrée de la plus vive douleur et de la plus tendre amour que l'on ait jamais senties; dans un temps où son idée est dans mon coeur comme la plus parfaite chose qui ait jamais été, et la plus parfaite à mon égard, je trouve que je me suis trompé et qu'elle ne mérite pas que je la pleure; cependant j'ai le même affliction de sa mort que si elle m'était fidèle et je sens son infidélité comme si elle n'était point morte. . . . je paye à une passion feinte qu'elle a eue pour moi, le meme tribut de douleur que je croyais devoir à une passion véritable. Je ne puis ni haïr, ni aimer sa mémoire; je ne puis me consoler ni m'affliger. (pp. 286-288)

[5] Jamais affliction n'a été si piquante et si vive . . . ce mal, qu'elle trouvait si insupportable, était la jalousie avec toutes les horreurs dont elle peut être accompagnée. (p. 310)

[6] Vous êtes amoureux, continua-t-elle, et, parce que vous ne vous fiez peut-être à personne, vous croyez que votre amour n'est pas su; mais il est connu, et même des personnes intéressées. On vous observe, on sait les lieux où vous voyez votre maîtresse, on a dessein de vous y surprendre. (p. 315)

[7] . . . ce prince était un chef-d'oeuvre de la nature; ce qu'il avait de moins admirable, c'était d'être l'homme du monde le mieux fait et le plus beau. (p. 243)

[8] —Pour moi, dit tout haut M. de Nemours, je suis l'homme du monde qui doit le moins y en avoir [belief in astrology]; et, se tournant vers Mme. de Clèves, auprès de qui il était: "On m'a prédit, lui dit-il tout bas, que je serais heureux par les bontés de la personne du monde pour qui j'aurais la plus violente et la plus respectueuse passion. Vous pouvez juger, madame, si je dois croire aux prédictions."

Mme. la Dauphine qui crut, par ce que M. de Nemours avait dit tout haut, que ce qu'il disait tout bas était quelque fausse prédiction qu'on lui avait faite, demanda à ce prince ce qu'il disait à Mme. de Clèves. S'il eût eu moins de présence d'esprit, il eût été surpris de cette demande. Mais prenant la parole sans hésiter.

—Je lui disais, madame, répondit-il, que l'on m'a prédit que je serais élevé à une si haute fortune que je n'oserais même y prétendre.

—Si l'on ne vous a fait que cette prédiction, répartit Mme. la Dauphine en souriant, et pensant à l'affaire d'Angleterre, je ne vous conseille pas de décrier l'astrologie, et vous pourriez trouver des raisons pour la soutenir.

Mme. de Clèves comprit bien ce que voulait dire Mme. la Dauphine; mais elle entendait bien aussi que la fortune dont M. de Nemours voulait parler, n'était pas d'être roi d'Angleterre. (pp. 297-298)

[9] L'on ne peut exprimer ce que sentirent M. de Nemours et Mme. de Clèves de se trouver seuls et en état de se parler pour la première fois. (p. 382)

[10] Un jour, entre autres, on se mit à parler de la confiance. Je dis qu'il n'y avait personne en qui j'en eusse une entière; que je trouvais que l'on se repentait toujours d'en avoir et que je savais beaucoup de choses dont je n'avais jamais parlé. La reine me dit qu'elle m'en estimait davantage; qu'elle n'avait trouvé personne en France qui eût du secret et que c'était ce qui l'avait le plus embarrassée, parce que cela lui avait ôté le plaisir de donner sa confiance; que c'était une chose nécessaire, dans la vie, que d'avoir quelqu'un à qui on pût parler, et surtout pour les personnes de son rang. (p. 314)

[11] —Il faut nous quitter, ma fille, lui dit-elle, en lui tendant la main; le péril où je vous laisse et le besoin que vous avez de moi augmentent le déplaisir que j'ai de vous quitter. Vous avez de l'inclination pour M. de Nemours; je ne vous demande point de me l'avouer: je ne suis plus en état de me servir de votre sincérité pour vous conduire. Il y a déjà longtemps que je me suis aperçue de cette inclination; mais je ne vous en ai pas voulu parler d'abord, de peur de vous en faire apercevoir vous-même. Vous ne la connaissez que trop présentement; vous êtes sur le bord du précipice: il faut de grands efforts et de grandes violences pour vous retenir. Songez ce que vous devez à votre mari; songez ce que vous vous devez à vous même, et pensez que vous allez perdre cette réputation que vous vous êtes acquise et que je vous ai tant souhaitée. Ayez de la force et du courage, ma fille, retirez-vous de la cour, obligez votre mari de vous emmener, ne craignez point de prendre des partis trop rudes et trop difficiles, quelque affreux qu'ils vous paraissent d'abord: ils seront plus doux dans les suites que les malheurs d'une galanterie. Si d'autres raisons que celles de la vertu et de votre devoir vous pouvaient obliger à ce que je souhaite, je vous dirais que, si quelque chose était capable de troubler le bonheur que j'espère en sortant de ce monde, ce serait de vous voir tomber comme les autres femmes; mais, si ce malheur vous doit arriver, je reçois la mort avec joie, pour n'en être pas le témoin. (pp. 277-278)

[12] —N'en doutez pas, madame, répliqua M. de Clèves, vous vous êtes trompée; vous avez attendu de moi des choses aussi impossibles que celles que j'attendais de vous. Comment pouviez-vous espérer que je conservasse de la raison? Vous aviez donc oublié que je vous aimais éperdument et que j'étais votre mari? L'un des deux peut porter aux extrémités: que ne peuvent point les deux ensemble? Eh! que ne [f]ont-ils aussi, continua-t-il; je n'ai que des sentiments violents et

incertains dont je ne suis pas le maître. Je ne me trouve plus digne de vous; vous ne me paraissez plus digne de moi. Je vous adore, je vous hais, je vous offense, je vous demande pardon; je vous admire, j'ai honte de vous admirer. Enfin il n'y a plus en moi ni de calme, ni de raison. (pp. 362-363)

[13] Ils s'enfermèrent pour y travailler; on donna ordre à la porte de ne laisser entrer personne et on renvoya tous les gens de M. de Nemours. Cet air de mystère et de confidence n'était pas d'un médiocre charme pour ce prince et même pour Mme. de Clèves. La présence de son mari et les intérêts du vidame de Chartre la rassuraient en quelque sorte sur ses scrupules. Elle ne sentait que le plaisir de voir M. de Nemours, elle en avait une joie pure et sans mélange qu'elle n'avait jamais sentie: cette joie lui donnait une liberté et un enjouement dans l'esprit que M. de Nemours ne lui avait jamais vus et qui redoublaient son amour. Comme il n'avait point eu encore de si agréables moments, sa vivacité en était augmentée; et quand Mme. de Clèves voulut commercer à se souvenir de la lettre et à l'écrire, ce prince, au lieu de lui aider sérieusement, ne faisait que l'interrompre et lui dire des choses plaisantes. Mme. de Clèves entra dans le même esprit de gaieté, de sorte qu'il y avait déjà longtemps qu'ils étaient enfermés, et on était déjà venu deux fois de la part de la reine dauphine pour dire à Mme. de Clèves de se dépêcher, qu'ils n'avaient pas encore fait la moitié de la lettre. (p. 328)

[14] Et qui est-il, madame, cet homme heureux qui vous donne cette crainte? Depuis quand vous plaît-il? Qu'a-t-il fait pour vous plaire? Quel chemin a-t-il trouvé pour aller à votre coeur? (p. 123)

[15] Mme. de Clèves n'était pas peu embarrassée. La raison voulait qu'elle demandât son portrait; mais, en le demandant publiquement, c'était apprendre à tout le monde les sentiments que ce prince avait pour elle, et, en le lui demandant en particulier, c'était quasi l'engager à lui parler de sa passion. Enfin elle jugea qu'il valait mieux le lui laisser, et elle fut bien aise de lui accorder une faveur qu'elle lui pouvait faire sans qu'il sût même qu'elle la lui faisait. (p. 302)

[16] Il vit qu'elle était seule; mais il la vit d'une si admirable beauté qu'à peine fut-il maître du transport que lui donna cette vue. Il faisait chaud, et elle n'avait rien, sur sa tête et sur sa gorge, que ses cheveux confusément rattachés. Elle était sur un lit de repos, avec une table devant elle, où il y avait plusieurs corbeilles pleines de rubans; elle en choisit quelques-uns, et M. de Nemours remarqua que c'étaient des mêmes couleurs qu'il avait portées au tournoi. Il vit qu'elle en faisait des noeuds à une canne des Indes, fort extraordinaire, qu'il avait portée quelque temps et qu'il avait donnée à sa soeur, à qui Mme. de

Clèves l'avait prise sans faire semblant de la reconnaître pour avoir été à M. de Nemours. Après qu'elle eut achevé son ouvrage avec une grâce et une douceur que répandaient sur son visage les sentiments qu'elle avait dans le coeur, elle prit un flambeau et s'en alla, proche d'une grande table, vis-à-vis du tableau du siège de Metz, où était le portrait de M. de Nemours; elle s'assit et se mit à regarder ce portrait avec une attention et une rêverie que la passion seule peut donner. (pp. 366-367)

[17] Car, enfin, elle m'aime, disait-il; elle m'aime, je n'en saurais douter; les plus grands engagements et les plus grandes faveurs ne sont pas des marques si assurées que celles que j'en ai eues. Cependant je suis traité avec la même rigueur que si j'étais haï; j'ai espéré au temps, je n'en dois plus rien attendre; je la vois toujours se défendre également contre moi et contre elle-même. Si je n'étais point aimé, je songerais à plaire; mais je plais, on m'aime, et on me le cache. Que puis-je donc espérer, et quel changement dois-je attendre dans ma destinée? Quoi! je serai aimé de la plus aimable personne du monde et je n'aurai cet excès d'amour que donnent les premières certitudes d'être aimé que pour mieux sentir la douleur d'être maltraité! Laissez-moi voir que vous m'aimez, belle princesse, s'écria-t-il, laissez-moi voir vos sentiments; pourvu que je les connaisse par vous une fois en ma vie, je consens que vous repreniez pour toujours ces reigueurs dont vous m'accabliez. Regardez-moi du moins avec ces mêmes yeux dont je vous ai vue cette nuit regarder mon portrait; pouvez-vous l'avoir regardé avec tant de douceur et m'avoir fui moi-même si cruellement? Que craignez-vous? Pourquoi mon amour vous est-il si redoutable? Vous m'aimez, vous me le cachez inutilement; vous même m'en avez donné des marques involontaires. Je sais mon bonheur; laissez-m'en jouir, et cessez de me rendre malheureux. (p. 369)

Orphans

La Vie de Marianne

[1] Son amie lui demande l'histoire de sa vie, et elle l'écrit à sa manière. Marianne n'a aucune forme d'ouvrage présente à l'esprit. Ce n'est point un auteur, c'est une femme qui pense, qui a passé par différents états, qui a beaucoup vu, enfin dont la vie est un tissu d'événements qui lui ont donné une certaine connaissance du coeur et du caractère des hommes. (p. 55)

[2] Et moi, je devinais la pensée de toutes ces personnes-là sans au-

cun effort; mon instinct ne voyait rien là qui ne fût de sa connaissance. (p. 59)

[3] Je me levai donc pour l'aller prendre; et dans le trajet qui n'était
que de deux pas, ce coeur si fier s'amollit, mes yeux se mouillèrent,
je ne sais comment, et je fis un grand soupir, ou pour moi, ou pour
Valville, ou pour la belle robe; je ne sais pour lequel des trois. (p. 132)

[4] . . . mais ne savez-vous pas que notre âme est encore plus superbe
que vertueuse, plus glorieuse qu'honnête, et par conséquent plus délicate sur les intérêts de sa vanité que sur ceux de son véritable honneur. (p. 71)

[5] Estimez mes qualités tant qu'il vous plaira, vous diraient tous les
hommes, vous me ferez grand plaisir, pourvu que vous m'honoriez,
moi qui les ai, et qui ne suis pas elles; car si vous me laissez là, si vous
négligez ma personne, je ne suis pas content, vous prenez à gauche;
c'est comme si vous me donniez le superflu et que vous me refusassiez le nécessaire; faites-moi vivre d'abord, et me divertissez apres.
(p. 87)

[6] Je n'étais rien, je n'avais rien qui pût me faire considérer; mais à
ceux qui n'ont ni rang, ni richesses qui en imposent, il leur reste une
âme, et c'est beaucoup; c'est quelquefois plus que le rang et la richesse, elle peut faire face à tout. (p. 178)

[7] . . . notre vie, pour ainsi dire, nous est moins chère que nous, que
nos passions. A voir quelquefois ce qui se passe dans notre instinct
là-dessus, on dirait que, pour être, il n'est pas nécessaire de vivre; que
ce n'est que par accident que nous vivons, mais que c'est naturellement que nous sommes. On dirait que, lorsqu'un homme se tue, par
exemple, il ne quitte la vie que pour se sauver, que pour se débarrasser d'une chose incommode; ce n'est pas de lui dont il ne veut plus,
mais bien du fardeau qu'il porte. (p. 129)

[8] . . . car enfin j'aimais un homme auquel il ne fallait plus penser;
et c'était là un sujet de douleur; mais, d'un autre côté, j'en étais
tendrement aimé, de cet homme, et c'est une grande douceur. Avec
cela on est du moins tranquille sur ce qu'on vaut; on a les honneurs
essentiels d'une aventure, et on prend patience du reste. (p. 191)

[9] Quand je dis que je vais vous faire le portrait de ces deux dames,
j'entends que je vous en donnerai quelques traits. On ne saurait
rendre ce que sont les personnes. (p. 166)

[10] J'ai vu une jolie femme dont la conversation passait pour un enchantement, personne au monde ne s'exprimait comme elle; c'était
la vivacité, c'était la finesse même qui parlait: les connaisseurs n'y
pouvaient tenir de plaisir. La petite vérole lui vint, elle en resta extrêmement marquée: quand la pauvre femme reparut, ce n'était plus
qu'une babillarde incommode. (p. 8)

[11] . . . j'ai à vous répondre une chose qui doit empêcher messieurs les parents d'être encore inquiets sur le mariage qu'ils appréhendent entre M. de Valville et moi; c'est que jamais il ne se fera; je le garantis, j'en donne ma parole et on peut s'en fier à moi; et si je ne vous en ai pas assuré avant que Mme. de Miran arrivât, vous aurez la bonté de m'excuser, Monseigneur; ce qui m'a empêché de le faire, c'est que je n'ai pas cru qu'il fût à propos, ni honnête à moi de renoncer à M. de Valville, pendant qu'on me menaçait pour m'y contraindre. (p. 335)

[12] Allez, mademoiselle, oubliez tout ce qui s'est passé ici; qu'il reste comme nul, et consolez-vous d'ignorer qui vous êtes. La noblesse de vos parents est incertaine, mais celle de votre coeur est incontestable, et je la préférerais, s'il fallait opter. (p. 357)

[13] Adieu, la petite aventurière; vous n'êtes encore qu'une fille de condition, nous dit-on, mais vous n'en demeurerez pas là, et nous serons bien heureuses, si au premier jour vous ne vous trouvez pas une princesse. (p. 338)

[14] Mais je n'ai pas eu besoin d'amour pour être charmé de vous, je n'ai eu besoin que de savoir les qualités de votre âme . . . Que m'importe à moi votre famille? Quand on la connaîtrait, fût-elle royale, ajouterait-elle quelque chose au mérite personnel que vous avez? Et puis les âmes ont-elles des parents? Ne sont-elles pas toutes d'une condition égale? Eh bien! ce n'est qu'à votre ame à qui j'en veux. (p. 423)

[15] Monsieur lui dis-je, savez-vous mon histoire?

Oui, mademoiselle, reprit-il, je la sais, voilà pourquoi vous me voyez ici; c'est elle qui m'a appris que vous valez mieux que tout ce que je connais dans le monde, c'est elle qui m'attache à vous. (p. 421)

Collision

Manon Lescaut

Source: Abbé Prévost, *Manon Lescaut*, eds. Deloffre and Picard (Paris: Garnier Frères, 1965).

[1] Touche au bout du monde, et mène-moi quelque part où je ne puisse jamais être séparé de Manon. (p. 106)

[2] J'y faisais entrer une maison écartée, avec un petit bois et un ruisseau d'eau douce au bout du jardin, une bibliothèque composée de livres choisis, un petit nombre d'amis vertueux et de bon sens, une table propre, mais frugale et modérée. J'y joignais un commerce de lettres avec un ami qui ferait son séjour à Paris, et qui m'informerait

des nouvelles publiques, moins pour satisfaire ma curiosité que pour me faire un divertissement des folies des hommes. (p. 40)

³ Quel passage, en effet, de la situation tranquille où j'avais été, aux mouvements tumultueux que je sentais renaître! J'en étais épouvanté. Je frémissais, comme il arrive lorsqu'on se trouve la nuit dans une campagne écartée: on se croit transporté dans un nouvel ordre de choses; on y est saisi d'une horreur secrète, dont on ne se remet qu'après avoir considéré longtemps tous les environs. (p. 45)

⁴ C'étaient des campagnes stériles et inhabitées, où l'on voyait à peine quelques roseaux et quelques arbres dépouillés par le vent. (p. 184)

⁵ Où fuir? dans un pays inconnu, désert, ou habité par des bêtes féroces, et par des sauvages aussi barbares qu'elles? (p. 193)

⁶ Nous avions à traverser, jusqu'à leurs colonies, de stériles campagnes de plusieurs journées de largeur, et quelques montagnes si hautes et si escarpées que le chemin en paraissait difficile aux hommes les plus grossiers et les plus vigoreux. (p. 197)

⁷ . . . avait fait sa déclaration en fermier général, c'est-à-dire en lui marquant dans une lettre que le payement serait proportionné aux faveurs. (p. 46)

⁸ Rien n'est plus admirable, et ne fait plus d'honneur à la vertu, que la confiance avec laquelle on s'adresse aux personnes dont on connaît parfaitement la probité. On sent qu'il n'y a point de risque à courir. Si elles ne sont pas toujours en état d'offrir du secours, on est sûr qu'on en obtiendra du moins de la bonté et de la compassion. Le coeur, qui se ferme avec tant de soin au reste des hommes, s'ouvre naturellement en leur présence, comme une fleur s'épanouit à la lumière du soleil, dont elle n'attend qu'une douce influence. (p. 57)

⁹ Notre entretien fut plein d'amitié. Il voulut être informé de mes dispositions. Je lui ouvris mon coeur sans réserve, excepté sur le dessein de ma fuite. Ce n'est pas à vos yeux, cher ami, lui dis-je, que je veux paraître ce que je ne suis point. (p. 90)

¹⁰ Un coeur de père est le chef-d'oeuvre de la nature; elle y règle elle-même tous les ressorts. (p. 163)

¹¹ Mon coeur s'ouvrit à mille sentiments de plaisir dont je n'avais jamais eu l'idée. Une douce chaleur se répandit dans toutes mes veines. (p. 21)

¹² . . . qui pût lui faire goûter parfaitement les douceurs de l'amour. (p. 61)

¹³ On le délivra de mes mains. J'avais presque perdu moi-même la force et la respiration. O Dieu! m'écriai-je, en poussant mille soupirs; justice du Ciel! Faut-il que je vive un moment, après une telle in-

famie? Je voulus me jeter encore sur le barbare qui venait de
m'assassiner. On m'arrêta. Mon désespoir, mes cris et mes larmes
passaient toute imagination. Je fis des choses si étonnantes, que tous
les assistants, qui en ignoraient la cause, se regardaient les uns les
autres avec autant de frayeur que de surprise. (p. 85)

¹⁴ Le commun des hommes n'est sensible qu'à cinq ou six passions, dans le cercle desquelles leur vie se passe, et où toutes leurs
agitations se réduisent. Otez-leur l'amour et la haine, le plaisir et la
douleur, l'espérance et la crainte, ils ne sentent plus rien. Mais les
personnes d'un caractère plus noble peuvent être remuées de mille
façons différentes; il semble qu'elles aient plus de cinq sens, et
qu'elles puissent recevoir des idées et des sensations qui passent les
bornes ordinaires de la nature. (p. 81)

¹⁵ Qu'ai-je à mettre en balance avec elle? Je n'y ai rien mis jusqu'à
présent. Elle me tient lieu de gloire, de bonheur, et de fortune. (p.
112)

¹⁶ Nous étions encore au lit, lorsqu'un exempt de police entra dans
notre chambre avec une demi-douzaine de gardes. (p. 78)

¹⁷ Nous étions dans le délire du plaisir, et le glaive était suspendu
sur nos têtes. (p. 151)

¹⁸ Nous étions prêts à nous mettre au lit. Il ouvre la porte, et il
nous glâce le sang par sa vue. O Dieu! c'est le vieux G.M. dis-je à
Manon. Je saute sur mon épée; elle était malheureusement embarrassée dans mon ceinturon. Les archers, qui virent mon mouvement,
s'approchèrent aussitôt pour me la saisir. Un homme en chemise est
sans résistance. (p. 152)

¹⁹ Il ne se trouva rien de manqué à son ajustement, excepté la culotte que j'avais malheureusement oubliée. L'oubli de cette pièce nécessaire nous eût, sans doute, apprêtés à rire si l'embarras où il nous
mettait eût été moins sérieux. J'étais au désespoir qu'une bagatelle de
cette nature fût capable de nous arrêter. Cependant, je pris mon parti,
qui fut de sortir moi-même sans culotte. Je laissai la mienne à
Manon. Mon surtout était long, et je me mis, à l'aide de quelques
épingles, en état de passer décemment à la porte. (pp. 105-106)

²⁰ Je te jure, mon cher Chevalier, que tu es l'idole de mon coeur,
et qu'il n'y a que toi au monde que je puisse aimer de la façon que je
t'aime; mais ne vois-tu pas, ma pauvre chère âme, que, dans l'état où
nous sommes réduits, c'est une sotte vertu que la fidélité? Crois-tu
qu'on puisse être bien tendre lorsqu'on manque de pain? (pp. 68-69)

²¹ Et puis, tu es une chimiste admirable, ajoutai-je en l'embrassant,
tu transformes tout en or.
Vous serez donc la plus riche personne de l'univers, me répondit-

elle, car, s'il n'y eut jamais d'amour tel que le vôtre, il est impossible aussi d'être aimé plus tendrement que vous l'êtes. (p. 187)

[22] Monsieur, c'est que nos deux chairs se touchent de bien proche. (pp. 59-60)

[23] Puissent votre fortune et votre argent périr sans ressource, et vous rester seul et nu, pour sentir la vanité des biens qui vous ont follement enivré! (p. 65)

[24] Nous nous assîmes au milieu d'une vaste plaine, sans avoir pu trouver un arbre pour nous mettre à couvert. (p. 198)

Die Leiden des jungen Werthers

Source: Johann Wolfgang Goethe, *Die Leiden des jungen Werthers*, in *Gedenkausgabe der Werke, Briefe und Gespräche*, ed. Ernst Beutler (Zurich: Artemis Verlag, 1953), Vol. IV.

[1] Sage das nicht weiter; es gibt Leute, die es mir verübeln würden. (p. 386)

[2] Und, mein Lieber! ist nicht vielleicht das Sehnen in mir nach Veränderung des Zustandes eine innere, unbehagliche Ungeduld, die mich überall hin verfolgen wird. (p. 433)

[3] . . . und gestern nacht, da ich zu Bette gehen wollte, und mit mir selbst allerlei schwatzte, sagte ich so auf einmal: Gute Nacht, lieber Werther, und mußte hernach selbst über mich lachen. (p. 469)

[4] Heute führte ich es schnell nach der Lippe, und die Zähne knisterten mir. (p. 419)

[5] Mein Tagebuch, das ich seit einiger Zeit vernachlässiget, fiel mir heut' wieder in die Hände, und ich bin erstaunt, wie ich so wissentlich in das alles, Schritt vor Schritt, hineingegangen bin! Wie ich über meinen Zustand immer so klar gesehen und doch gehandelt habe, wie ein Kind, jetzt noch so klar sehe und es noch keinen Anschein zur Besserung hat. (p. 422)

[6] Daß ihr Menschen rief ich aus, um von einer Sache zu reden, gleich sprechen müßt: das ist töricht, das ist klug, das ist gut, das ist bös! Und was will das alles heißen? Habt ihr deswegen die inneren Verhältnisse einer Handlung erforscht? Wißt ihr mit Bestimmtheit die Ursachen zu entwickeln, warum sie geschah, warum sie geschehen mußte? (p. 425)

[7] Ich könnte jetzt nicht zeichnen, nicht einen Strich, und bin nie ein größerer Malerer gewesen, als in diesen Augenblicken. (p. 384)

[8] Wenn das liebe Tal um mich dampft und die hohe Sonne an der Oberfläche der undurchdringlichen Finsternis meines Waldes ruht

und nur einzelne Strahlen sich in das innere Heiligtum stehlen, ich
dann im hohen Grase am fallenden Bache liege und näher an der
Erde tausend mannigfaltige Gräschen mir merkwürdig werden;
wenn ich das Wimmeln der kleinen Welt zwischen Halmen, die un-
zähligen, unergründlichen Gestalten der Würmchen, der Mückchen
näher an meinem Herzen fühle, und fühle die Gegenwart des All-
mächtigen, der uns nach seinem Bilde schuf, das Wehen des Alllie-
benden der uns in ewiger Wonne schwebend trägt und erhält—mein
Freund, wenn's dann um meine Augen dämmert und die Welt um
mich her und der Himmel ganz in meiner Seele ruhn, wie die Gestalt
einer Geliebten; dann sehne ich mich oft und denke: ach, könntest du
dem Papier das einhauchen, was so voll, so warm in dir lebt, daß es
würde der Spiegel deiner Seele, wie deine Seele ist der Spiegel des
unendlichen Gottes. (pp. 384-385)

⁹ . . . wenn ich dann die Vögel um mich den Wald beleben hörte,
und die Millionen Mückenschwärme im letzten roten Strahle der
Sonne mutig tanzten, und ihr letzter zuckender Blick den summen-
den Käfer aus seinem Grase befreite; und das Schwirren und Weben
um mich auf den Boden aufmerksam machte und das Moos, das
meinem harten Felsen seine Nahrung abzwingt, und das Geniste, das
den dürren Sandhügel hinunter wächst, mir das innere, glühende, heilige Leben der Natur eröffnete: wie faßte ich das alles in mein
warmes Herz, fühlte mich in der überfließenden Fülle wie vergöttert,
und die herrlichen Gestalten der unendlichen Welt bewegten sich all-
belebend in meiner Seele. (p. 431)

¹⁰ Ungeheure Berge umgaben mich, Abgründe lagen vor mir, und
Wetterbäche stürzten herunter, die Flüsse strömten unter mir, und
Wald und Gebirg erklang; und ich sah sie wirken und schaffen inein-
ander in den Tiefen der Erde, alle die unergründlichen Kräfte . . . (p.
431)

¹¹ . . . und die Menschen dann sich in Häuslein zusammen sichern
und sich annisten und herrschen in ihrem Sinne über die weite Welt!
Armer Tor, der du alles so gering achtest, weil du so klein bist! (p.
431)

¹² Vom unzugänglichen Gebirge über die Einöde, die kein Fuß be-
trat, bis ans Ende des unbekannten Ozeans weht der Geist des Ewig-
schaffenden und freut sich jedes Staubes, der ihn vernimmt und lebt.
—Ach, damals, wie oft habe ich mich mit Fittichen eines Kranichs,
der über mich hinflog, zu dem Ufer des ungemessenen Meeres ge-
sehnt, aus dem schäumenden Becher des Unendlichen jene schwel-
lende Lebenswonne zu trinken und nur einen Augenblick, in der ein-
geschränkten Kraft meines Busens, einen Tropfen der Seligkeit des

Wesens zu fühlen, das alles in sich und durch sich hervorbringt. (p. 431)

[13] Kannst du sagen: Das ist! da alles vorübergeht? da alles mit der Wetterschnelle vorüberrollt, so selten die ganze Kraft seines Daseins ausdauert, ach! in den Strom fortgerissen, untergetaucht und an Felsen zerschmettert wird? Da ist kein Augenblick, der nicht dich verzehrte und die Deinigen um dich her, kein Augenblick, da du nicht ein Zerstörer bist, sein mußt. Der harmloseste Spaziergang kostet tausend armen Würmchen das Leben, es zerrüttet ein Fußtritt die mühseligen Gebäuden der Ameisen und stampft eine kleine Welt in ein schmäliches Grab. Ha! nicht die große, seltene Not der Welt, diese Fluten, die eure Dörfer wegspülen, diese Erdbeben, die eure Städte verschlingen, rühren mich; mir untergräbt das Herz die verzehrende Kraft, die in all der Natur verbergen liegt, die nichts gebildet hat, das nicht seinen Nachbar, nicht sich selbst zerstörte. Und so taumle ich beängstigt! Himmel und Erde und ihre webenden Kräfte um mich her: ich sehe nichts als ein ewig verschlingendes, ewig wiederkäuendes Ungeheuer. (p. 432)

[14] O meine Freunde! warum der Strom des Genies so selten ausbricht, so selten in hohen Fluten hereinbraust und eure staunende Seele erschüttert?—Liebe Freunde, da wohnen die gelassenen Herren auf beiden Seiten des Ufers, denen ihre Gartenhäuschen, Tulpenbeete und Krautfelder zu Grunde gehen würden und die daher in Zeiten mit Dämmen und Ableiten der knüftig drohenden Gefahr abzuwehren wissen. (p. 392)

[15] Die Natur findet keinen Ausweg aus dem Labyrinthe der verworrenen und widersprechenden Kräfte, und der Mensch muß sterben. (p. 429)

[16] Wenn ich bei ihr gesessen bin, zwei, drei Stunden, und mich an ihrer Gestalt, an ihrem Betragen, an dem himmlischen Ausdruck ihrer Worte geweidet habe, und nun so nach und nach alle meine Sinnen aufgespannt werden, mir es düster vor den Augen wird, ich kaum noch höre und es mich an die Gürgel faßt, wie ein Meuchelmörder, dann mein Herz in wilden Schlägen den bedrängten Sinnen Luft zu machen sucht uhd ihre Verwirrung nur vermehrt—Wilhelm, ich weiß oft nicht, ob ich auf der Welt bin! Und—wenn mich manchmal die Wehmut das Übergewicht nimmt und Lotte mir den elenden Trost erlaubt, auf ihrer Hand meine Beklemmung auszuweinen, —so muß ich fort! muß hinaus! und schweife dann weit im Feld umher. Einen gähen Berg zu klettern, ist dann meine Freude, durch einen unwegsamen Wald einen Pfad durchzuarbeiten, durch die Hecken, die mich verletzen, durch die Dornen, die mich

zerreißen ... O Wilhelm! die einsame Wohnung einer Zelle, das härene Gewand und der Stachelgürtel wären Labsale, nach denen meine Seele schmachtet. Adieu! Ich sehe dieses Elendes kein Ende als das Grab. (pp. 434-435)

17 Ja, es ist so, wie die Natur sich zum Herbste neigt, wird es Herbst in mir und um mich her. Meine Blätter werden gelb, und schon sind the Blätter der benachbarten Bäume abgefallen. (p. 488)

18 Und dies Herz ist jetzt tot, aus ihm fließen keine Entzückungen mehr, meine Augen sind trocken, und meine Sinnen, die nicht mehr von erquickenden Tränen gelabt werden, ziehen ängstlich meine Stirn zusammen. Ich leide viel, denn ich habe verloren, was meines Lebens einzige Wonne war, die heilige belebende Kraft, mit der ich Welten um mich schuf; sie ist dahin! (p. 467)

19 Ich will sterben. —Es ist nicht Verzweiflung, es ist Gewißheit, daß ich ausgetragen habe und daß ich mich opfere für dich. (p. 489)

20 '. . . aber, Werther, sollen wir uns wiederfinden? wiedererkennen? Was ahnen Sie? was sagen Sie?' (p. 437)

21 Siehe, wir träumen, wenn wir vom Tode reden. Ich habe manchen sterben sehen; aber so eingeschränkt ist die Menschheit, daß sie für ihres Daseins Anfang und Ende keinen Sinn hat. Jetzt noch mein, dein! dein, o Geliebte! Und einen Augenblick—getrennt, geschieden—vielleicht auf ewig? —Nein, Lotte, nein—wie kann ich vergehen? wie kannst du vergenen? Wir *sind* ja! —Vergehen! —Was heißt das? Das ist wieder ein Wort, ein leerer Schall! ohne Gefühl für mein Herz. Tot, Lotte! eingescharrt der kalten Erde, so eng! so finster! (p. 501-502)

22 . . . iche habe das Herz gefühlt, die große Seele, in deren Gegenwart ich mir schien mehr zu sein, als ich war, weil ich alles war, was ich sein konnte. Guter Gott! blieb da eine einzige Kraft meiner Seele ungenutzt? Konnt' ich nicht vor ihr das ganze wunderbare Gefühl entwickeln, mit dem mein Herz die Natur umfaßt? War unser Umgang nicht ein ewiges Weben von der feinsten Empfindung, dem schärfsten Witze, dessen Modifikationen bis zur Unart alle mit dem Stempel des Genies bezeichnet waren? (p. 387)

23 '. . . daß du nights vermagst mit deinem ganzen Vermögen, und die Angst dich inwendig krampft, daß du alles hingeben möchtest, dem untergehenden Geschöpfe einen Tropfen Stärkung, einen Funken Mut einflößen zu können.' (p. 412)

24 Guter Herr, ach, mein Hans ist mir gestorben! Es war der jüngste ihrer Knaben. Ich war stille. Und mein Mann, sagte sie, ist aus der Schweiz zurück und hat nichts mitgebracht, und ohne gute Leute hätte er sich herausbetteln müssen, er hatte das Fieber unterwegs gekriegt. (p. 457)

[25] Es ist nichts, worum sie einander nicht bringen. Gesundheit, guter Name, Freudigkeit, Erholung! . . . Manchmal möcht' ich sie auf den Knien bitten, nicht so rasend in ihre eigenen Eingeweide zu wüten. (pp. 446-447)

[26] Ich hörte sie leise reden; sie erzählten einander unbedeutende Sachen, Stadtneuigkeiten: wie diese heiratet, wie jene krank, sehr krank ist—sie hat einen trockenen Husten, die Knochen stehn ihr zum Gesichte heraus, und kriegt Ohnmachten; ich gebe keinen Kreuzer für ihr Leben, sagte die eine. —Der N.N. ist auch so übel dran, sagte Lotte. —Er ist schon geschwollen, sagte die andere. — Und meine lebhafte Einbildungskraft versetzte mich ans Bett dieser Armen; ich sah sie, mit welchem Widerwillen sie dem Leben den Rücken wandten, wie sie—Wilhelm! und meine Weibchen redeten davon, wie man eben davon redet—daß ein Fremder stirbt. (p. 465)

[27] Ich möchte mir oft die Brust zerreißen und das Gehirn einstoßen, daß man einander so wenig sein kann. Ach, die Liebe, Freude, Wärme und Wonne, die ich nicht hinzubringe, wird mir der andere nicht geben, und mit einem ganzen Herzen voll Seligkeit werde ich den andern nicht beglücken, der kalt und kraftlos vor mir steht. (p. 466)

[28] Der Tisch ward gedeckt, und eine gute Freundin, die nur etwas zu fragen kam, gleich gehen wollte—und blieb, machte die Unterhaltung bei Tische erträglich; man zwang sich, man redete, man erzählte, man vergaß sich. (p. 506)

[29] Denn nur insofern wir mitempfinden, haben wir Ehre, von einer Sache zu reden. (p. 427)

[30] Vergebens, daß der gelassene, vernünftige Mensch den Zustand des Unglücklichen übersieht, vergebens, daß er ihm zuredet! Ebenso wie ein Gesunder, der am Bette des Kranken steht, ihm von seinen Kräften nicht das geringste einflößen kann. (p. 427)

[31] "Ein gutes junges Geschöpf, das in dem engen Kreis häuslicher Beschäftigungen, wöchentlicher bestimmter Arbeit herangewachsen war, das weiter keine Aussicht von Vergnügen kannte, als etwa sonntags in einem nach und nach zusammengeschafften Putz mit ihresgleichen um die Stadt spazieren zu gehen, vielleicht alle hohe Feste einmal zu tanzen und übrigens mit aller Lebhaftigkeit des herzlichsten Anteils manche Stunde über den Anlaß eines Gezänkes, einer üblen Nachrede mit einer Nachbarin zu verplaudern. —Deren feurige Natur fühlt nun endlich innigere Bedürfnisse, die durch die Schmeicheleien der Männer vermehrt werden; ihre vorigen Freuden werden ihr nach und nach unschmackhaft, bis sie endlich einen Menschen antrifft, zu dem ein unbekanntes Gefühl sie unwiderstehlich hinreißt, auf den sie nun alle ihre Hoffnungen wirft, die Welt

rings um sich vergißt, nichts hört, nichts sieht, nichts fühlt, als ihn, den einzigen, sich nur sehnt nach ihm, dem einzigen. . . ." (pp. 427-428)

[32] Ja, ich müßte die Gabe des größten Dichters besitzen, um dir zugleich den Ausdruck seiner Gebärden, die Harmonie seiner Stimme, das heimliche Feuer seiner Blicke lebendig darstellen zu können. (pp. 394-395)

[33] . . . unüberwindlich bemächtigte sich die Teilnehmung seiner, und es ergriff ihn eine unsägliche Begierde, den Menschen zu retten. Er fühlte ihn so unglücklich, er fand ihn als Verbrecher selbst so schuldlos, er setzte sich so tief in seine Lage, daß er gewiß glaubte, auch andere davon zu überzeugen. (pp. 479-480)

[34] *Ihr könnt seinem Geist und seinem Charakter eure Bewunderung und Liebe, seinem Schicksale eure Tränen nicht versagen.* (p. 382)

Les Liaisons dangereuses

Source: Choderlos de Laclos, *Les Liaisons dangereuses*, ed. Yves Le Hir (Paris: Editions Garnier Frères, 1952).

[1] Tout en me consolant, une main était restée dans la mienne; le joli corps était appuyé sur mon bras, et nous étions extrêmement rapprochés. Vous avez sûrement remarqué combien, dans cette situation, à mesure que la défense mollit, les demandes et les refus se passent de plus près; comment la tête se détourne et les regards se baissent, tandis que les discours, toujours prononcés d'une voix faible, deviennent rares et entrecoupés. Ces symptômes précieux annoncent, d'une manière non équivoque, le consentement de l'âme. (p. 277)

[2] Ah! sans doute il faut séduire sa fille: mais ce n'est pas assez, il faut la perdre; et puisque l'âge de cette maudite femme la met à l'abri de mes coups, il faut la frapper dans l'objet de ses affections. (p. 94)

[3] . . . je ne connais rien de si plat que cette facilité de bêtise, qui se rend sans savoir ni comment ni pourquoi, uniquement parce qu'on l'attaque et qu'elle ne sait pas résister. Ces sortes de femmes ne sont absolument que des machines à plaisir.

Vous me direz qu'il n'y a qu'à n'en faire que cela, et que c'est assez pour nos projets. A la bonne heure! mais, n'oublions pas que de ces machines-là, tout le monde parvient bientôt à en connaître les ressorts et les moteurs; ainsi, que pour se servir de celle-ci sans danger, il faut se dépêcher, s'arrêter de bonne heure, et la briser ensuite. (p. 249)

⁴ J'ai dirigé sa promenade de manière qu'il s'est trouvé un fossé à franchir; et, quoique fort leste, elle est encore plus timide: vous jugez bien qu'une prude craint de sauter le fossé. Il a fallu se confier à moi. J'ai tenu dans mes bras cette femme modeste. Nos préparatifs et le passage de ma vieille tante avaient fait rire aux éclats la folâtre dévote: mais dès que je me fus emparé d'elle, par une adroite gaucherie, nos bras s'enlacèrent mutuellement. Je pressai son sein contre le mien; et, dans ce court intervalle, je sentis son coeur battre plus vite. L'aimable rougeur vint colorer son visage, et son modeste embarras m'apprit assez *que son coeur avait palpité d'amour et non de crainte.* Ma tante cependant s'y trompa comme vous, et se mit à dire: "L'enfant a eu peur"; mais la charmante candeur de l'enfant ne lui permit pas le mensonge, et elle répondit naïvement: "Oh non, mais . . ." Ce seul mot m'a éclairé. (p. 18)

⁵ Je me relevai alors; et gardant un moment le silence, je jetais sur elle, comme au hasard, des regards farouches qui, pour avoir l'air d'être égarés, n'en étaient pas moins clairvoyants et observateurs. Le maintien mal assuré, la respiration haute, la contraction de tous les muscles, les bras tremblants, et à demi élevés, tout me prouvait assez que l'effet était tel que j'avais voulu le produire . . . (p. 296)

⁶ Cette utile curiosité, en servant à m'instruire, m'apprit encore à dissimuler; forcée souvent de cacher les objets de mon attention aux yeux de ceux qui m'entouraient, j'essayai de guider les miens à mon gré; j'obtins dès lors de prendre à volonté ce regard distrait que vous avez loué si souvent. Encouragée par ce premier succès, je tâchai de régler de même les divers mouvements de ma figure. Ressentais-je quelque chagrin, je m'étudiais à prendre l'air de la sérénité, même celui de la joie; j'ai porté le zèle jusqu'à me causer des douleurs volontaires, pour chercher pendant ce temps l'expression du plaisir. Je me suis travaillée avec le même soin et plus de peine, pour réprimer les symptômes d'une joie inattendue. C'est ainsi que j'ai su prendre, sur ma physionomie, cette puissance dont je vous ai vu quelquefois si étonné. (p. 175)

⁷ . . . une occasion d'expérience: douleur et plaisir, j'observai tout exactement, et ne voyais dans ces diverses sensations, que des faits à recueillir et à méditer. (p. 176)

⁸ . . . nos yeux parlèrent beaucoup. Je dis nos yeux: je devrais dire les siens; car les mieux n'eurent qu'un langage, celui de la surprise. Il dut penser que je m'étonnais et m'occupais excessivement de l'effet prodigieux qu'il faisait sur moi. . . .

Etranger dans ma société, qui ce soir-là était peu nombreuse, il me devait les soins d'usage; aussi, quand on alla souper, m'offrit-il la main. J'eus la malice, en l'acceptant, de mettre dans la mienne un

léger frémissement, et d'avoir, pendant ma marche, les yeux baissés
et la respiration haute. (pp. 190-191)

⁹ Ah! gardez vos conseils et vos craintes pour ces femmes à délire,
et qui se disent *à sentiment*; dont l'imagination exaltée ferait croire que
la nature a placé leurs sens dans leur tête; qui, n'ayant jamais réfléchi,
confondent sans cesse l'amour et l'amant; qui, dans leur folle illusion,
croient que celui-là seul avec qui elles ont cherché le plaisir, en est
l'unique dépositaire, et vraies superstitieuses, ont pour le prêtre, le
respect et la foi qui n'est dû qu'à la divinité. (p. 174)

¹⁰ Descendue dans mon coeur, j'y ai étudié celui des autres. J'y ai
vu qu'il n'est personne qui n'y conserve un secret qu'il lui importe
qu'il ne soit point dévoilé . . . (p. 179)

¹¹ Vous écrivez toujours comme un enfant. Je vois bien d'où cela
vient; c'est que vous dites tout ce que vous pensez, et rien de ce que
vous ne pensez pas. Cela peut passer ainsi de vous à moi, que devons
n'avoir rien de caché l'une pour l'autre: mais avec tout le monde!
avec votre amant surtout! vous auriez toujours l'air d'une petite
sotte. Vous voyez bien que, quand vous écrivez à quelqu'un, c'est
pour lui et non pas pour vous: vous devez donc moins chercher à lui
dire ce que vous pensez, que ce qui lui plaît davantage. (p. 247)

¹² C'est après une nuit orageuse, et pendant laquelle je n'ai pas
fermé l'oeil; c'est après avoir été sans cesse ou dans l'agitation d'une
ardeur dévorante, ou dans l'entier anéantissement de toutes les facultés de mon âme, que je viens chercher auprès de vous, Madame,
un calme dont j'ai besoin, et dont pourtant je n'espère pas jouir encore. En effet, la situation où je suis en vous écrivant, me fait connaître plus que jamais, la puissance irrésistible de l'amour; j'ai peine
à conserver assez d'empire sur moi pour mettre quelque ordre dans
mes idées; et déjà je prévois que je ne finirai pas cette lettre, sans être
obligé de l'interrompre. Quoi! ne puis-je donc espérer que vous par-
tagerez quelque jour le trouble que j'éprouve en ce moment? J'ose
croire cependant que, si vous le connaissiez bien, vous n'y seriez pas
entièrement insensible. Croyez-moi, Madame, la froide tranquillité,
le sommeil de l'âme, image de la mort, ne mènent point au bonheur;
les passions actives peuvent seules y conduire; et malgré les tour-
ments que vous me faites éprouver, je crois pouvoir assurer sans
crainte, que, dans ce moment, je suis plus heureux que vous. En vain
m'accablez-vous de vos rigueurs désolantes, elles ne m'empêchent
point de m'abandonner entièrement à l'amour et d'oublier, dans le
délire qu'il me cause, le désespoir auquel vous me livrez. C'est ainsi
que je veux me venger de l'exil auquel vous me condamnez. Jamais
je n'eus tant de plaisir en vous écrivant; jamais je ne ressentis, dans

cette occupation, une émotion si douce et cependant si vive. Tout semble augmenter mes transports: l'air que je respire est plein de volupté; la table même sur laquelle je vous écris, consacrée pour la première fois à cet usage, devient pour moi l'autel sacré de l'amour; combien elle va s'embellir à mes yeux! j'aurai tracé sur elle le serment de vous aimer toujours! Pardonnez, je vous en prie, au désordre de mes sens. Je devrais peut-être m'abandonner moins à des transports que vous ne partagez pas: il faut vous quitter un moment pour dissiper une ivresse qui s'augmente à chaque instant, et qui devient plus forte que moi. (pp. 100-101)

13 Je suis encore trop plein de mon bonheur, pour pouvoir l'apprécier, mais je m'étonne du charme inconnu que j'ai ressenti. . . . Quand même la scène d'hier m'aurait, comme je le crois, emporté un peu plus loin que je ne comptais; quand j'aurais, un moment, partagé le trouble et l'ivresse que je faisais naître: cette illusion passagère serait dissipée à présent; et cependant le même charme subsiste. J'aurais même, je l'avoue, un plaisir assez doux à m'y livrer, s'il ne me causait quelque inquiétude. Serai-je donc, à mon âge, maîtrisé comme un écolier, par un sentiment involontaire et inconnu? Non: il faut, avant tout, le combattre et l'approfondir. (p. 262)

14 . . . de penser que je puisse dépendre en quelque manière de l'esclave même que je me serais asservie; que je n'aie pas en moi seul la plénitude de mon bonheur; et que la faculté de m'en faire jouir dans toute son énergie soit réservée à telle ou telle femme, exclusivement à toute autre. (p. 293)

15 J'ai besoin de me faire violence pour me distraire de l'impression qu'elle m'a faite; c'est même pour m'y aider, que je me suis mis à vous écrire. (p. 225)

16 Enfin, même après nous être séparés, son idée ne me quittait point, et j'ai eu besoin de me travailler pour m'en distraire. (p. 300)

17 Ce fut avec cette candeur naïve ou sublime, qu'elle me livra sa personne et ses charmes, et qu'elle augmenta mon bonheur en le partageant. L'ivresse fut complète et réciproque; et, pour la première fois, la mienne survécut au plaisir. Je ne sortis de ses bras que pour tomber à ses genoux, pour lui jurer un amour éternel; et, il faut tout avouer, je pensais ce que je disais. (pp. 299-300)

18 Jusque-là, ma belle Amie, vous me trouverez, je crois, une pureté de méthode qui vous fera plaisir; et vous verrez que je ne me suis écarté en rien des vrais principes de cette guerre, que nous avons remarqué souvent être si semblable à l'autre. (p. 298)

19 Figurez-vous une femme assise, d'une raideur immobile, et d'une figure invariable; n'ayant l'air ni de penser, ni d'écouter, ni d'entendre; dont les yeux fixes laissent échapper des larmes assez continues, mais qui coulent sans effort. Telle était Madame de Tourvel, pendant mes discours; mais si j'essayais de ramener son attention vers moi par une caresse, par le geste même le plus innocent, à cette apparente apathie succédaient aussitôt la terreur, la suffocation, les convulsions, les sanglots, et quelques cris par intervalle, mais sans un mot articulé. (p. 299)

[20] Il fallait donc trouver, pour mon observation, une femme délicate et sensible, qui fît son unique affaire de l'amour, et qui, dans l'amour même, ne vît que son amant; dont l'émotion, loin de suivre la route ordinaire, partît toujours du coeur, pour arriver aux sens ... Enfin, il fallait qu'elle réunît encore cette candeur naturelle, devenue insurmontable par l'habitude de s'y livrer, et qui ne lui permet de dissimuler aucun des sentiments de son coeur. Or, vous en conviendrez, de telles femmes sont rares; et je puis croire que sans celle-ci, je n'en aurais peut-être jamais rencontré. (pp. 315-316)

[21] Tout ce que je puis dire, c'est que, placée par M. de Valmont entre sa mort ou son bonheur, je me suis décidée pour ce dernier parti. Je ne m'en vante, ni ne m'en accuse: je dis simplement ce qui est. . . .

C'est donc à votre neveu que je me suis consacrée; c'est pour lui que je me suis perdue. Il est devenu le centre unique de mes pensées, de mes sentiments, de mes actions. Tant que ma vie sera nécessaire à son bonheur, elle me sera précieuse, et je la trouverai fortunée. (p. 305)

[22] Je l'avouerai, je lui trouvais auparavant un air de réflexion, de réserve, qui l'abandonnait rarement et qui souvent me ramenait, malgré moi, aux fausses et cruelles impressions qu'on m'avait données de lui. Mais depuis qu'il peut se livrer sans contrainte aux mouvements de son coeur, il semble deviner tous les désirs du mien. Qui sait si nous n'étions pas nés l'un pour l'autre! si ce bonheur ne m'était pas réservé, d'être nécessaire au sien! . . . Et, je le sens par moi-même; ce bonheur qu'on fait naître, est le plus fort lien, le seul qui attache véritablement. (pp. 313-314)

[23] Impitoyable dans sa vengeance, il [le ciel] m'a livrée à celui-là même qui m'a perdue. C'est à la fois, pour lui et par lui que je souffre. Je veux le fuir, en vain, il me suit; il est là; il m'obsède sans cesse. Mais qu'il est différent de lui-même! Ses yeux n'expriment plus que la haine et le mépris. Sa bouche ne profère que l'insulte et le reproche. Ses bras ne m'entourent que pour me déchirer. Qui me sauvera de sa barbare fureur?

Mais quoi! c'est lui . . . Je ne me trompe pas; c'est lui que je revois. Oh! mon aimable ami! reçois-moi dans tes bras; cache-moi dans ton sein: oui, c'est toi, c'est bien toi! Quelle illusion funeste m'avait fait te méconnaître? combien j'ai souffert dans ton absence! Ne nous séparons plus, ne nous séparons jamais. Laisse-moi respirer. Sens mon cœur, comme il palpite! Ah! ce n'est plus de crainte, c'est la douce émotion de l'amour. Pourquoi te refuser à mes tendres caresses? Tourne vers moi tes doux regards! Quels sont ces liens que tu cherches à rompre? Pourquoi prépares-tu cet appareil de mort? qui peut altérer ainsi tes traits? que fais-tu? Laisse-moi: je frémis! Dieu! c'est ce monstre encore! (p. 369)

The Life as Book

Le Neveu de Rameau

Source: Denis Diderot, *Le Neveu de Rameau*, in *Oeuvres Romanesques*, ed. Henre Bénac (Paris: Garnier Frères, 1959), pp. 395-492.

[1] . . . un composé de hauteur et de bassesse, de bon sens et de déraison. (p. 396)

[2] Ils m'arrêtent une fois l'an, quand je les rencontre, parce que leur caractère tranche avec celui des autres, et qu'ils rompent cette fastidieuse uniformité que notre éducation, nos conventions de société, nos bienséances d'usage, ont introduite. S'il en paraît un dans une compagnie, c'est un grain de levain qui fermente et qui restitue à chacun une portion de son individualité naturelle. Il secoue, il agite, il fait approuver ou blâmer; il fait sortir la vérité; il fait connaître les gens de bien; il démasque les coquins; c'est alors que l'homme de bon sens écoute, et démêle son monde. (p. 397)

[3]   LUI

. . . Vous croyez que le même bonheur est fait pour tous. Quelle étrange vision! Le vôtre suppose un certain tour d'esprit romanesque que nous n'avons pas, une âme singulière, un goût particulier. Vous décorez cette bizarrerie du nom de la vertu, vous l'appelez philosophie. Mais la vertu, la philosophie sont-elles faites pour tout le monde? En a qui peut, en conserve qui peut. Imaginez l'univers sage et philosophe; convenez qu'il serait diablement triste. (p. 428)

[4]   LUI

. . . boire de bons vins, se gorger de mets délicats, se rouler sur de jolies femmes, se reposer dans des lits biens mollets. Excepté cela, le reste n'est que vanité. (p. 429)

⁵
LUI

Vanité! Il n'y a plus de patrie: je ne vois d'un pôle à l'autre que des tyrans et des esclaves. (p. 429)

⁶
LUI

. . . La reconnaissance est un fardeau, et tout fardeau est fait pour être secoué. (p. 429)

⁷
LUI

Vanité! Qu'importe qu'on ait un état ou non, pourvu qu'on soit riche, puisqu'on ne prend un état que pour le devenir. Remplir ses devoirs, à quoi cela mènera-t-il? à la jalousie, au trouble, à la persécution. Est-ce ainsi qu'on s'avance? Faire sa cour, morbleu! faire sa cour, voir les grands, étudier leurs goûts, se prêter à leurs fantaisies, servir leurs vices, approuver leurs injustices: voilà le secret.

MOI

Veiller à l'éducation de ses enfants?

LUI

Vanité! C'est l'affaire d'un précepteur.

MOI

Mais si ce précepteur, pénétré de vos principes, néglige ses devoirs, qui est-ce qui en sera châtié?

LUI

Ma foi, ce ne sera pas moi, mais peut-être un jour le mari de ma fille ou la femme de mon fils.

MOI

Mais si l'un et l'autre se précipitent dans la débauche et les vices?

LUI

Cela est de leur état.

MOI

S'ils se déshonorent?

LUI

Quoi qu'on fasse, on ne peut se déshonorer quand on est riche. (pp. 429-430)

⁸
MOI

De Socrate ou du magistrat qui lui fit boire la ciguë, quel est aujourd'hui le déshonoré?

LUI

Le voilà bien avancé! en a-t-il été moins condamné? en a-t-il moins été mis à mort? (p. 461)

⁹
LUI

. . . toute l'Europe en a été émerveillée, et il n'y a pas un courtisan dont elle n'ait excité l'envie . . . (p. 439)

10
LUI

. . . Lors, par exemple, qu'il y a partage entre les sentiments, que
la dispute s'est élevée à son dernier degré de violence, qu'on ne
s'entend plus, que tous parlent à la fois, il faut être placé à l'écart,
dans l'angle de l'appartement le plus éloigné du champ de bataille,
avoir préparé son explosion par un long silence, et tomber subite-
ment, comme une comminge, au milieu des contendants. Personne
n'a eu cet art comme moi. Mais où je suis surprenant, c'est dans
l'opposé: j'ai des petits tons que j'accompagne d'un sourire, une va-
riété infinie de mines approbatives; là, le nez, la bouche, le front, les
yeux entrent en jeu; j'ai une souplesse de reins, une manière de con-
tourner l'épine du dos, de hausser ou de baisser les épaules, d'étendre
les doigts, d'incliner la tête, de fermer les yeux et d'être stupéfait
comme si j'avais entendu descendre du ciel une voix angélique et divine. C'est là ce qui flatte. Je ne sais si vous saisissez bien toute
l'énergie de cette dernière attitude là. Je ne l'ai point inventée, mais
personne ne m'a surpassé dans l'exécution. Voyez, voyez. (p. 438)

11
MOI

Il est vrai que cela est unique. (p. 438)

12
MOI

. . . Il faut convenir que vous avez porté le talent de faire des fous
et de s'avilir aussi loin qu'il est possible. (p. 439)

13
MOI

Je commençais à supporter avec peine la présence d'un homme qui
discutait une action horrible, un exécrable forfait, comme un con-
naisseur en peinture ou en poésie examine les beautés d'un ouvrage
de goût, ou comme un moraliste ou un historien relève et fait éclater
les circonstances d'une action héroïque. Je devins sombre malgré
moi. (p. 462)

14
MOI

J'avoue que je ne saurais démêler si c'est de bonne foi ou mécham-
ment que vous parlez. Je suis un bon homme; ayez la bonté d'en user
avec moi plus rondement et de laisser là votre art. (p. 443)

15
LUI

. . . «Il me semble qu'il y a pourtant là quelque chose; mais j'ai beau
frapper, secouer, il ne sort rien.» (p. 481)

16
LUI

. . . Seul, je prends la plume, je veux écrire; je me ronge les ongles,
je m'use le front. Serviteur; bon soir, le dieu est absent. (p. 481)

17
MOI

. . . Dites-moi comment il est arrivé qu'avec la facilité de sentir, de retenir et de rendre les plus beaux endroits des grands maîtres, avec l'enthousiasme qu'ils vous inspirent et que vous transmettez aux autres, vous n'ayez rien fait qui vaille. (pp. 479-480)

[18]   LUI

Le quelque chose qui est là et qui me parle me dit: Rameau, tu voudrais bien avoir fait ces deux morceaux-là; si tu avais fait ces deux morceaux-là, tu en ferais bien deux autres; et quand tu en aurais fait un certain nombre, on te jouerait, on te chanterait partout; quand tu marcherais, tu aurais la tête droite, la conscience te rendrait témoignage à toi-même de ton propre mérite, les autres te désigneraient du doigt. On dirait: C'est lui qui a fait les jolies gavottes (et il chantait les gavottes; puis, avec l'air d'un homme touché qui nage dans la joie et qui en a les yeux humides, il ajoutait en se frottant les mains): Tu aurais une bonne maison (et il en mesurait l'étendue avec ses bras), un bon lit (et il s'y étendait nonchalamment), de bons vins (qu'il goûtait en faisant claquer sa langue contre son palais), un bon équipage (et il levait le pied pour y monter), de jolies femmes (à qui il prenait déjà la gorge et qu'il regardait voluptueusement). (p. 406)

[19] Il [Lui] entassait en brouillant ensemble trente airs italiens, français, tragiques, comiques, de toutes sortes de caractères; tantôt avec une voix de basse-taille il descendait jusqu'aux enfers, tantôt s'égosillant et contrefaisant le fausset, il déchirait le haut des airs, imitant de la démarche, du maintien, du geste, les différents personnages chantants; successivement furieux, radouci, impérieux, ricaneur. Ici c'est une jeune fille qui pleure, et il en rend toute la minauderie; là, il est prêtre, il est roi, il est tyran, il menace, il commande, il s'emporte; il est esclave, il obéit. Il s'apaise, il se désole, il se plaint, il rit; jamais hors de ton, de mesure, du sens des paroles et du caractère de l'air. Tous les poussebois avaient quitté leurs échiquiers et s'étaient rassemblés autour de lui. Les fenêtres du café étaient occupées en dehors par les passants qui s'étaient arrêtés au bruit. On faisait des éclats de rire à entrouvrir le plafond. Lui n'apercevait rien; il continuait, saisi d'une aliénation d'esprit, d'un enthousiasme si voisin de la folie qu'il est incertain qu'il en revienne, s'il ne faudra pas le jeter dans un fiacre et le mener droit aux Petites-Maisons. . . .

Mais vous vous seriez échappé en éclats de rire à la manière dont il contrefaisait les différents instruments. Avec des joues renflées et bouffies, et un son rauque et sombre, il rendait les cors et les bassons; il prenait un son éclatant et nasillard pour les hautbois; précipitant sa voix avec une rapidité incroyable pour les instruments à corde dont il cherchait les sons les plus approchés; il sifflait les petites flûtes, il recoulait les traversières, criant, chantant, se démenant comme un forcené, faisant lui seul les danseurs, les danseuses, les chanteurs, les chanteuses, tout un orchestre, tout un théâtre lyrique, et se divisant en vingt rôles divers; courant, s'arrêtant avec l'air d'un énergumène; étincelant des yeux, écumant de la bouche. Il faisait une chaleur à périr, et la sueur qui suivait les plis de son front et la longueur de ses joues, se mêlait à la poudre de ses cheveux, ruisselait et sillonnait le haut de son habit. Que ne lui vis-je pas faire? Il pleurait, il riait, il soupirait, il regardait ou attendri ou tranquille, ou furieux; c'était une femme qui se pâme de douleur, c'était un malheureux livré à tout son désespoir; un temple qui s'élève; des oiseaux qui se taisent au soleil couchant; des eaux ou qui murmurent dans un lieu solitaire et frais, ou qui descendent en torrent du haut des montagnes; un orage, une tempête, la plainte de ceux que vont périr, mêlée au sifflement des vents, au fracas du tonnerre; c'était la nuit avec ses ténèbres, c'était l'ombre et le silence, car le silence même se peint par des sons. Sa tête était tout à fait perdue. (pp. 468-469)

[20]   **MOI**

Le souverain? Encore y a-t-il quelque chose à dire. Et croyez-vous qu'il ne se trouve pas de temps en temps à côté de lui un petit pied, un petit chignon, un petit nez qui lui fasse faire un peu de la panto-mime? Quiconque a besoin d'un autre est indigent et prend une posi-tion. Le roi prend une position devant sa maîtresse et devant Dieu; il fait son pas de pantomime. Le ministre fait le pas de courtisan, de flatteur, de valet ou de gueux devant son roi. La foule des ambitieux danse vos positions, en cent manières plus viles les unes que les autres, devant le ministre. L'abbé de condition, en rabat et en man-teau long, au moins une fois la semaine, devant le dépositaire de la feuille des bénéfices. Ma foi, ce que vous appelez la pantomime des gueux est le grand branle de la terre; chacun a sa petite Hus et son Bertin. (p. 487)

[21] Qu'il fasse beau, qu'il fasse laid, c'est mon habitude d'aller sur les cinq heures du soir me promener au Palais Royal. C'est moi qu'on voit toujours seul, rêvant sur le banc d'Argenson. Je m'entretiens avec moi-même de politique, d'amour, de goût ou de philosophie. J'abandonne mon esprit à tout son libertinage. Je le laisse maître de suivre la première idée sage ou folle qui se présente, comme on voit, dans l'allée de Foy, nos jeunes dissolus marcher sur les pas d'une courtisane à l'air éventé, au visage riant, à l'oeil vif, au nez retroussé, quitter celle-ci pour une autre, les attaquant toutes et ne s'attachant à aucune. Mes pensées ce sont mes catins. (p. 395)

Les Confessions

Source: Jean-Jacques Rousseau, *Les Confessions*, ed. Jacques Voisine (Paris: Garnier Frères, 1964).

[1] Là fut le terme de la sérénité de ma vie enfantine. Dès ce moment je cessai de jouir d'un bonheur pur, et je sens aujourd'hui même que le souvenir des charmes de mon enfance s'arrête là. Nous restâmes encore à Bossey quelques mois. Nous y fûmes comme on nous représente le premier homme encore dans le paradis terrestre, mais ayant cessé d'en jouir. C'était en apparence la même situation, et en effet une tout autre manière d'être. L'attachement, le respect, l'intimité, la confiance, ne liaient plus les élèves à leurs guides; nous ne les regardions plus comme des dieux qui lisaient dans nos coeurs; nous étions moins honteux de mal faire et plus craintifs d'être accusés: nous commencions à nous cacher, à nous mutiner, à mentir. (p. 21)

[2] Je revenais avec deux camarades. A demi-lieue de la ville, j'entends sonner la retraite; je double le pas, j'entends battre la caisse, je cours à toutes jambes: j'arrive essouflé, tout en nage; le coeur me bat; je vois de loin les soldats à leur poste; j'accours, je crie d'une voix étouffée. Il était trop tard. A vingt pas de l'avancée je vois lever le premier pont. Je frémis en voyant en l'air ces cornes terribles, sinistre et fatal augure du sort inévitable que ce moment commençait pour moi. (pp. 44-45)

[3] Le parti que j'ai pris d'écrire et de me cacher est précisément celui qui me convenait. (p. 129)

[4] J'allais chercher des allées sombres, des réduits cachés, où je pusse m'exposer de loin aux personnes du sexe dans l'état où j'aurais voulu pouvoir être auprès d'elles. Ce qu'elles voyaient n'était pas l'objet obscène, je n'y songeais même pas; c'était l'objet ridicule. Le sot plaisir que j'avais de l'étaler à leurs yeux ne peut se décrire. Il n'y avait qu'un pas à faire pour sentir le traitement désiré, et je ne doute pas que quelque résolue, en passant, ne m'en eût donné l'amusement, si j'eusse eu l'audace d'attendre. (p. 96-97)

[5] En un moment je fus atteint et saisi par un grand homme portant une grande moustache, un grand chapeau, un grand sabre . . . (p. 97)

[6] En cherchant vainement la cause de cette unanime animosité, je fus prêt à croire que tout le monde était devenu fou. Quoi! le rédacteur de la *Paix perpétuelle* souffle la discorde; l'éditeur du *Vicaire savoyard* est un impie; l'auteur de *la Nouvelle Héloïse* est un loup; celui de l'*Emile* est un enragé! (pp. 697-698)

⁷ J'approche de la boutique d'un pâtissier, j'aperçois des femmes au comptoir; je crois déjà les voir rire et se moquer entre elles du petit gourmand. Je passe devant une fruitière, je lorgne du coin de l'oeil les belles poires, leur parfum me tente; deux ou trois jeunes gens tout près de là me regardent; un homme qui me connaît est devant sa boutique; je vois de loin venir une fille; n'est-ce point la servante de la maison? Ma vue courte me fait mille illusions. Je prends tous ceux qui passent pour des gens de connaissance; partout je suis intimidé, retenu par quelque obstacle . . . (pp. 39-40)

⁸ . . . elle vient se jeter à ma tête, à moi qu'elle sait qui n'ai rien, à moi dont le mérite, qu'elle ne peut connaître, doit être nul à ses yeux. Il y a là quelque chose d'inconcevable. (p. 378)

⁹ Elle m'avait donné cette confiance dont le défaut m'a presque toujours empêché d'être moi. Je le fus alors. Jamais mes yeux, mes sens, mon coeur et ma bouche n'ont si bien parlé. (p. 291)

¹⁰ Je l'ai déja dit, c'était de l'amour cette fois, et l'amour dans toute son énergie et dans toutes ses fureurs. (p. 526)

¹¹ Ce seul baiser, ce baiser funeste, avant même de le recevoir, m'embrasait le sang à tel point, que ma tête se troublait, un éblouissement m'aveuglait, mes genoux tremblants ne pouvaient me soutenir; j'étais forcé de m'arrêter, de m'asseoir; toute ma machine était dans un désordre inconcevable: j'étais prêt à m'évanouir. (p. 526)

¹² Jouir! Ce sort est-il fait pour l'homme? Ah! si jamais une seule fois dans ma vie j'avais goûté dans leur plénitude toutes les délices de l'amour, je n'imagine pas que ma frêle existence y eût pu suffire; je serais mort sur le fait. (p. 253)

¹³ . . . car enfin, quelque fidèle, quelque estimable que fût Mme. d'Houdetot, elle était femme; il était absent; les occasions étaient fréquentes, les tentations étaient vives, et il lui eût été bien difficile de se défendre toujours avec le même succès contre un homme plus entreprenant. C'était assurément beaucoup pour elle et pour moi, dans une pareille situation, d'avoir pu poser des limites que nous ne nous soyons jamais permis de passer. (p. 546)

¹⁴ Ce fut dans ce bousquet, qu'assis avec elle sur un banc de gazon, sous un acacia tout chargé de fleurs, je trouvai, pour rendre les mouvements de mon coeur, un langage vraiment digne d'eux. Ce fut la première et l'unique fois de ma vie; mais je fus sublime, si l'on peut nommer ainsi tout ce que l'amour le plus tendre et le plus ardent peut porter d'aimable et de séduisant dans un coeur d'homme. (p. 525)

¹⁵ J'entendais autour de moi un chuchotement de femmes qui me

semblaient belles comme des anges, et qui s'entredisaient à demi-voix: Cela est charmant, cela est ravissant; il n'y a pas un son là qui ne parle au coeur. (p. 448)

¹⁶ Le plaisir de donner de l'émotion à tant d'aimables personnes m'émut moi-même jusqu'aux larmes; et je ne les pus contenir au premier duo en remarquant que je n'étais pas seul à pleurer. . . . Je me livrai bientôt pleinement et sans distraction au plaisir de savourer ma gloire. Je suis pourtant sûr qu'en ce moment la volupté du sexe y entrait beaucoup plus que la vanité d'auteur; et surement s'il n'y eût là que des hommes, je n'aurais pas été dévoré, comme je l'étais sans cesse, du désir de recueillir de mes lèvres les délicieuses larmes que je faisais couleur. (pp. 448-449)

¹⁷ . . . les femmes surtout s'enivrèrent du livre et de l'auteur, au point qu'il y en avait peu, même dans les hauts rangs, dont je n'eusse fait la conquête, si je l'avais entrepris. (II, p. 313)

¹⁸ Quiconque, en lisant ces deux lettres, ne sent pas amollir et fondre son coeur dans l'attendrissement qui me les dicta, doit fermer le livre . . . (p. 519)

¹⁹ Etre éternel, rassemble autour de moi l'innombrable foule de mes semblables; qu'ils écoutent mes confessions, qu'ils gémissent de mes indignités, qu'ils rougissent de mes misères. Que chacun d'eux découvre à son tour son coeur aux pieds de ton trône avec la même sincérité; et puis qu'un seul te dise, s'il l'ose: *Je fus meilleur que cet homme-là.* (pp. 4-5)

²⁰ Moments précieux et si regrettés! ah! recommencez pour moi votre aimable cours, coulez plus lentement dans mon souvenir, s'il est possible, que vous ne fîtes réellement dans votre fugitive succession. Comment ferai-je pour prolonger à mon gré ce récit si touchant et si simple, pour redire toujours les mêmes choses, et n'ennuyer pas plus mes lecteurs en les répétant que je ne m'ennuyais moi-même en les recommençant sans cesse? (p. 259)

²¹ Encore si tout cela consistait en faits, en actions, en paroles, je pourrais le décrire et le rendre en quelque façon; mais comment dire ce qui n'était ni dit, ni fait, ni pensé même, mais goûté, mais senti, sans que je puisse énoncer d'autre objet de mon bonheur que ce sentiment même? (p. 259)

²² J'ai donc fort peu possédé, mais je n'ai pas laissé de jouir beaucoup à ma manière, c'est-à-dire par l'imagination. (I, p. 55)

²³ Mes sens émus depuis longtemps me demandaient une jouissance dont je savais pas même imaginer l'objet. J'étais aussi loin du véritable que si je n'avais point eu de sexe; et, déjà pubère et sensible, je pensais quelquefois à mes folies, mais je ne voyais rien au delà.

Dans cette étrange situation, mon inquiète imagination prit un parti qui me sauva de moi-même et calma ma naissante sensualité; ce fut de se nourrir des situations qui m'avaient intéressé dans mes lectures, de les rappeler, de les varier, de les combiner, de me les approprier tellement que je devinsse un des personnages que j'imaginais, que je me visse toujours dans les positions les plus agréables selon mon goût, enfin que l'état fictif où je venais à bout de me mettre, me fît oublier mon état réel dont j'étais si mécontent. Cet amour des objets imaginaires et cette facilité de m'en occuper achevèrent de me dégoûter de tout ce qui m'entourait, et déterminèrent ce goût pour la solitude qui m'est toujours resté depuis ce temps-là. On verra plus d'une fois dans la suite les bizarres effets de cette disposition si misanthrope et si sombre en apparence, mais qui vient en effet d'un coeur trop affectueux, trop aimant, trop tendre, qui, faute d'en trouver d'existants qui lui ressemblent, est forcé de s'alimenter de fictions. (pp. 43-44)

[24] Comment se pouvait-il qu'avec une âme naturellement expansive, pour qui vivre, c'était aimer, je n'eusse pas trouvé jusqu'alors un ami tout à moi, un véritable ami, moi qui me sentais si bien fait pour l'être? Comment se pouvait-il qu'avec des sens si combustibles, avec un coeur tout pétri d'amour, je n'eusse pas du moins une fois brûlé de sa flamme pour un objet déterminé? Dévoré du besoin d'aimer, sans jamais l'avoir pu bien satisfaire, je me voyais atteindre aux portes de la vieillesse, et mourir sans avoir vécu.

Ces réflexions tristes, mais attendrissantes, me faisaient replier sur moi-même avec un regret qui n'était pas sans douceur. Il me semblait que la destinée me devait quelque chose qu'elle ne m'avait pas donné. A quoi bon m'avoir fait naître avec des facultés exquises, pour les laisser jusqu'à la fin sans emploi? (p. 504)

[25] L'impossibilité d'atteindre aux êtres réels me jeta dans le pays des chimères, et ne voyant rien d'existant qui fût digne de mon délire, je le nourris dans un monde idéal, que mon imagination créatrice eut bientot peuplé d'êtres selon mon coeur. (II, p. 183)

[26] Il me semblait que dans cette île je serais plus séparé des hommes, plus à l'abri de leurs outrages, plus oublié d'eux, plus livré, en un mot, aux douceurs du désoeuvrement et de la vie contemplative. J'aurais voulu être tellement confiné dans cette île, que je n'eusse plus de commerce avec les mortels . . . (p. 758)

Index

Library of Congress Cataloging in Publication Data

Weinstein, Arnold, 1940-
   Fictions of the self, 1550-1800.   .

   Includes index.
    1.   European fiction—History and criticism.
2.   Characters and characteristics in literature.
I.   Title.
PN3491.W4   809.3'927   80-7558
ISBN 0-691-06448-2
ISBN 0-691-10107-8 (pbk.)